"Save the Family" Promise Book

By Marilyn Hickey

Selected verses from Psalms and Proverbs

SAVE THE FAMILY PROMISE BOOK

**Copyright © 1991 by
Marilyn Hickey Ministries
P.O. Box 17340
Denver, CO 80217
All Rights Reserved**
ISBN 1-56441-020-X

Scripture quotations are taken from
either the *New King James Version*
or the *King James Version*
of the Bible.

CONTENTS

I. WISDOM: STARTING PLACE FOR REVERSING THE CURSE 1
A. True Wisdom Is God's Wisdom 6
B. Wisdom Is Priceless 8
C. Wisdom Is Practical 10

II. GODLY PARENTS BRING GODLY BLESSINGS 13
A. By Enjoying the Marriage Relationship .. 18
B. By Being Prepared for Changes 19
C. By Training Their Children 21
D. By Disciplining Their Children 24
E. Survive Their Children's Teen Years ... 26
F. Restore Wayward Children 28
G. Come to Grips With Their Own Mortality 30

III. THE GODLY HUSBAND 33
A. Is Not Slothful 36
B. Resists Temptations 38
C. Honors His Wife 41
D. Disciplines His Children 42
E. Seeks God's Wisdom 43
F. Is Honest 45
G. Controls His Tongue 47

IV. THE GODLY WIFE 49
A. Is From the Lord 52
B. Honors Her Husband 53
C. Is Industrious 54
D. Is Talented 55
E. Is Morally Pure 56
F. Should Be Rewarded 57

V. CHILDREN: WISE AND OTHERWISE 59
A. Wise Children Make Their Parents Happy 62
B. Wise Children Obey Their Parents 64

- C. Foolish Children Bring Sorrow........65
- D. Foolish Children Keep the Wrong Kinds of Friends.................67
- E. Foolish Children Receive Punishment...69
- F. Foolish Children Sow Discord in the Home....................71
- G. Foolish Children Are Lazy...........73

VI. HOPE FOR PARENTS WHO HAVE FAILED............75

- A. God Loves Divorced People..........78
- B. God Forgives Past Mistakes.........79
- C. God Gives Wisdom.................80
- D. God Answers Prayer...............81

VII. SINGLE AND SPIRITUAL..83

- A. The Single Adult.................89
- B. The Divorced Person..............91
- C. The Widow and the Widower........93

VIII. WARNINGS TO THE WISE CAN BREAK A CURSE........95

- A. The Foolish Woman................99
- B. The Results of Immorality.........100
- C. Wisdom for Finances..............103
- D. Substance Abuse.................106

IX. BUILD A HEALTHY FAMILY.........................109

- A. By Trusting God.................114
- B. Through Knowing God's Word......115
- C. By Choosing To Forgive...........117
- D. By Building Godly Self-esteem.....118

X. GOD'S PROMISES FOR YOUR FAMILY...................119

- A. Safety..........................123
- B. Peace...........................125
- C. Guidance 127
- D. Blessings 129
- E. When a Crisis Hits...............131
- F. When a Loved One Dies...........133
- G. Wisdom for an Unsaved Spouse......135
- H. Household Salvation..............137

I. WISDOM: STARTING PLACE FOR REVERSING THE CURSE

YOU CAN HAVE GOD'S WISDOM FOR THE FUTURE

Have you noticed that when things start looking hopeless, people either wring their hands and sob, or they fold their hands and pray? We need to stop *worrying* and start *praying*; we need to quit thinking that God is going to fail us. We should pray for our children and believe that they will never conform to the world.

By faith we can bless our children's future. Let's use wisdom, not worry, to secure the blessing, the inheritance, and the victory that God has for our future and our children's future. Only by putting our future and the future of our children in the hands of God will we ever experience total peace and security.

The Bible gives us some very practical wisdom for securing future blessings, future inheritance, and future victory. You can secure future blessings for yourself and your children by praying God's Word over your situations and over your children.

Before Abraham died, he blessed Isaac and gave him all he had. By so doing he secured his future and Isaac's future. Did it work? Look at Genesis 25:11: *"And it came to pass after the death of Abraham, that God blessed his son Isaac; . . . ."* **God blessed Isaac**—but Abraham was the one who had sown the seeds for that blessing.

When you sow the seed of God's Word for yourself and your children, that's using wisdom for the future! And it takes faith to *secure* God's blessings—faith in the accomplished work of Jesus Christ on the Cross. You receive blessings through the Cross of Jesus Christ. It doesn't matter what you are in the natural. At the Cross you receive a new nature, and that's what God blesses.

Your future is secure, and the future of your children and your grandchildren is secure because of the Cross. Start confessing the blessings of the Cross over your life, your circumstances, your children, and their children. The death and resurrection of Jesus is more than sufficient to provide blessings today, tomorrow, and forever.

A. TRUE WISDOM IS GOD'S WISDOM

O LORD, how manifold are Your works! In wisdom You have made them all. The earth is full of Your possessions.
Psalms 104:24

To Him who by wisdom made the heavens, For His mercy endures forever.
Psalms 136:5

Wisdom calls aloud outside; She raises her voice in the open squares. She cries out in the chief concourses, At the openings of the gates in the city She speaks her words: "How long, you simple ones, will you love simplicity? For scorners delight in their scorning, And fools hate knowledge."
Proverbs 1:20-22

My son, if you receive my words, And treasure my commands within you, So that you incline your ear to wisdom, And apply your heart to understanding; Yes, if you cry out for discernment, And lift up your voice for understanding, If you seek her as silver, And search for her as for hidden treasures; Then you will understand the fear of the LORD, And find the knowledge of God. For the LORD gives wisdom; From His mouth come knowledge and understanding.
Proverbs 2:1-6

The LORD by wisdom founded the earth; By understanding He established the heavens; By His knowledge the depths were broken up, And clouds drop down the dew.
Proverbs 3:19,20

B. WISDOM IS PRICELESS

So teach us to number our days, That we may gain a heart of wisdom.
Psalms 90:12

The law of Your mouth is better to me Than thousands of shekels of gold and silver.
Psalms 119:72

Happy is the man who finds wisdom, And the man who gains understanding; For her proceeds are better than the profits of silver, And her gain than fine gold. She is more precious than rubies, And all the things you may desire cannot compare with her. Length of days is in her right hand, In her left hand riches and honor. Her ways are ways of pleasantness, And all her paths are peace. She is a tree of life to those who take hold of her, And happy are all who retain her.

Proverbs 3:13-18

Receive my instruction, and not silver, And knowledge rather than choice gold; For wisdom is better than rubies, And all the things one may desire cannot be compared with her.

Proverbs 8:10,11

How much better it is to get wisdom than gold! And to get understanding is to be chosen rather than silver.

Proverbs 16:16

C. WISDOM IS PRACTICAL

My son, let them not depart from your eyes—Keep sound wisdom and discretion; So they will be life to your soul And grace to your neck. Then you will walk safely in your way, And your foot will not stumble. When you lie down, you will not be afraid; Yes, you will lie down and your sleep will be sweet. Do not be afraid of sudden terror, Nor of trouble from the wicked when it comes; For the LORD will be your confidence, And will keep your foot from being caught.

Proverbs 3:21-26

I love those who love me, And those who seek me diligently will find me. Riches and honor are with me,

Enduring riches and righteousness. My fruit is better than gold, yes, than fine gold, And my revenue than choice silver. I traverse the way of righteousness, In the midst of the paths of justice, That I may cause those who love me to inherit wealth, That I may fill their treasuries.

Proverbs 8:17-21

The fear of the LORD is the beginning of wisdom, And the knowledge of the Holy One is understanding. For by me your days will be multiplied, And years of life will be added to you. If you are wise, you are wise for yourself, And if you scoff, you alone will bear it.

Proverbs 9:10-12

The mouth of the righteous speaks wisdom, And his

tongue talks of justice. The law of his God is in his heart; None of his steps shall slide.
Psalms 37:30,31

II. GODLY PARENTS BRING GODLY BLESSINGS

SOLOMON'S WISDOM

Solomon has a great deal to say about the physical aspects of marriage. He is very honest and helpful in this respect. At the beginning of Proverbs 5, Solomon speaks of a physical relationship as being wisdom: *"My son, attend unto my wisdom, and bow thine ear to my understanding"* (Proverbs 5:1). To have a good, strong physical relationship—one that is refreshing, one that is continuing—is wisdom!

He then goes on to set forth the guidelines and the boundaries of the physical relationship: *"Live joyfully with the wife whom thou lovest all the days of the life of thy vanity, which he* [God] *hath given thee under the sun . . . "* (Ecclesiastes 9:9). Live joyfully with her! Marriage should be a delightful relationship, not a drag. It should be great!

Solomon paints a beautiful picture of the marital relationship in Proverbs 5:15-19: *"Drink waters out of thine own cistern, and running waters out of thine own well. Let thy fountains be dispersed abroad, and rivers of waters in the streets. Let them be only thine own, and not strangers' with thee. Let thy fountain be blessed: and rejoice with the wife of thy youth. Let her be as the loving hind and pleasant roe; let her breasts satisfy thee at all times; and be thou ravished always with her love."*

Straightforward, isn't he? The physical relationship in marriage is to be refreshing—as refreshing as a good drink of cold water when you are really thirsty. The physical relationship is to be a fountain that flows all the time, and it is to be a wonderful thing.

You don't give up drinking water when you reach the age of 35, do you? No, you drink water until you die. Physical love can last a lifetime. The Bible says that Moses' natural force was not abated, nor his eye dim when he was 120 years old (see Deuteronomy 34:7). People don't have to lose their sex life as they grow older. We're to live joyfully all the days of our lives.

God is watching your physical relationship with your mate. *"For the ways of man are before the eyes of the Lord, and he pondereth all his goings"* (Proverbs 5:21). A marital relationship should be tremendous! Each partner should be wild over the other.

I can hear someone saying, "I don't think my marriage is like that." Then start claiming these scriptures so that it will be! God is concerned about your physical relationship because He knows it is important.

A. BY ENJOYING THE MARRIAGE RELATIONSHIP

Drink water from your own cistern, And running water from your own well. Should your fountains be dispersed abroad, Streams of water in the streets? Let them be only your own, And not for strangers with you. Let your fountain be blessed, And rejoice with the wife of your youth. As a loving deer and a graceful doe, Let her breasts satisfy you at all times; And always be enraptured with her love. For why should you, my son, be enraptured by an immoral woman, And embraced in the arms of a seductress?

Proverbs 5:15-20

B. BY BEING PREPARED FOR CHANGES

Cast your burden on the LORD, And He shall sustain you; He shall never permit the righteous to be moved.

Psalms 55:22

Whenever I am afraid, I will trust in You.

Psalms 56:3

In You, O LORD, I put my trust; Let me never be put to shame.

Psalms 71:1

The preparations of the heart belong to man, But the answer of the tongue is from the LORD.

Proverbs 16:1

The lot is cast into the lap,

But its every decision is from the LORD.

Proverbs 16:33

There are many plans in a man's heart, Nevertheless the LORD'S counsel—that will stand.

Proverbs 19:21

C. BY TRAINING THEIR CHILDREN

Come, you children, listen to me; I will teach you the fear of the LORD.

Psalms 34:11

Give ear, O my people to my law; Incline your ears to the words of my mouth. I will open my mouth in a parable; I will utter dark sayings of old, Which we have heard and known, And our fathers have told us. We will not hide them from their children, Telling to the generation to come the praises of the LORD, And His strength and His wonderful works that He has done. For He established a testimony in Jacob, And appointed a law in Israel, Which He commanded our fathers, That they should make them known to their children; That the generation to come might know them, The children who would be born, That they may arise and declare them to their children, That they may set their hope in God, And not forget the works of God, But keep His commandments.

Psalms 78:1-7

Hear, my son, and receive my sayings, And the years of your life will be many.

Proverbs 4:10

Do not enter the path of the wicked, And do not walk in the way of evil.

Proverbs 4:14

A wise son heeds his father's instruction, But a scoffer does not listen to rebuke.

Proverbs 13:1

Train up a child in the way he should go, And when he is old he will not depart from it.
Proverbs 22:6

D. BY DISCIPLINING THEIR CHILDREN

If his sons forsake My law And do not walk in My judgments, If they break My statutes And do not keep My commandments, Then I will visit their transgression with the rod, And their iniquity with stripes.

Psalms 89:30-32

Blessed is the man whom You instruct, O LORD, And teach out of Your law.

Psalms 94:12

He who spares his rod hates his son, But he who loves him disciplines him promptly.

Proverbs 13:24

Chasten your son while there is hope, And do not set your

heart on his destruction.

Proverbs 19:18

Foolishness is bound up in the heart of a child, But the rod of correction will drive it far from him.

Proverbs 22:15

The rod and reproof give wisdom, But a child left to himself brings shame to his mother.

Proverbs 29:15

Correct your son, and he will give you rest; Yes, he will give delight to your soul.

Proverbs 29:17

E. SURVIVE THEIR CHILDREN'S TEEN YEARS

I have been young, and now am old; Yet I have not seen the righteous forsaken, Nor his descendants begging bread. He is ever merciful, and lends; And his descendants are blessed.

Psalms 37:25,26

But the mercy of the LORD is from everlasting to everlasting On those who fear Him, And His righteousness to children's children.

Psalms 103:17

His descendants will be mighty on earth; The generation of the upright will be blessed.

Psalms 112:2

My son, eat honey because it is good, And the honeycomb

which is sweet to your taste; So shall the knowledge of wisdom be to your soul; If you have found it, there is a prospect, And your hope will not be cut off.

Proverbs 24:13,14

F. RESTORE WAYWARD CHILDREN

Restore to me the joy of Your salvation, And uphold me with Your generous Spirit, Then I will teach transgressors Your ways, And sinners shall be converted to You.

Psalms 51:12,13

The children of Your servants will continue, And their descendants will be established before You.

Psalms 102:28

Hear, my son, and receive my sayings, And the years of your life will be many. I have taught you in the way of wisdom; I have led you in right paths. When you walk, your steps will not be hindered. And when you

run, you will not stumble.
Proverbs 4:10-13

He who despises the word will be destroyed, But he who fears the commandment will be rewarded. The law of the wise is a fountain of life, To turn one away from the snares of death.
Proverbs 13:13,14

Deliver those who are drawn toward death, And hold back those stumbling to the slaughter. If you say, "Surely we did not know this," Does not He who weighs the hearts consider it?
Proverbs 24:11,12

G. COME TO GRIPS WITH THEIR OWN MORTALITY

Yea, though I walk through the valley of the shadow of death, I will fear no evil; For You are with me; Your rod and Your staff, they comfort me.

Psalms 23:4

LORD, make me to know my end, And what is the measure of my days, That I may know how frail I am.

Psalms 39:4

Precious in the sight of the LORD Is the death of His saints.

Psalms 116:15

My son, do not forget my law, But let your heart keep my commands; For length of days and long life And peace they will add to you.

Proverbs 3:1,2

The fear of the LORD prolongs days, But the years of the wicked will be shortened.
Proverbs 10:27

The silver-haired head is a crown of glory, If it is found in the way of righteousness.
Proverbs 16:31

Children's children are the crown of old men, And the glory of children is their father.
Proverbs 17:6

Listen to counsel and receive instruction, That you may be wise in your latter days.
Proverbs 19:20

The glory of young men is their strength, And the splendor of old men is their gray head.
Proverbs 20:29

Listen to your father who begot you, And do not despise your mother when she is old.
Proverbs 23:22

III. THE GODLY HUSBAND

HIS LEADERSHIP ABILITY

Some men are natural leaders and express this in almost every situation in which they are placed. Others are more passive and better followers. However, every man must be a leader in some area. It is built into him by God. God gave man dominion over the fish of the sea and over all the earth (see Genesis 1:26). Though this dominion was also extended to the woman, there is a sense that God ordained for man to be the leader. He said, "... *the husband is the head of the wife* ..." (Ephesians 5:23).

Whether this leadership is expressed or not, man has a basic desire to be a leader—especially in his home. This desire and responsibility was given to him by God. A responsible husband first comes under the headship of the Lord Jesus Christ. His leadership in the home is then expressed by following Biblical mandates regarding that role. The husband leads by loving his wife first (see Colossians 3:19) and fostering freedom and dignity in his family. He bestows honor, deals wisely, and acts as the head of the home. All this entails leadership. This leadership should be initiated by the husband and gratefully relinquished by the wife.

A. IS NOT SLOTHFUL

And let the beauty of the LORD our God be upon us, And establish the work of our hands for us; Yes, establish the work of our hands.

Psalms 90:17

Man goes out to his work And to his labor until the evening.

Psalms 104:23

Go to the ant, you sluggard! Consider her ways and be wise, Which, having no captain, Overseer or ruler, Provides her supplies in the summer, And gathers her food in the harvest. How long will you slumber, O sluggard? When will you rise from your sleep? A little sleep, A little slumber, A little folding of the hands to sleep—So shall your poverty come on you like a robber, And your need like an armed man.

Proverbs 6:6-11

The way of the slothful man is like a hedge of thorns, But the way of the upright is a highway.

Proverbs 15:19

He who is slothful in his work Is a brother to him who is a great destroyer.

Proverbs 18:9

As a door turns on its hinges, So does the slothful turn on his bed. The sluggard is wiser in his own eyes Than seven men who can answer sensibly.

Proverbs 26:14,16

B. RESISTS TEMPTATIONS

LORD, who may abide in Your tabernacle? Who may dwell in Your holy hill? He who walks uprightly, And works righteousness, And speaks the truth in his heart.

Psalms 15:1,2

Keep back Your servant also from presumptuous sins; Let them not have dominion over me. Then I shall be blameless, And I shall be innocent of great transgression.

Psalms 19:13

When wisdom enters your heart, And knowledge is pleasant to your soul, Discretion will preserve you; Understanding will keep you.

Proverbs 2:10,11

To deliver you from the immoral woman, From the seductress who flatters with her words, Who forsakes the companion of her youth, And forgets the covenant of her God.

Proverbs 2:16,17

To keep you from the evil woman, From the flattering tongue of a seductress. Do not lust after her beauty in your heart, Nor let her allure you with her eyelids. For by means of a harlot A man is reduced to a crust of bread; And an adulteress will prey upon his precious life. Can a man take fire to his bosom, And his clothes not be burned? Can one walk on hot coals, And his feet not be seared? So is he who goes in to his neighbor's wife; Whoever touches her shall not be innocent.

Proverbs 6:24-29

A foolish woman is clamorous; She is simple, and knows nothing. For she sits at the door of her house, On a seat by the highest places of the city, To call to those who pass by, Who go straight on their way: "Whoever is simple let him turn in here"; And as for him who lacks understanding, she says to him, "Stolen water is sweet, And bread eaten in secret is pleasant." But he does not know that the dead are there, That her guests are in the depths of hell.

Proverbs 9:13-18

C. HONORS HIS WIFE

Your wife shall be like a fruitful vine In the very heart of your house, Your children like olive plants All around your table. Behold, thus shall the man be blessed who fears the LORD.

Psalms 128:3,4

Her children rise up and call her blessed; Her husband also, and he praises her.

Proverbs 31:28

D. DISCIPLINES HIS CHILDREN

If they break My statutes And do not keep My commandments, Then I will visit their transgression with the rod, And their iniquity with stripes.
Psalms 89:31,32

My son, do not despise the chastening of the LORD, Nor detest His correction; For whom the LORD loves He corrects, Just as a father the son in whom he delights.
Proverbs 3:11,12

Do not withhold correction from a child, For if you beat him with a rod, he will not die. You shall beat him with a rod, And deliver his soul from hell.
Proverbs 23:13,14

E. SEEKS GOD'S WISDOM

Blessed is the man Who walks not in the counsel of the ungodly, Nor stands in the path of sinners, Nor sits in the seat of the scornful; But his delight is in the law of the LORD, And in His law he meditates day and night.

Psalms 1:1,2

Behold, You desire truth in the inward parts, And in the hidden part You will make me to know wisdom.

Psalms 51:6

So teach us to number our days, That we may gain a heart of wisdom.

Psalms 90:12

Receive my instruction, and not silver, And knowledge

rather than choice gold.
Proverbs 8:10

Give instruction to a wise man, and he will be still wiser; Teach a just man, and he will increase in learning.
Proverbs 9:9

Listen to counsel and receive instruction, That you may be wise in your latter days.
Proverbs 19:20

F. IS HONEST

I have hated those who regard vain idols; But I trust in the LORD.

Psalms 31:6

He who works deceit shall not dwell within my house; He who tells lies shall not continue in my presence.

Psalms 101:7

A false balance is an abomination to the LORD, But a just weight is His delight.

Proverbs 11:1

Wealth gained by dishonesty will be diminished, But he who gathers by labor will increase.

Proverbs 13:11

He who is greedy for gain troubles his own house, But he who hates bribes will live.

Proverbs 15:27

A good name is to be chosen rather than great riches, Loving favor rather than silver and gold.

Proverbs 22:1

Better is the poor who walks in his integrity Than one perverse in his ways, though he be rich.

Proverbs 28:6

Two things I request of You (Deprive me not before I die): Remove falsehood and lies far from me; Give me neither poverty nor riches—Feed me with the food You prescribe for me; Lest I be full and deny You, And say, "Who is the LORD?" Or lest I be poor and steal And profane the name of my God.

Proverbs 30:7-9

G. CONTROLS HIS TONGUE

Let the words of my mouth and the meditation of my heart Be acceptable in Your sight, O LORD, my strength and my redeemer.

Psalms 19:14

The mouth of the righteous speaks wisdom, And his tongue talks of justice.

Psalms 37:30

My mouth shall speak wisdom, And the meditation of my heart shall bring understanding.

Psalms 49:3

Put away from you a deceitful mouth, And put perverse lips far from you.

Proverbs 4:24

A wholesome tongue is a tree of life, But perverseness in it breaks the spirit.

Proverbs 15:4

The heart of the wise teaches his mouth, And adds learning to his lips.

Proverbs 16:23

He who has a deceitful heart finds no good, And he who has a perverse tongue falls into evil.

Proverbs 17:20

Death and life are in the power of the tongue, And those who love it will eat its fruit.

Proverbs 18:21

Do you see a man hasty in his words? There is more hope for a fool than for him.

Proverbs 29:20

IV. THE GODLY WIFE

YOU CAN DO IT!

Woman was the very last thing God created—the crowning touch of all His creation. Adam was formed from the dust of the earth. Eve was fashioned from a part of Adam with a very special purpose—to be his helpmeet (helpmate). What a marriage. What a honeymoon! Two perfect people in paradise! How long this honeymoon lasted we don't know, but we do know it ended when sin entered their lives.

Sin has spoiled marriages and honeymoons ever since. Wouldn't you like to do something about it? Well, you can! Jesus took care of the sin problem, and gave you His righteousness and His mind. Loving God with all your being equips you to love yourself, then to equally love your husband, causing the honeymoon to go on and on. Now you really do have the power to make your marriage a perpetual honeymoon. No, not an unrealistic state of bliss, but a practical, joyful, relationship that gets better and more romantic as the years go by.

A. IS FROM THE LORD

Houses and riches are an inheritance from fathers, But a prudent wife is from the LORD.
Proverbs 19:14

Who can find a virtuous wife? For her worth is far above rubies.
Proverbs 31:10

B. HONORS HER HUSBAND

A man will be satisfied with good by the fruit of his mouth, And the recompense of a man's hands will be rendered to him.

Proverbs 12:14

The heart of her husband safely trusts her; So he will have no lack of gain. She does him good and not evil All the days of her life.

Proverbs 31:11,12

Her husband is known in the gates, When he sits among the elders of the land.

Proverbs 31:23

C. IS INDUSTRIOUS

And let the beauty of the LORD our God be upon us, And establish the work of our hands for us; Yes, establish the work of our hands.
Psalms 90:17

She seeks wool and flax, And willingly works with her hands.
Proverbs 31:13

She also rises while it is yet night, And provides food for her household, And a portion for her maidservants.
Proverbs 31:15

She perceives that her merchandise is good, And her lamp does not go out by night.
Proverbs 31:18

She watches over the ways of her household, And does not eat the bread of idleness.
Proverbs 31:27

D. IS TALENTED

She considers a field and buys it; From her profits she plants a vineyard.

Proverbs 31:16

She stretches out her hands to the distaff, And her hand holds the spindle.

Proverbs 31:19

She makes linen garments and sells them, And supplies sashes for the merchants.

Proverbs 31:24

E. IS MORALLY PURE

With the pure You will show Yourself pure; And with the devious You will show Yourself shrewd.

Psalms 18:26

Your testimonies are very sure; Holiness adorns Your house, O LORD, forever.

Psalms 93:5

I will behave wisely in a perfect way. Oh, when will You come to me? I will walk within my house with a perfect heart.

Psalms 101:2

A gracious woman retains honor, But ruthless men retain riches.

Proverbs 11:16

"Many daughters have done well, But you excel them all."

Proverbs 31:29

F. SHOULD BE REWARDED

For exaltation comes neither from the east Nor from the west nor from the south. But God is the Judge: He puts down one, And exalts another.
Psalms 75:6,7

Her children rise up and call her blessed; Her husband also, and he praises her.
Proverbs 31:28

Charm is deceitful and beauty is vain, But a woman who fears the LORD, she shall be praised. Give her of the fruit of her hands, And let her own works praise her in the gates.
Proverbs 31:30,31

V. CHILDREN: WISE AND OTHERWISE

CHILDREN WHO HIT THE MARK

From the beginning of time, children have needed love, understanding, and guidance in order to overcome temptation and to win in life. Psalms 127:4 tells us that children are, *"as arrows in the hand of a mighty man."*

Your children have a God-given hunger and ability to acquire knowledge and learn about the Lord. With encouragement, instruction, and prayer, even the smallest child can grow intellectually and spiritually.

Although times and cultures change, God's unchanging Word has an answer for every problem and circumstance.

The Bible demonstrates that the Word will never fail anyone who stands firm on God's promises. Take the Word into every situation, and be an overcomer. Today you may need divine instruction and intervention in one or more areas of your life. You, or another, may need healing, deliverance, a financial breakthrough, or a relationship reconciled. Let me assure you that the Lord can redeem every situation!

A. WISE CHILDREN MAKE THEIR PARENTS HAPPY

Behold, how good and how pleasant it is For brethren to dwell together in unity!
Psalms 133:1

A wise son makes a father glad, But a foolish man despises his mother.
Proverbs 15:20

The father of the righteous will greatly rejoice, And he who begets a wise child will delight in him. Let your father and your mother be glad, And let her who bore you rejoice.
Proverbs 23:24,25

My son, be wise, and make my heart glad, That I may answer him who reproaches me.
Proverbs 27:11

Whoever loves wisdom makes his father rejoice, But a companion of harlots wastes his wealth.

Proverbs 29:3

B. WISE CHILDREN OBEY THEIR PARENTS

How can a young man cleanse his way? By taking heed according to Your word.
Psalms 119:9

Both young men and maidens; Old men and children. Let them praise the name of the LORD, For His name alone is exalted; His glory is above the earth and heaven.
Psalms 148:12,13

A fool despises his father's instruction, But he who receives reproof is prudent.
Proverbs 15:5

My son, give me your heart, And let your eyes observe my ways.
Proverbs 23:26

C. FOOLISH CHILDREN BRING SORROW

Do not be like the horse or like the mule, Which have no understanding, Which must be harnessed with bit and bridle, Else they will not come near you. Many sorrows shall be to the wicked; But he who trusts in the LORD, mercy shall surround him.

Psalms 32:9,10

He who begets a scoffer does so to his sorrow, And the father of a fool has no joy.

Proverbs 17:21

A foolish son is a grief to his father, And bitterness to her who bore him.

Proverbs 17:25

A foolish son is the ruin of his father, And the contentions of a wife are a continual dripping.

Proverbs 19:13

He who mistreats his father and chases away his mother Is a son who causes shame and brings reproach.

Proverbs 19:26

Whoever keeps the law is a discerning son, But a companion of gluttons shames his father.

Proverbs 28:7

D. FOOLISH CHILDREN KEEP THE WRONG KINDS OF FRIENDS

Blessed is the man Who walks not in the counsel of the ungodly, Nor stands in the path of sinners, Nor sits in the seat of the scornful.

Psalms 1:1

I have not sat with idolatrous mortals, Nor will I go in with hypocrites. I have hated the congregation of evildoers, And will not sit with the wicked.

Psalms 26:4,5

He who walks with wise men will be wise, But the companion of fools will be destroyed.

Proverbs 13:20

Thorns and snares are in the way of the perverse; He who guards his soul will be far from them.

Proverbs 22:5

Make no friendship with an angry man, And with a furious man do not go, Lest you learn his ways And set a snare for your soul.

Proverbs 22:24,25

Whoever is a partner with a thief hates his own life; He swears to tell the truth, but reveals nothing.

Proverbs 29:24

E. FOOLISH CHILDREN RECEIVE PUNISHMENT

For the LORD knows the way of the righteous, But the way of the ungodly shall perish.
Psalms 1:6

The face of the LORD is against those who do evil, To cut off the remembrance of them from the earth.
Psalms 34:16

Wisdom is found on the lips of him who has understanding, But a rod is for the back of him who is devoid of understanding.
Proverbs 10:13

Judgments are prepared for scoffers, And beatings for the backs of fools.
Proverbs 19:29

A whip for the horse, A bridle for the donkey, And a rod for the fool's back.

Proverbs 26:3

F. FOOLISH CHILDREN SOW DISCORD IN THE HOME

The words of his mouth are wickedness and deceit; He has ceased to be wise and to do good. He devises wickedness on his bed; He sets himself in a way that is not good; He does not abhor evil.

Psalms 36:3,4

These six things the LORD hates, Yes, seven are an abomination to Him: A proud look, A lying tongue, Hands that shed innocent blood, A heart that devises wicked plans, Feet that are swift in running to evil, A false witness who speaks lies, and one who sows discord among brethren.

Proverbs 6:16-19

He who loves transgression loves strife, And he who exalts his gate seeks destruction.

Proverbs 17:19

A fool's lips enter into contention, And his mouth calls for blows.

Proverbs 18:6

It is honorable for a man to stop striving, Since any fool can start a quarrel.

Proverbs 20:3

Where there is no wood, the fire goes out; And where there is no talebearer, strife ceases.

Proverbs 26:20

He who is of a proud heart stirs up strife, But he who trusts in the LORD will be prospered.

Proverbs 28:25

G. FOOLISH CHILDREN ARE LAZY

He who deals with a slack hand becomes poor, But the hand of the diligent makes one rich. He who gathers in summer is a wise son, But he who sleeps in harvest is a son who causes shame.

Proverbs 10:4,5

He who tills his land will be satisfied with bread, But he who follows frivolity is devoid of understanding.

Proverbs 12:11

VI. HOPE FOR PARENTS WHO HAVE FAILED

POWER TO TRANSFORM THE PAST

God's transforming power can correct situations which may have resulted from improper parenting. Let's face it. No matter how good our intentions may be, sometimes we parents promote failure in our children rather than faith.

One day my son Mike said, "Mother, if you and Dad had put half as much into me as you put into Sarah, I would be much further down the road." I almost responded defensively; but the Lord said, "Don't do that; don't be defensive at all; just admit where you blew it." So instead of reading my son the riot act, I said, "Michael, you're right; there were things that we did wrong. Can you find it in your heart to forgive us?"

He said, "Of course I do."

Perhaps you have made some mistakes raising your children. But is God going back on His Word just because you may have blown it? No, because God's transforming power can undo any mistakes we may have made in raising our children. Although it was certainly unintentional, I failed my son in some areas; but I never failed to love him. And I know God is going to bring Michael through despite my mistakes.

A. GOD LOVES DIVORCED PEOPLE

For the LORD God is a sun and shield; The LORD will give grace and glory; No good thing will He withhold From those who walk uprightly.

Psalms 84:11

For You, Lord, are good, and ready to forgive, And abundant in mercy to all those who call upon You.

Psalms 86:5

For as the heavens are high above the earth, So great is His mercy toward those who fear Him.

Psalms 103:11

B. GOD FORGIVES PAST MISTAKES

But there is forgiveness with You, That You may be feared.
Psalms 130:4

Hatred stirs up strife, But love covers all sins.
Proverbs 10:12

He who covers a transgression seeks love, But he who repeats a matter separates the best of friends.
Proverbs 17:9

The discretion of a man makes him slow to anger, And it is to his glory to overlook a transgression.
Proverbs 19:11

He who covers his sins will not prosper, But whoever confesses and forsakes them will have mercy.
Proverbs 28:13

C. GOD GIVES WISDOM

Behold, You desire truth in the inward parts, And in the hidden part You will make me to know wisdom.

Psalms 51:6

Incline your ear and hear the words of the wise, And apply your heart to my knowledge; For it is a pleasant thing if you keep them within you; Let them all be fixed upon your lips, So that your trust may be in the LORD; I have instructed you today, even you.

Proverbs 22:17-19

D. GOD ANSWERS PRAYER

The LORD has heard my supplication; The LORD will receive my prayer.

Psalms 6:9

Blessed be the LORD, Because He has heard the voice of my supplications!

Psalms 28:6

But certainly God has heard me; He has attended to the voice of my prayer. Blessed be God, Who has not turned away my prayer, Nor His mercy from me!

Psalms 66:19,20

He shall regard the prayer of the destitute, And shall not despise their prayer.

Psalms 102:17

The sacrifice of the wicked is an abomination to the LORD, But the prayer of the upright is His delight. The way of the wicked is an abomination to the LORD, But He loves him who follows righteousness.
Proverbs 15:8,9

The LORD is far from the wicked, But He hears the prayer of the righteous.
Proverbs 15:29

VII. SINGLE AND SPIRITUAL

DEALING WITH LONELINESS

If you are single, there may have been times when you felt lonely. Loneliness is defined as "sadness due to a lack of sympathy or friendship." This is quite different from *being* alone. It is the sadness of *feeling* alone, friendless, left out, uncared for, or not special. Perhaps it comes quite uninvited and stays too long.

How can you handle loneliness? Let's look at these symptoms.

1. You feel friendless?

Usually you can count many friends, but sometimes you *feel* as if there are none. This is a feeling and not the truth. You do have a Friend that sticks closer than a brother (see Proverbs 18:24). Talk to your closest Friend! Then call someone and *be* a friend—maybe he/she is feeling lonely too. Develop your existing friendships, and then force yourself to reach out to others.

2. Uncared for?

Nobody cares? You know, people really do—you just don't *feel* as if they do. The Lord wants you to cast loneliness and all your burdens on Him because He cares for you (see I Peter 5:7).

3. Not special?

Again, this is a feeling, because you *are* special. You

were chosen to be part of the Bride of Christ before the foundation of the world, and you are blessed with every spiritual blessing (see Ephesians 1:3,4).

4. Left out?

You are not left out! God knows all about you, your needs, and your innermost desires. God has good plans for all His children, including you. You may not have received all His good things yet, but they are waiting for you. God doesn't withhold them from those that walk uprightly (see Psalms 84:11).

Then how do you handle this lonely feeling? The same way you handle any other negative emotion: you talk to the Lord about it, and then refuse to allow it to govern your actions! You see, right at the heart of loneliness is the error of expecting people to meet all your emotional needs. There is only one relationship that totally meets all your emotional needs and that is fellowship with Jesus Christ. Spend an hour talking to Him, loving Him, pouring out your heart to Him, and confessing His Word back to Him. Focus your attention on the One Who loves you and cares more than any mate ever could!

You know, loneliness is not confined to the single—there are lonely people everywhere. Cheerful people are not the married, nor those who have not known loneliness. They are those who have learned to conquer it. You can conquer it because you are a conqueror (see Romans 8:37).

A. THE SINGLE ADULT

Wait on the LORD; Be of good courage, And He shall strengthen your heart; Wait, I say on the LORD!

Psalms 27:14

God sets the solitary in families; He brings out those who are bound into prosperity; But the rebellious dwell in a dry land.

Psalms 68:6

Because you have made the LORD, who is my refuge, Even the Most High, your habitation, No evil shall befall you, Nor shall any plague come near your dwelling; For He shall give His angels charge over you, To keep you in all your ways.

Psalms 91:9-11

Because he has set his love upon Me, therefore I will deliver him; I will set him on high, because he has known My name. He shall call upon Me, and I will answer him; I will be with him in trouble; I will deliver him and honor him. With long life I will satisfy him, And show him My salvation.
Psalms 91:14-16

Houses and riches are an inheritance from fathers, But a prudent wife is from the LORD.
Proverbs 19:14

He who loves purity of heart And has grace on his lips, The king will be his friend.
Proverbs 22:11

B. THE DIVORCED PERSON

Turn Yourself to me, and have mercy on me, For I am desolate and afflicted. The troubles of my heart have enlarged; Oh, bring me out of my distresses! Look on my affliction and my pain, And forgive all my sins.

Psalms 25:16-18

Trust in the LORD with all your heart, And lean not on your own understanding; In all your ways acknowledge Him, And He shall direct your paths.

Proverbs 3:5,6

When a man's ways please the LORD, He makes even his enemies to be at peace with him.

Proverbs 16:7

Happy is the man who is always reverent, But he who hardens his heart will fall into calamity.

Proverbs 28:14

C. THE WIDOW AND THE WIDOWER

A father of the fatherless, a defender of widows, Is God in His holy habitation.

Psalms 68:5

The LORD watches over the strangers; He relieves the fatherless and widow; But the way of the wicked He turns upside down.

Psalms 146:9

The LORD will destroy the house of the proud, But He will establish the boundary of the widow.

Proverbs 15:25

VIII. WARNINGS TO THE WISE CAN BREAK A CURSE

THE WORD WORKS!

You could read the Bible—backwards and forwards—and still never know how to mix it with faith. It would never be profitable to you. If you will take a scripture, however, and begin to pray it and quote it and confess it and stand uncompromisingly on it, you will find that the Word works! When you begin to get into the Scriptures, you begin to see that nothing is impossible to you with the Word of God.

Take the Word into your family situations. One time I began to pray Proverbs 10:1 for my son: "... *A wise son maketh a glad father* ...." I began to confess, "Mike is a wise son, and he pleases his father." Mike never had good grades in school. I was praying that scripture, not particularly with his grades in mind, but that he would make wise decisions. I prayed that he would please his earthly father and his heavenly Father.

Some time later Mike's math teacher called me and, as we were visiting together, said, "My, your son is certainly outstanding in math. He's always been good in math, hasn't he?"

"No, not really. It's always been his poorest subject."

"Really?" the instructor said. "He's good in math. He has quite a bit of talent in that area."

I said to the Lord later, "That was such a shock to me."

"Why?" the Lord replied. "You've been praying that he would be a wise son. What did you expect?"

I guess I didn't expect it in that area. But you see, **when you begin to pray the Word, it works in all areas.** If we pray the Word, we should expect to receive what we request in Jesus' name.

A. THE FOOLISH WOMAN

As a ring of gold in a swine's snout, So is a lovely woman who lacks discretion.

Proverbs 11:22

It is better to dwell in a corner of a housetop, Than in a house shared with a contentious woman.

Proverbs 21:9

A continual dripping on a very rainy day And a contentious woman are alike; Whoever restrains her restrains the wind, And grasps oil with his right hand.

Proverbs 27:15,16

B. THE RESULTS OF IMMORALITY

"An evil disease," they say, "clings to him. And now that he lies down, he will rise up no more."

Psalms 41:8

For by means of a harlot A man is reduced to a crust of bread; And an adulteress will prey upon his precious life. Can a man take fire to his bosom, And his clothes not be burned? Can one walk on hot coals, And his feet not be seared? So is he who goes in to his neighbor's wife; Whoever touches her shall not be innocent.

Proverbs 6:26-29

People do not despise a thief If he steals to satisfy himself when he is starving. Yet when he is found, he must restore sevenfold; He may have to give up all the substance of his house. Whoever commits adultery with a woman lacks understanding; He who does so destroys his own soul. Wounds and dishonor he will get, And his reproach will not be wiped away. For jealousy is a husband's fury; Therefore he will not spare in the day of vengeance. He will accept no recompense, nor will he be appeased though you give many gifts.

Proverbs 6:30-35

My son, give me your heart, And let your eyes observe my ways. For a harlot is a deep pit, And a seductress is a narrow well. She also lies in wait as for a victim, And increases the unfaithful among men.

Proverbs 23:26-28

Whoever loves wisdom makes his father rejoice, But a companion of harlots wastes his wealth.

Proverbs 29:3

C. WISDOM FOR FINANCES

A good man deals graciously and lends; He will guide his affairs with discretion.

Psalms 112:5

Honor the LORD with your possessions, And with the firstfruits of all your increase; So your barns will be filled with plenty, And your vats will overflow with new wine.

Proverbs 3:9,10

He who deals with a slack hand becomes poor, But the hand of the diligent makes one rich.

Proverbs 10:4

He who trusts in his riches will fall, But the righteous will

flourish like foliage.
Proverbs 11:28

Wealth gained by dishonesty will be diminished, But he who gathers by labor will increase.
Proverbs 13:11

The plans of the diligent lead surely to plenty, But those of everyone who is hasty, surely to poverty.
Proverbs 21:5

By humility and the fear of the LORD Are riches and honor and life.
Proverbs 22:4

The rich rules over the poor, And the borrower is servant to the lender.
Proverbs 22:7

Through wisdom a house is built, And by understanding it is established; By knowledge

the rooms are filled With all precious and pleasant riches.
Proverbs 24:3,4

D. SUBSTANCE ABUSE

They reel to and fro, and stagger like a drunken man, And are at their wits' end.
Psalms 107:27

Wine is a mocker, Intoxicating drink arouses brawling, And whoever is led astray by it is not wise.
Proverbs 20:1

He who loves pleasure will be a poor man; He who loves wine and oil will not be rich.
Proverbs 21:17

Hear, my son, and be wise; And guide your heart in the way. Do not mix with winebibbers, or with gluttonous eaters of meat.
Proverbs 23:19,20

Who has woe? Who has sorrow? Who has contentions? Who has complaints? Who has wounds without cause? Who has redness of eyes? Those who linger long at the wine, Those who go in search of mixed wine.

Proverbs 23:29,30

It is not for kings, O Lemuel, It is not for kings to drink wine, Nor for princes intoxicating drink; Lest they drink and forget the law, And pervert the justice of all the afflicted.

Proverbs 31:4,5

IX. BUILD A HEALTHY FAMILY

THE HOUSE OF RIGHTEOUSNESS

I'm sure you want your children and your children's children to inherit only blessings from you! So what can you do *right now* to ensure that? You can begin by examining your own priorities. What is your number-one priority? God's Word tells us clearly what it should be: *"But seek ye first the kingdom of God, and his righteousness; and all these things shall be added unto you"* (Matthew 6:33).

But if the pursuit of riches and wealth, fame and power, and public acceptance and popularity is more important to you than seeking first the kingdom of God, then you are into idolatry—and idolatry is a terrible sin.

The Bible tells us what will happen to idolaters and warns us of the curses that idolatry will bring. God tells us that He is a jealous God and that the iniquity of the fathers will be passed down to the third and fourth generations (see Deuteronomy 5:7,9). He also warns us in Deuteronomy 28:20 that idolatry brings specific curses, among them *"The LORD shall send upon thee cursing, vexation, and rebuke, in all that thou settest thine hand unto for to do, until thou be destroyed, and until thou perish quickly; because of the wickedness of thy doings, whereby thou hast forsaken me."*

These are the sort of curses that come upon you if you turn to idolatry. The curses will come upon your children and your children's children too because they will inherit your weaknesses. Your future generations will be prey to the familiar spirits who are watching and waiting to strike. Most likely, your children will be seven times worse than you are: *"Whosoever rewardeth evil for good, evil shall not depart from his house"* (Proverbs 17:13).

Do you want to be free from generation curses? Do you want to clean up your act right now? Then you must forgive those who have gone before you and passed down their curses to you. Forgive those people who have hurt you today, pray for them rather than be bitter against them, and begin earnestly to seek the kingdom of God.

A. BY TRUSTING GOD

But let all those rejoice who put their trust in You; Let them ever shout for joy, because You defend them; Let those also who love Your name Be joyful in You.

Psalms 5:11

How precious is Your lovingkindness, O God! Therefore the children of men put their trust under the shadow of Your wings.

Psalms 36:7

Trust in the LORD with all your heart, And lean not on your own understanding; In all your ways acknowledge Him, And He shall direct your paths.

Proverbs 3:5,6

B. THROUGH KNOWING GOD'S WORD

To know wisdom and instruction, To perceive the words of understanding, To receive the instruction of wisdom, Justice, judgment, and equity; To give prudence to the simple, To the young man knowledge and discretion—A wise man will hear and increase learning, And a man of understanding will attain wise counsel, To understand a proverb and an enigma, The words of the wise and their riddles.

Proverbs 1:2-6

Turn at my reproof; Surely I will pour out my spirit on you; I will make my words known to you.

Proverbs 1:23

Now therefore, listen to me, my children, For blessed are those who keep my ways. Hear instruction and be wise, And do not disdain it. Blessed is the man who listens to me, Watching daily at my gates, Waiting at the posts of my doors. For whoever finds me finds life, And obtains favor from the LORD; But he who sins against me wrongs his own soul; All those who hate me love death.

Proverbs 8:32-36

C. BY CHOOSING TO FORGIVE

For You, Lord, are good, and ready to forgive, And abundant in mercy to all those who call upon You.

Psalms 86:5

A friend loves at all times, And a brother is born for adversity.

Proverbs 17:17

The discretion of a man makes him slow to anger, And it is to his glory to overlook a transgression.

Proverbs 19:11

D. BY BUILDING GODLY SELF-ESTEEM

What is man that You are mindful of him, And the son of man that You visit him? For You have made him a little lower than the angels, And You have crowned him with glory and honor.

Psalms 8:4,5

I said, "You are gods, And all of you are children of the Most High."
Psalms 82:6

Know that the LORD, He is God; It is He who has made us, and not we ourselves; We are His people and the sheep of His pasture.

Psalms 100:3

Behold, children are a heritage from the LORD, The fruit of the womb is His reward.
Psalms 127:3

X. GOD'S PROMISES FOR YOUR FAMILY

HOW DO YOU BUILD YOUR HOUSE?

If you are not giving the Word to your children, you are not building your house in wisdom and instruction. Fill your house with the Word, and the house will fill up with riches and wealth. Proverbs tells us, *"Through wisdom is an house builded; and by understanding it is established: and by knowledge shall the chambers be filled with all precious and pleasant riches. Lay not wait, O wicked man, against the dwelling of the righteous; spoil not his resting place"* (Proverbs 24:3,4,15).

Get the Word into your children when they are young. Pray and confess the Word *to* them, *over* them, and *with* them. Get your children to confess that "they can do all things through Christ Who strengthens them" (see Philippians 4:13).

The Bible has more to say about your household: *"The house of the wicked shall be overthrown: but the tabernacle of the upright shall flourish"* (Proverbs 14:11). The wicked can't touch the house of the righteous because the Word is there. Our families are in covenant relationship with God. We overcome the devil by the blood of the Lamb and the word of our testimony (see Revelation 12:11). The blood and the Word put our families over!

Finally, don't ever be satisfied until your children are

Spirit-filled. Do you remember Cornelius in the book of Acts? He sowed alms and prayed; he was a devout man. When Peter was sent there to preach, Cornelius and his household received the Holy Spirit (Acts 10:1-48). Expect the same for your household: *"For the promise is unto you, and to your children, and to all that are afar off, even as many as the Lord our God shall call"* (Acts 2:39).

A. SAFETY

The LORD is my rock and my fortress and my deliverer; My God, my strength, in whom I will trust; My shield and the horn of my salvation, my stronghold.

Psalms 18:2

You are my hiding place; You shall preserve me from trouble; You shall surround me with songs of deliverance.

Psalms 32:7

You who love the LORD, hate evil! He preserves the souls of His saints; He delivers them out of the hand of the wicked.

Psalms 97:10

When the whirlwind passes by, the wicked is no more, But the righteous has an everlasting foundation.

Proverbs 10:25

The way of the LORD is strength for the upright, But destruction will come to the workers of iniquity.

Proverbs 10:29

In the fear of the LORD there is strong confidence, And His children will have a place of refuge.

Proverbs 14:26

The highway of the upright is to depart from evil; He who keeps his way preserves his soul.

Proverbs 16:17

The name of the LORD is a strong tower; The righteous run to it and are safe.

Proverbs 18:10

The fear of man brings a snare, But whoever trusts in the LORD shall be safe.

Proverbs 29:25

B. PEACE

I will both lie down in peace, and sleep; For You alone, O LORD, make me dwell in safety.
Psalms 4:8

The LORD will give strength to His people; The LORD will bless His people with peace.
Psalms 29:11

But the meek shall inherit the earth, And shall delight themselves in the abundance of peace.
Psalms 37:11

Great peace have those who love Your law, And nothing causes them to stumble.
Psalms 119:165

The righteous eats to the satisfying of his soul, But the stomach of the wicked shall be in want.
Proverbs 13:25

The backslider in heart will be filled with his own ways, But a good man will be satisfied from above.

Proverbs 14:14

The fear of the LORD leads to life, And he who has it will abide in satisfaction; He will not be visited with evil.

Proverbs 19:23

C. GUIDANCE

The LORD is my shepherd; I shall not want. He makes me to lie down in green pastures; He leads me beside the still waters.
Psalms 23:1,2

The humble He guides in justice, And the humble He teaches His way.
Psalms 25:9

I will instruct you and teach you in the way you should go; I will guide you with My eye.
Psalms 32:8

For this is God, Our God forever and ever; He will be our guide Even to death.
Psalms 48:14

Do good, O LORD, to those who are good, And to those who are upright in their hearts. As for such as turn aside to

their crooked ways, The LORD shall lead them away With the workers of iniquity.
Psalms 125:4,5

Trust in the LORD with all your heart, And lean not on your own understanding; In all your ways acknowledge Him, And He shall direct your paths.
Proverbs 3:5,6

Commit your works to the LORD, And your thoughts will be established.
Proverbs 16:3

A man's heart plans his way, But the LORD directs his steps.
Proverbs 16:9

D. BLESSINGS

For You, O LORD, will bless the righteous; With favor You will surround him as with a shield.

Psalms 5:12

He grants the barren woman a home, Like a joyful mother of children.

Psalms 113:9

May the LORD give you increase more and more, You and your children.

Psalms 115:14

The curse of the LORD is on the house of the wicked, But He blesses the habitation of the just.

Proverbs 3:33

My son, give attention to my words; Incline your ear to my sayings. Do not let them depart

from your eyes; Keep them in the midst of your heart; For they are life to those who find them, And health to all their flesh.
Proverbs 4:20-22

E. WHEN A CRISIS HITS

The LORD also will be a refuge for the oppressed, A refuge in times of trouble.

Psalms 9:9

They confronted me in the day of my calamity, But the LORD was my support.

Psalms 18:18

May the LORD answer you in the day of trouble; May the name of the God of Jacob defend you.

Psalms 20:1

Hear my prayer, O LORD, And let my cry come to You. Do not hide Your face from me in the day of my trouble; Incline Your ear to me; In the day that I call, answer me speedily.

Psalms 102:1,2

Those who sow in tears Shall reap in joy.

Psalms 126:5

A prudent man foresees evil and hides himself, But the simple pass on and are punished.

Proverbs 22:3

F. WHEN A LOVED ONE DIES

Surely goodness and mercy shall follow me All the days of my life; And I will dwell in the house of the LORD Forever.
Psalms 23:6

Precious in the sight of the LORD Is the death of His saints.
Psalms 116:15

The fear of the LORD prolongs days, But the years of the wicked will be shortened. The hope of the righteous will be gladness, But the expectation of the wicked will perish.
Proverbs 10:27,28

The wicked is banished in his wickedness, But the righteous has a refuge in his death.
Proverbs 14:32

The way of life winds upward for the wise, That he may turn away from hell below.
Proverbs 15:24

G. WISDOM FOR AN UNSAVED SPOUSE

Salvation belongs to the LORD. Your blessing is upon Your people.

Psalms 3:8

Whoever offers praise glorifies Me; And to him who orders his conduct aright I will show the salvation of God.

Psalms 50:23

For God is my King from of old, Working salvation in the midst of the earth.

Psalms 74:12

Remember me, O LORD, with the favor You have toward Your people; Oh, visit me with Your salvation.

Psalms 106:4

My soul faints for Your salvation, But I hope in Your word.

Psalms 119:81

The fruit of the righteous is a tree of life, And he who wins souls is wise.

Proverbs 11:30

A brother offended is harder to win than a strong city, And contentions are like bars of a castle.

Proverbs 18:19

H. HOUSEHOLD SALVATION

All the ends of the world Shall remember and turn to the LORD, And all the families of the nations Shall worship before You.

Psalms 22:27

Delight yourself also in the LORD, And He shall give you the desires of your heart.

Psalms 37:4

The fruit of the righteous is a tree of life, And he who wins souls is wise.

Proverbs 11:30

In the way of righteousness is life, And in its pathway there is no death.

Proverbs 12:28

MY PRAYER LIST

MY PRAYER LIST

MY PRAYER LIST

MY PRAYER LIST

MY PRAYER LIST

MY PRAYER LIST

MY PRAYER LIST

MY PRAYER LIST

MY PRAYER LIST

PERSONAL STUDY NOTES

PERSONAL STUDY NOTES

PERSONAL STUDY NOTES

PERSONAL STUDY NOTES

PERSONAL STUDY NOTES

PERSONAL STUDY NOTES

PERSONAL STUDY NOTES

PERSONAL STUDY NOTES

PERSONAL STUDY NOTES

THE METHOD OF S. SULPICE

THE
METHOD OF S. SULPICE

FOR THE ORGANISING OF

CATECHISMS

WITH

PLANS OF INSTRUCTION FOR THE VARIOUS CATECHISMS

TRANSLATED INTO ENGLISH

LONDON
GRIFFITH FARRAN BROWNE & CO. LIMITED
39 CHARING CROSS ROAD

The Rights of Translation and Reproduction are Reserved

TRANSLATOR'S PREFACE

THE widespread interest with which Bishop Dupanloup's *Ministry of Catechising* has been received makes it certain that the Clergy will not long be satisfied without having the fountain-head to draw from. With this view the present translation of the *Method of S. Sulpice* has been made, as the necessary complement to Bishop Dupanloup's work, which is entirely founded upon it.

It is scarcely necessary to say that it contains a few things not suitable for English children, or for our branch of the Catholic Church, but they are not many, and may safely be left to the discretion of our Clergy.

THE TRANSLATOR.

Michaelmas, 1896.

TABLE OF CONTENTS

	PAGE
INTRODUCTION	1

PART I

RULES AND OBSERVATIONS COMMON TO ALL CATECHISMS

OBJECT OF PART I. 16

CHAPTER I

ON THE BEST PLACE FOR THE EXERCISES OF THE CATECHISM

It is better to hold the catechism in separate chapels than to hold it in the body of the church 17
Plan on which chapels of the catechism should be built—Importance of a good form 19
Light and ventilation of the chapels 21
Altar and pulpit 21
Benches—Their form 22
Arrangement of benches—Division of the catechism into quarters 23

CHAPTER II

ON THE CHILDREN WHO ARE TO BELONG TO THE CATECHISM, AND ON THE MANNER OF ARRANGING THEM

Separate catechisms should be held for boys and girls . . 25
Boys and girls to be divided into several classes, according to their age 26

CONTENTS

	PAGE
How to place the children who belong to a catechism	26
Much preliminary care to be taken in the placing	27
Provisionary arrangement—Manner of doing it	28
Free children—Children belonging to boarding-schools	29
Order to be kept during the departure of the children belonging to schools	29
Card on which to enter the children's names, etc.	31
Order to be observed while the names are being entered	32
Final placing—How to make out the chart of places	33
Announcement of places—Importance of this	33
Warning given after the announcement of places	34
Reference-book of the places—Catechist who has charge of it	34
Plan for the cards of the heads of forms	34
Arrangement of places for the dignitaries	35
Arrangement of places for the catechists	36

CHAPTER III

GENERAL EXERCISES OF THE CATECHISMS

Article I—*Singing of Hymns*

Advantages of hymn-singing—it refreshes the children, instructs them, helps to keep them quiet	38

Article II—*Entry into the Chapel*

Importance of order and silence	41
List of hymns	42
Prayer before the catechism—Use of the *claquoir*	43

Article III—*Questioning*

How to conduct the questioning — Children to be called by their Christian names and surnames	44
Names not to be wrongly pronounced	44
Names which are laughable not to be called out	44
If a child does not answer, pass on generally to another without repeating the question	44
Not allow the children to make excuses out loud	45
Question on all points of the catechism	45
Question quickly and with animation	45
Question a great many children	45

CONTENTS

	PAGE
How should vain or frivolous children be questioned?	46
Way to question timid children	46
First way to interest children in the questioning—Praises	47
Second way to make the questioning interesting—Marking with a number	48

Article IV—*Game of the Good Point*

Third way to make the interrogation interesting—The game of the good point	49
First way of playing the good point	50
What is meant by a good point	50
Another way of playing the game of the good point	50
Preparation for the game of the good point	51
While the game of the good point is going on, the catechist needs great presence of mind	52
Means of acquiring this presence of mind	52
The catechist ought to speak very little during the game of the good point	53
Always give the same proofs, and in the same terms	53

Article V—*Recitation of the Gospel*

Importance and success of this practice	55
Billets of the Gospel	56
Manner of reciting the Gospel	56
How to encourage the children to learn the Gospel by heart	56

Article VI—*Report of the Analyses* . . . 57

Article VII—*On the Instruction*

Importance and difficulty of the instruction	59
The instruction should be given in a familiar and conversational manner	60
The catechist ought to be perfectly at his ease, and to interest the children	60

Article VIII—*Notices, Counsels, and the Homily* . 60

Article IX—*Good Points given—Break-up of the Catechism* 62

CONTENTS

CHAPTER IV

ON THE INSTRUCTION OF THE CHILDREN

Article I—*Brevity and Clearness in the Instruction*

	PAGE
First quality requisite in the instruction—Brevity	66
Second condition of instruction—Clearness	67
Clearness of thought	67
Clearness in expression—Figurative or very refined expressions are to be avoided	68
Technical expressions are to be avoided	69
Come down to such language as children can understand—Study their characters	70
Avoid the other extreme in imitating the children's language	70
Periphrases sometimes to be used	70
Clearness in the method	71
The children should understand the divisions	72
Order in the proofs	73

Article II—*On the Proofs which should be employed in the Instruction*

Qualities of a proof	73
Source of proofs—Proofs drawn from Holy Scripture	74
Proofs drawn from the holy Fathers	75
Proofs drawn from reason	75
Necessity of proofs drawn from visible things—Comparisons or illustrations	76
Comparisons with visible things arrest the attention of children	77
Jesus Christ and saints who were catechists have made use of comparisons	77
Qualities of comparisons—Brevity	78
Second quality of comparisons—Appropriateness	78
Third quality of comparisons—Clearness	79
Sources from whence to draw comparisons	79
Faults to be avoided in comparisons	81
Proofs drawn from examples	82
Historical examples—Where to find them	83
Qualities of a historical example	84
Manner of giving examples from history	85
On parables	87

CONTENTS

Article III—*Manner of giving Instruction*

	PAGE
First mode of giving instruction—By means of a continuous discourse	89
Another mode—Putting questions	90
Accustom the children to speak of God with reverence	92
Questions should be short, clear, and profitable	92
Vary the manner	93
Questions should be well put	93
Questions should be adapted to the majority	93
Circumstances in which it is not well to use questions	94
Mode of questioning on the histories given	94
Important observation	95
How to question when the subject is difficult	95
Morals to be explained in a practical way	96
Example	97
If the children do not understand anything it must be repeated	98
The catechist must prepare and be master of his subject	98
The instruction not to be learned by heart	99
How to know the mistakes we may make	99

CHAPTER V

OF THE SANCTIFICATION OF THE CHILDREN

Children who are being virtuously trained easily receive good impulses	101
Need of the help of God for this work to be fruitful	102

Article I—*Virtues necessary for the Catechist if he is to labour profitably for the Sanctification of the Children*

Gentleness and Love for the Children

The catechist must seek to win the children's heart	103
Men are not persuaded by force, but by gentleness	104
Children also are won by gentleness	104
Gentleness of Jesus Christ in dealing with souls	105
Gentleness of Jesus Christ towards children	105
Love of Gerson for children	105
Effects of love and gentleness shown to children	108

CONTENTS

Zeal for the Salvation of the Children

	PAGE
Necessity and character of true zeal	109
Zeal should be wise and enlightened	109
Bad effects of impetuous zeal	110
Observations on the difference of behaviour towards boys and towards girls	111
True zeal has not respect of persons	111
Ordinary results of respect of persons	111
Practical rules for avoiding even the shadow of respect of persons	112
Behaviour towards the rich and the poor	112
True zeal should be persevering, strong, and generous	113
Necessity of this zeal, drawn from the dangers to which children are exposed	113
Necessity of this zeal, drawn from the value of the children's souls	113
Example of Gerson, the model of true zeal	114
If the children are still innocent, it is necessary to maintain them in innocence	115
If they have been corrupted, it is necessary to make them holy	116
Even if they remain hardened, it is necessary to labour for their sanctification	117
Excellence of the ministry of a catechist	118

The Spirit of Piety and Prayer necessary in a Catechist

Necessity of a spirit of piety and prayer	118
Talents will not take the place of piety in a catechist	119
Piety will supply what is wanting in talents	119
Example of M. d'Argenteuil	119
Certain pious practices suggested to the catechists of S. Sulpice	120
Purity of intention necessary in a catechist	122
Special examination and prayer should sometimes be made on the duties of a catechist	123
Advantage of prayer—It obtains for us that which is lacking in us	124
Prayer a means for obtaining the conversion of the children	124
Conclusion: Gentleness and zeal, love of the work, and piety are necessary for the catechist	125
Perfection consists in the exercise of these four virtues	125

CONTENTS

Article II—Of certain means employed in the Catechisms of S. Sulpice towards the Sanctification of the Children

The Homily

	PAGE
Object of the homily	127
To teach the children to know the nature of their duties	127
Qualities of the homily	128
Character of outward action	129
Outward action ought to be natural in the catechist	129
Outward action should be suitable to the subject, to any figures used, and to feelings expressed	129
Importance of the impression made by movements—The children are affected by it more than by words	131
Action should be noble	133
Outward action should be such as befits a man of God	134

Confession

Advantages of confession—Rules of S. Sulpice regarding confession	134
How to warn the children against false shame	135
Find out those children who have no confessor	136
Tickets for the confessors—Reason for these tickets	137
How to fill up these tickets and give them to the children	138
Certificates of confession—Certain things to guard against	138
How to get the children to be regular in confessing	140
Excuse for breaking the rule—My confessor does not wish me to confess every month	141
Another excuse—My confessor did not give me a certificate	141
Another excuse—I have lost my certificate	142
Prepare the children for absolution	143

General and Special Admonitions

General admonitions—How to give them	144
When must the general admonitions be given?	145
Private admonitions: in what circumstances must they be given?	145
Knowledge of the temperament of the children necessary for giving good advice—Children of a sanguine temperament	146
Phlegmatic children	146
Children of a bilious temperament	147
Children of a melancholy temperament	147

CHAPTER VI

ON THE NECESSITY OF MAKING THE CATECHISM PLEASANT TO THE CHILDREN, AND SOME MEANS FOR ATTAINING THIS OBJECT

	PAGE
Necessity of making instruction and goodness pleasant to children	149
The Councils recommend that instruction should be made easy and pleasant to the children	150
It is easier than people think to make the catechism pleasant to the children	151

Article I—*Rewards*

Rewards excite the children to do well	152
Rewards engrave the instructions in the children's memory	152
Synods recommend the practice of giving rewards	153
What rewards should be given?	153
In what proportion should they be given?	154
When should the rewards be distributed?	154

Article II—*Festivals of the Catechisms* . 155

Article III—*Recitation and Explanation of* Billets

Advantage of the recitation and explanation of *billets*	156
Origin of this practice	156
Qualifications of those who recite, and of the catechist who explains the *billets*	157
Rehearsal of this exercise	157
How the *billets* should be recited	158

Article IV—*Dialogues*

Advantages of dialogues—Difficulty of finding good ones	158
Children who recite the dialogues to be carefully chosen	159
Rehearsal of dialogues	159
How to place the children who recite the dialogues	160
Children to have prompters	160

Article V—*Conférences*

Advantages of *conférences*	160
Three important rules to be observed	161

CONTENTS

	PAGE
Preparation for the *conférence*—Advice to those who take part in it	161

Article VI—*Processions* . . . 162

Article VII—*Singing Vespers and the* Salut

Make much of singing the vesper psalms	163
Manner of singing them	163
Of the *Salut*	164

Article VIII—*Stories*

Value of stories—How to relate them	164

CHAPTER VII

HOW TO TURN THE CATECHISM INTO EXERCISES OF EMULATION

Children are susceptible of emulation	166
We must sometimes not be afraid to expose the children to the risk of vanity	167
Different ways of exciting emulation	167

Article I—*Dignities of the Catechism*

Advantages of dignities	169
Special behaviour towards the dignitaries	169
Dignitaries—The Intendent	170
Functions and privileges of the Intendent	170
The Assistants	171
The Secretaries	171
The Aspirants	171
The Heads of Forms	172
Promotion of dignitaries	172
Meetings and list of dignitaries	174

Article II—*Diligences (or Analyses)*

Motives which may lead the children to make analyses	174
Report of the analyses—One way of inducing the children to make analyses	175
Report of the analyses—One means of leading the children on to piety	175

		PAGE
How to treat those children whose analyses do not follow the instruction or if made by their parents	. . .	178
Correction of the analyses		179
Advantage which the catechist may derive from the correction of the analyses		180
Advantages which the children derive from the analyses—Advantages while the catechism is going on . . .		180
Advantages at home—Religious advantages . . .		180
Literary advantages		181
Advantages for all the rest of life		182

Article III—*Distribution of Pictures*

How to distribute the pictures	183
Persons employed in the distribution . . .	183
Programme of the distribution	184
The children to roll up their pictures, etc. . .	185
The distribution should be the last thing . .	185
The distribution is an opportunity for the catechist .	186

Article IV—*Solemn Distribution of Prizes*

Importance of this distribution—It should be surrounded with a certain state	187
Number of prizes and different kinds . . .	187
Manner of distributing them	188

Article V—*Visitations of the Catechisms*

Advantages of an annual visitation	190
Ceremonial and order of the visit	190
Object of the visit	191
Fruits of the visit	192

Article VI—*Punishments*

Punishment should only be rare	193
Punishment, to be profitable, must not be given hastily .	194
Warn the child in private before punishing him .	194
If he must be publicly reproved, it must be still with gentleness	194
Sometimes a child must be rebuked on the spot and severely .	195
If the child is angry, take no particular notice . .	195
After the catechism, he must be spoken to privately .	196
Punishments should be slight in themselves . .	197

CONTENTS

	PAGE
Punishments in use at S. Sulpice—Bad marks	197
Dismissal from the catechism—Must be done wisely and discreetly	198
On what condition should a child be received back who has been dismissed?	198

CHAPTER VIII

HOW TO MAINTAIN GOOD ORDER AND ENSURE THE SUCCESS OF THE CATECHISMS

Article I—*Silence*

Methods of preserving silence—Warn at the right moment	201
Make them cross their arms or join their hands	202
Give the children the example of keeping silent	202

Article II.—*On Punctuality in coming to the Catechism at the exact time*

Advantages of being careful to come at the exact time	203
Punishments for careless children	203
The catechists should set the example for this punctuality	204
Always begin the catechism exactly at the hour	205

Article III—*How to Prevent Absences* . . 205

Article IV—*Keeping the Registers*

Knowledge of details necessary in a good catechist	206
The success of the catechism depends in great measure on the exact keeping of the registers	206
Sometimes the spiritual welfare of the children depends upon it—Example	207
Another example	207
Regularity in confession depends on the keeping of the registers	208
The same catechist should enter the names of the children throughout the year	209
The day, the month, and the year of admission should be entered	210
How to enter the surname	212
Importance of learning the right spelling of the surname	213
How to enter the baptismal name	213
How to know the children's age	214

CONTENTS

	PAGE
It is important to know the confessor to whom each child belongs	215
How to collect the certificates of confession	216
These certificates to be put in a box at once	217
How to enter these certificates in the great register	217
It is important to know where the children live	218
How to enter the absences in the great register	219
How to prevent absences	219
Register of analyses	221
Different kinds of seals	222

PART II

RULES AND OBSERVATIONS RELATING TO EACH CATECHISM

CHAPTER I

ON THE LITTLE CATECHISMS

Article I—Of what Children the Little Catechisms are composed

Importance of the little catechisms	226
At what age the children should come to the little catechism	226

Article II—Rule of the Little Catechisms

Order of the catechism	227
General discipline of the little catechism	228
Rewards and punishments	231
Dignitaries	232

Article III—On the Instruction of the Children in the Little Catechism

What should be taught to the youngest children	236
Explanation of the letter of the little catechism	237
Historical instructions on religion	238
General plan and programme of historical instructions	239

Article IV—Ways for Training the young Children in Piety

The piety of the children may be roused by histories and stories	245
Festivals of the little catechisms	245

CHAPTER II

ON THE CATECHISMS OF FIRST COMMUNION

	PAGE
At what age children are admitted to the catechism of first Communion	247

Article I—Rule of the Catechisms of First Communion

Discipline of the catechism	248
Rewards and punishments	250
Dignities	254

Article II—On the Instruction of the Children

With what care the children who attend this catechism must be instructed	255
Programme of instructions for the catechism of first Communion Game of the good point	256
Special instruction to be given to some children	258

CHAPTER III

WEEK-DAY CATECHISMS

What is meant at S. Sulpice by week-day catechisms	260

Article I—Necessary conditions for admission to the Week-day Catechisms

What children are admitted to the week-day catechisms	261
Children who do not fulfil the desired conditions not to be admitted without very good reasons	262

Article II—Exercises of the Week-day Catechisms

Order to be followed in the week-day catechisms	263

Article III—Plan of Admonitions and Instructions for the Week-day Catechism

Great care in tracing for oneself a scheme of admonitions	266
Advantage of this scheme of admonitions—Different ways of giving them	267
Programme of instructions	268

Article IV—Special Meetings of the Week-day Catechisms

How the examination of the children is conducted	273
Notes of the examination	274

CONTENTS

	PAGE
Announcement of the examination list	275
Rules to be followed in the exclusion of certain children whose conduct is bad	276
It is not always well to put off the Communion of the children to the next year	277
Why the first act of contrition was instituted	279
Advantages resulting from it both for the children and for their confessors	280
Another means of stimulating the children's piety—Devotion to the Blessed Virgin	281

Article V—*Last Meetings of the Week-day Catechisms*

Explain to the children the rule of life	282
Give advice to the children as to how they must be dressed on the day of first Communion	283
Advise them by their alms to help the poor children to be suitably dressed	284

Article VI—*Retreat of the First Communion*

Notice for the retreat	285
The children who are poor to be taken care of during the retreat	287
Order of the exercises	288
Rules to be followed in the meditations and discourses	288
Second act of contrition	289
Communion blanche; its disadvantages	290
Certificates of confession, countersigned by the chief of the catechism	291
Various customs relating to candles and the offering for first Communion; the parents' blessing	291
Last counsels given to the children on the eve of the first communion	292

Article VII—*First Communion*

Ceremony of the first Communion	293
Watch over the children during the ceremony to help them to keep recollected	293
How the ceremony of first Communion is ended	294
Meeting again in the evening—Renewal of baptismal promises	295
Consecration to the Holy Virgin	295

CONTENTS

Article VIII—Catechisms of Confirmation

	PAGE
It is well to put some interval between the first Communion and Confirmation	297
Exercises for preparing the children for Confirmation	299
Ceremony of Confirmation	299

Article IX—Distribution of Memorials of First Communion and of Confirmation

A very ancient custom to give children memorials of first Communion and of Confirmation 300

CHAPTER IV

CATECHISMS OF PERSEVERANCE

Article I—How important it is to institute Catechisms of Perseverance

Advantages of catechisms of perseverance	303
Public parochial functions do not take the place of catechisms of perseverance	303
Difficulties which may be raised against the institution of a catechism of perseverance	304
It is a great advantage to the children to attend the catechism of perseverance for several years	305

Article II—Rule of the Catechisms of Perseverance

Exercises of catechisms of perseverance	307
Character of the instructions	308
Proofs too much reasoned out, not suitable for young people	309
How to propose and meet objections	309

Article III—Scheme of Instructions for the Catechism of Perseverance

Three years sufficient for a course of instruction	310
Programme of instructions for a course of three years	312

Article IV—Means of Sanctification employed in Catechisms of Perseverance

How to train young people in sound piety	340

	PAGE
Counsels	340
Monthly Communions	341
Order of the monthly Communion	342
Important observation	343
Celebration of festivals	343

Article V—*Retreats*

Advantages of retreats	344
Quinquagesima retreat	345
Retreat of the time of first Communion	346

Article VI—*Associations*

On the members of the association	347
Object of the association	348
Ceremony employed at the reception of associates and aspirants	349
Dignitaries of the association	350
Advantages of such an association	352
Association in the boys' catechism	353

Article VII—*Works of Charity instituted in the Catechisms of Perseverance*

Advantages derived by the catechisms from works of charity	355
Petite Œuvre	355
Councils for the administration of the *Petite Œuvre*	356
Interior management of the house belonging to the *Œuvre*	356
Dignitaries of the *Œuvre*	356
Petite Conférence of S. Vincent de Paul	363
Duties of the members	363
Dignitaries of the *Petite Conférence*	365
Meetings of the *Petite Conférence*	367

THE METHOD OF S. SULPICE

INTRODUCTION

OF all the decrees passed by the Church in the Council of Trent, perhaps there was none more necessary than that which enjoins on every pastor the obligation of carefully teaching the elements of the Christian faith to children. In those days, unhappily, the function of catechist had fallen into contempt, and many pastors entirely neglected this part of their duty. But hardly had the Church made her voice heard, than on all sides a wonderful zeal for the Christian instruction of childhood was awakened. A number of councils published the decree of Trent; men of the first order desired themselves to carry it into practice; and, in order to perpetuate the blessed effects of it in the Church, companies were formed with the sole object of giving Christian instruction to children.

In Italy, S. Carlo Borromeo published this decree in his first Provincial Council, and in concert with the bishops of his province, ordered that the children should be called together by the sound of a bell.

The first Synod of Sienna, that of Camerino in Umbria; the Synods of Monza, of Cesene and Forli; those of Parma, of Albano, of Montefiascone, and a number of others, followed the same example. The Synod of Brescia in Lombardy exhorted the clergy to give rewards to the children, so that they might have an affection for these wholesome exercises, and exhorts them to speak to the children, and to feel for them as a mother.

Spain showed equal zeal and eagerness. The Provincial Council of Valencia and that of Tarragona published the decree of Trent, and at the same time ordered the clergy to conduct the catechism in the vulgar tongue.

In the kingdom of Naples, the Provincial Council of Salerno desired, as at Milan, that the children should be called together at the sound of a bell.

The North, animated by the same spirit, made similar rules. In Germany, many towns made a grant out of the public money, for the sake of furthering the success of so holy an institution, and specially for a distribution of prizes every year. The Council of Constance even directed the clergy to make the catechism so pleasant, that it would be looked on by the children more as a sort of amusement than a serious occupation. The Synod of Antwerp made the same recommendation; that of Augsburg added wise advice on the way to make the catechism fruitful.

In Savoy, the catechisms were brought into an honourable position by the Statutes of Tarantaise, and chiefly by those of Annecy.

France could not see all these happy reforms without taking part in them herself. The Council of Besançon, in 1571, formed rules for the catechisms; the Council of Bourges, the Synods of Metz, of Rouen, and of Orléans, the Statutes of Troyes, of Angers, and of all our dioceses without exception, enjoined on the curés the practice of the catechism.

While on all sides the councils were occupying themselves with the great object of the Christian instruction of children, bishops, ecclesiastics of high rank, saints honoured with the gift of miracles, were seen taking on themselves the function of catechists, and thus by their great example most effectually impressing on the Christian world the importance of it. Italy could show two illustrious cardinals, S. Carlo Borromeo and the learned and pious Bellarmin. Bellarmin, being Archbishop of Capua, assembled the children in his cathedral, gave them the catechism himself, and distributed rewards to those who had answered best. Having once found an old man, nearly one hundred years of age, among the twelve poor whose feet it was his office to wash on Holy Thursday, he asked him to repeat the Apostles' Creed. "I have never known it," said the old man; "no one has ever taught it to me." At these words the holy archbishop changed colour, and for some moments could not speak. Then, with a deep sigh, and amid a torrent of tears, he exclaimed, "What! in a hundred years has not one man been found who would teach this poor Christian the articles of the faith? Woe, woe, to such negligent pastors!"

This circumstance redoubled his zeal for the exercise of the catechism; he commended it still more earnestly to his curés; and with this object, he gathered them together in his palace, and in special conferences traced out for them the rules to be observed in their public catechising; more than this, he went to the several parishes, and gave the catechism himself to the children. It is said that he explained it in so fatherly a manner, that all were touched and softened by it. As soon as the archbishop's catechism was announced, people of every age hastened to it with the children, and Bellarmin took advantage of this to give them good advice.

S. François de Sales gave the same example to his curés. Every Sunday in the year, and on Saturdays in Lent, this holy bishop took the catechism alternately with his canons. To make it pleasanter to the children, *cantiques* were sung sometimes with the voice alone, sometimes with organ accompaniment; and he always had a number of rewards with him. Twice a year he went with his children in solemn procession through the town.

In Portugal, Dom Barthélemi des Martyrs, Archbishop of Braga, gave himself entirely, particularly after he had resigned his pastoral charge, to this work. S. Ignatius, on returning to his own country, resolved to hold the catechism for the children; and when he was told no one would come to hear him, he replied, "If I had only one to teach, I should think myself well rewarded for my trouble." The high esteem in which he held the office of catechist led him to devote himself, he and his first companions, to this branch of ministry. When he became General of his Order, he began his new duties by giving the catechism in a church in Rome, where not only children crowded to hear him, but theologians, canonists, and people of rank. Though his language was somewhat barbarous and full of Spanish idioms, his exhortations made a great impression on his audience; having listened to him, every one went away in silence, tears in their eyes, compunction in their hearts. He kept up this exercise forty-six days in the same church; and it is from his example that the superiors of the Company of Jesus always conduct a catechism for forty days as their first work.

S. Francis Borgia went about the country, a little bell in his hand, calling the children and teaching them the Christian doctrine. In India, S. Francis Xavier talked to the children in childish language, and taught them the first elements of the Christian faith. "He went through the town of Goa, and with a loud voice besought the parents for the love of God to send their children and their slaves to the catechism." It was the belief of the holy man, adds the author of his Life, "that if only the Portuguese youth were well instructed in the principles of religion, and early trained to the practice of virtue, in a very short time Christianity would revive in Goa. . . . And it was, in fact, by means of the children that the town did begin to assume a new aspect."

France produced more great examples of this sort than the other parts of the Christian world. The pious Bishop of Cahors, M. Alain de Solminiac, never left a parish till he had held a catechism in the vulgar tongue, and his love always suggested to him some new way of making the instruction interesting and pleasant to his hearers. M. le Nobletz, who had been a catechist since he was fourteen, carried on this ministry up to his death with wonderful success. He knew how to attach the children to himself by rewards wisely given, and by his sweet and winning manner; he even sometimes brought with him a young lad, placing him amongst the children, so that his example should induce the others to answer the various questions he put to them. Père Romilion, founder of the Ursulines in France, feeling that his vocation was to catechise children, began to exercise this ministry at *l' Isle*, in the *Comtat Venaissin*, and with most wonderful results. He so attached the children to his catechism by the rewards which he distributed each time, and by all the pious devices which his apostolic zeal could suggest, that he kept them for two or three hours following without their feeling the slightest weariness.

If it needed such grand examples of zeal effectually to arouse the clergy, it needed also, so that these examples should be perpetuated in the Church, that associations should be founded devoted to the Christian instruction of youth. The holy Pope Pius V., raised up by God to restore the ruins of the Church, instituted at Rome a confraternity of catechists under the name of the *Christian Doctrine*. A great number of persons hastened to join it, and bound themselves to hold the catechism on Sundays and festivals in the churches which the Supreme Pontiff assigned to them. Seeing the great fruit produced by their instructions, the Pope granted indulgences to those who exercised this work of charity, and to those who came to the catechism to be instructed. He did more: by an express bull, he exhorted all the patriarchs, archbishops, bishops, and prelates to introduce this holy and salutary practice into their churches. S. Carlo Borromeo established the confraternity of *Christian Doctrine* at Milan, and strove to propagate it throughout his diocese. The change it wrought was soon apparent. Not a Sunday came round which did not bring to the churches in town or country multitudes of the faithful, some teaching and the rest listening; and at the close all joining together in singing litanies, psalms, hymns, and sacred *cantiques*. These exercises attracted a great crowd of people, and above all the artisans, who willingly left games, dances, and other worldly diversions to take part in these gatherings. It was a pleasure to the holy archbishop to visit them, and his presence was a new subject for joy and public edification. When he died, there were, in the town and diocese of Milan, more than 40,000 people under instruction, about 740 catechisms, and more than 3000 catechists.

S. François de Sales, as soon as he became bishop, also instituted the confraternity of *Christian Doctrine* at Annecy, and fixed the Statutes for its order and regulation, and for ensuring its duration.

In France, César de Bus, in the first place, exercised his zeal in the *Comtat Venaissin*, where he earned the title, the *Apostle of the Children*. To attract them to his catechisms, he gave them rewards, and made them sing *cantiques* and recite dialogues. He even took the trouble to prepare individually the children who were to answer in public, so that the instruction should not drag or go badly. He conceived the plan of establishing a congregation, the essential spirit, the indispensable duty, the constant and principal function of which should be the teaching of Christian doctrine, and which should form in the church an order of catechists, as that of S. Dominic was an order of preachers. This Society began in 1592 under the name of Priests of the Christian Doctrine, and was confirmed by Clement VIII. in 1597.

Soon after, S. Vincent de Paul laid the foundation of another congregation, which embraced the same subject, the Christian instruction of children. In the missions which his priests preached to the country people, he enjoined them to teach the little catechism at noon and the great catechism in the evening, and he desired that part of the time should be occupied in questioning the children. Once, having heard that one of his priests had departed from these instructions, he wrote to him in these words: "I have been much disturbed to find that, instead of teaching the great catechism in the evenings, you have preached sermons in your mission. This ought not to be, . . . because the people have more need of the catechism, and they profit more by it ; and also because it is our custom, and it has pleased our Lord to give great blessings to this practice ; and also it gives greater opportunity for the exercise of humility."

No one has so deeply experienced the effect of these benedictions, neither has anyone contributed so effectually to the revival and spread of the work of catechisms in France, as M. Olier, the disciple and friend of S. Vincent de Paul. It is well known in what a condition the parish of S. Sulpice, in Paris, was, when this parish, of greater importance than any, was, according to the records of the time, the very sink, not only of the capital, but of all France. Ungodly men, libertines, atheists, everything that was most corrupt was to be found there.

M. Olier did not despair of the mercy of God ; in the first place, he consecrated the parish to the Holy Virgin, and then, with a view to its reformation, he set himself to evangelise it by the means of catechisms, for in this parish the depravity of morals was quite equalled by the ignorance of religion. "I begin," he wrote, "to understand what is God's design for the reformation of this parish ; He wills that first we should help the young by giving them Christian principles, and teaching them the fundamental maxims of salvation, and this by means of the young students of the seminary, who will go through all the district carrying this instruction." A great catechism and many lesser ones were established in the church of S. Sulpice, and about twelve others in different parts of the parish. Each of these catechisms was given over to the zeal of two ecclesiastics from the seminary, one of whom went about the streets and into the houses with a little bell to call the children to the catechism; the other gave the instructions. As it was an unusual thing to see the priests thus going about in the parish, it was a most edifying sight; and it was most comforting to M. Olier to see what a change was wrought everywhere by this well-organised scheme for dispensing the bread of the word, in which about four thousand children took part. This good shepherd himself held the catechism for the very youngest children on Sundays and festivals, in the parish church.

Besides these catechisms, M. Olier set on foot several others; two for first Communion, one at Easter, and the other at Whitsuntide,—these were called week-day catechisms (*catéchismes de semaine*); a third for Confirmation; and he appointed confessors to hear the children's general confessions. During Lent, three times a week, he held a catechism for the pages and young footmen; another for the beggars, to bring them on to the sacraments of Penitence and the Eucharist. To these, after the catechism, alms were distributed according to the good answers they had made. And lastly, another catechism was held every Friday for the old people.

The zeal for the instruction of children which burnt so brightly in M. Olier, did not die out with this man of God. Under M. de Bretonvilliers and M. de Poussé, his successors in the cure of S.

Sulpice, the catechisms increased considerably. M. Tronson, superior of the seminary, though burdened with a multitude of important affairs, entered into the smallest details concerning the instruction of the children, and constantly strove to inspire his pupils with a great esteem for this work. He even took the trouble of reading and correcting the little addresses they would have to give, particularly at the openings. He had given the general administration of the catechisms to one of the directors of the seminary, M. Baüin, who seemed to reproduce, together with the virtues and example of M. Olier, his zeal for the instruction and the sanctification of the children.

We read in a manuscript life of this holy priest: "The charity of M. Baüin particularly shone out towards the children in the parish of S. Sulpice. He went from time to time to visit the catechisms, to see if everything was going on in order; and as he knew that God largely blessed this work, he established fixed rules with a view to bring it to its highest perfection. He planned them together with M. Tronson and the oldest directors of the seminary. He either established or matured several practices of the catechisms of S. Sulpice, such as the recitation of *billets*, the good or bad points, the rewards, the discussions between the children, the heads of the form, the office of the various dignitaries, the charts of the form, the excuses in case of absence, the monthly communions, the chanting of vespers, the *cantiques*, etc."

By this time the faubourg Saint-Germain had

assumed a wholly new appearance. "I wish," says a writer of the time,[1] "that I could represent the parish of S. Sulpice in the condition in which it was about fifty years ago when the seminary was established, and compare that abominable Babylon, the very sink and drain of every abomination, with it as it now is, after the labours of the communities of the seminary and the presbytery. It is enough to say that, in the church of S. Sulpice alone, every year 200,000 communions are made, although there are thirty communities in this parish." This happy renovation was the fruit of the zeal with which the children were prepared for their first Communion. Not one was allowed to be absent from the *Sunday catechism*; and every year, so that no one could plead ignorance, the parents and the masters and mistresses of schools were given public notice, and warned that their children would be shut out from their first Communion, unless they sent them regularly and punctually. Neither was anyone exempt from attending the *week-day catechism*; M. Baüin was inflexible on this point. "If we admit the children to their first Communion without making them go through the week-day catechism, they will all their life know much less about the greatness of the sacraments, and of the right dispositions in which they should receive them. In our catechisms, we strive to inspire them with an extreme horror of sin, with a great respect for the sacraments, and a very great fear of approaching

[1] See *Mémoires historiques sur l'Eglise de Saint-Sulpice*, 12mo, pp. 598 and 611.

them without right preparation. We are not satisfied with instructing them in things absolutely necessary to salvation, which yet they would hardly learn from even the best-disposed parents; but we do what we can to touch their hearts, to constrain them to be wholly converted, to root out their bad habits, and to make good confessions."

The catechisms of S. Sulpice are to this day much as they were when founded by these venerable priests; the same rules, the same customs, consecrated by long experience, are preserved; the changes which in course of time have been introduced are only very slight. And if they still do much good in the parish, we owe it more than anything else to this respect for the traditions. The good is not limited to the single parish of S. Sulpice, it extends besides to a very great number of parishes in different dioceses of France and even of foreign countries, for the pupils of the seminary, who during their clerical education have been trained to the work of the catechisms, are eager to establish it on the model they had under their own eyes, when, on return to their dioceses, as curés or in any other capacity, they are put in charge of the religious instruction of youth.

It is not to be supposed that catechisms can be organised in the same manner everywhere in all particulars. Different localities have to be taken into account, as well as the different efficiency of individual catechists, and the aptitude of the children; but if the accessory is carefully distinguished from the fundamental, that which is primary in well-ordered catechisms, distinguished from certain practices which may give more interest to the work, but yet are not essential to it, it will be easy to follow the method of S. Sulpice, even in country parishes.

PART I

RULES AND OBSERVATIONS COMMON TO ALL CATECHISMS

OF all the advice which the author of the *Catéchisme de Bourges*[1] gives to catechists, perhaps there is nothing wiser than the way in which he sets forth what is the real cause of that dislike to the catechism which is so common in most parishes. "Many ecclesiastics," says this author, "say that it is useless for them to exhort their people to come to the catechism, or to send their children to it, for that still no one comes; but the reason is this: they do not seriously apply themselves to this exercise, . . . they do not prepare for it, . . . they do not think of any incentives, such as giving images or other things; or of having the forms well arranged, so that the children can sit comfortably. They do not go to the smallest expense for all this, . . . they do not choose a convenient place, or a convenient hour, . . . they do not go to their own houses to exhort them, to write down their names, and to persuade them to come; . . . and very often these

[1] M. de la Chétardie, formerly catechist of S. Sulpice.

are the real reasons for no one coming to the catechism."[1]

In fact, experience shows of what extreme importance to the success of the catechisms are all these means, which are so necessary and yet so neglected. It is by these means, and several others we shall speak of hereafter, that to this day is owing the reputation of the catechisms of S. Sulpice; if they were employed elsewhere, as far as local circumstances would allow, they would produce similar results, and would teach the catechist the secret of holding the children's attention for several consecutive hours,[2] and making them feel a constant fresh interest in Christian instruction.

The first part of the *Method* of S. Sulpice has for its object the explanation in detail of these various means. It will treat—1. On the place where the catechism should be held; 2. Of the different members of a catechism; 3. Of the exercises of the catechism; 4. The instruction of the children; 5. The edification of the children; 6. The necessity of making the catechism pleasant to the children, with some hints for attaining that end; 7, How to make the exercises of the catechism exercises of emulation; 8. and last, The way to keep the register of the catechism.

[1] *Catéchisme de Bourges,* vol. i. preface, part 2, No. 34.
[2] S. François de Sales fixed the time of the catechism for two hours: "Adeò mature, ut catechismus duas horas habere possit, æstivis præsertim diebus. Modus catechismi, etc." (*Opuscules de S. François de Sales,* vol. ii. p. 26. Ed. 12mo, 1767).

CHAPTER I

THE BEST PLACE FOR THE EXERCISES OF THE CATECHISM

IF we only look at what is the practice in the greater number of parishes, we should suppose that the middle of the nave was the best place for the exercises of the catechism. But not so judged the founders of the catechisms of S. Sulpice. They were convinced, and it is still acknowledged, that it is very difficult to keep up the constant attention of the children if they are assembled in the middle of the nave of a parish church. In fact, the attention of children in a catechism cannot be secured unless they are spoken to in an easy, natural tone of voice, as in ordinary conversation; but if a catechist, stationed in the middle of the nave, tries to speak in this tone, and yet loud enough for all the children to hear him, he will very soon find himself exhausted. Besides, it is absolutely necessary that silence should reign in the catechism, and that the children, naturally so restless, should not be distracted by outward objects; but if they are seated in the nave, will they not every moment be distracted by people passing in and out, or perhaps coming near to see or hear, to say nothing of the funeral processions and other religious ceremonies which may often interrupt the silence? And further, in the nave of the church, many children in the greater catechisms, particularly the girls, will be ashamed to answer the questions put to them, and the fear of being humiliated before strangers will drive them away much more than the desire of showing off will attract them. Sometimes even the catechist will not feel himself so free as he should to praise or blame the children, to question them, or even to give them familiar instruction, particularly in the little catechisms; for the fear of appearing too simple to the grown-up people who are listening, will often lead him to forget that he is instructing children. It is true that in several parishes where the catechism is held in the middle of the nave, it is found that grown-up people take advantage of the instructions; but it must be granted that the children, for whom the catechism is intended, suffer by this. Why not have a special catechism for these people? They would profit more, and not spoil the children's instruction. It was to obviate this evil that the Council of Besançon, held in the year 1571, forbade, on pain of excommunication, any adult to enter the church while the curé was holding the catechism for the little children: *Ne per grandiorum superbiam et insolentiam curatus perturbetur, aut altiora tractare cogatur.*[1] To remedy this evil the founders of the catechisms of S. Sulpice were led to have chapels built, specially devoted to this work,

[1] *Concilia Germaniæ*, vol. viii. p. 190.

OF THE PLACE FOR THE CATECHISM

and entirely separated from the church. Many parishes in the capital follow the same practice. There is hardly any in which it would not be easy to arrange it; it is but to set apart one of the chapels for the catechism, and to divide it off from the church by a partition eight or ten feet high. And this would be quite sufficient.

But, in order that the chapels should be fit for the exercises of the catechism, they must be so arranged that the children can easily hear the catechist, and also hear each other from any point in the place where they are assembled. It is also necessary that the catechist should be able to watch the children, and have them all under his eye without being obliged to change his position. Hence it is easy to see that the form of the chapel has a great deal to do with the success of the catechism.

Experience proves that a chapel in the form of a long square has few advantages, for if it is beyond a certain length, the catechist, who must always be at one end, so that he may have all his audience in view, will have great difficulty in keeping watch over the children at the opposite end. These children will have a difficulty in hearing him, and they themselves will with difficulty be heard by the children at the other end. There is another inconvenience. The places which are farthest off from the catechist, in fact nearly half the forms, are looked on by the children as very inferior to the others; and in the arrangement of places this is a constant subject of discontent, complaint, and grumbling.

If a chapel is in the form of a semicircle, the

catechist is easily heard ; but it may be that the children at one end can scarcely hear the children at the opposite end. The catechist, if he is placed in the centre, will not be able to see all his audience without changing his position, and as, in order to keep up the children's attention, he is obliged to put his questions to all corners of the catechism, and to look from one side to another, he will be obliged to turn himself sometimes to the right, sometimes to the left, and be perpetually in motion.

Chapels which are circular in form do not present the same disadvantages, and the same may be said for those which are oval in form, if the catechist takes his place where the diameter is smallest. But the best of all is the quarter of a circle ; it is best for the catechist, for, remaining in his place, he has his eye on the whole catechism ; and it is best for the attention of the children, who, wherever they may be placed, see easily, and in front of them, the altar, the pulpit, and the head of the catechism.

The chapels devoted to the catechism should be sufficiently high and well ventilated, so that the children should not suffer from want of air. It would be well even to have one or two large windows in the upper part, which could be easily opened. It would be desirable also to have several doors for exit, or that at least the one door should be large enough to allow of the children going away quickly and without confusion.

Every part of these chapels should be light, if possible, and the light should come from a little above, otherwise the children would come in each other's light. In the same way, if the catechism goes on when the day is closing, lamps should be so arranged that everyone can see without being a hindrance to his neighbours. The chapel of the catechism should have a sacristy adjoining, but it should have an entrance independent of the catechism.

In the principal part of the chapel, and opposite the children, should be placed a picture or a statue of a kind that will edify and impress them, or even an altar, with its usual ornaments. The restlessness of children is held in check by the sight of these religious objects; and, moreover, they help to fix their attention during prayer. Quite close to the place where the catechist is, there should be a small platform, from which he speaks to the children when he gives them an instruction or explains to them the Gospel. They will listen to him with more respect and attention; and the catechist will find that, being a little above them, he can be better heard, and he will be able more easily to keep watch on his audience, of whom he should never lose sight. It is related of S. François de Sales, that when he conducted the catechism in his cathedral, he took up his position on a platform, from whence he commanded all the children. This lovable and truly good father was seated on a throne raised up about five steps; all the army of children surrounded him. . . . It was a delight beyond anything to hear how familiarly he explained the rudiments of our faith: on each point, a wealth of illustrations seemed to flow from him in explanation; he looked on his little world and his little world looked on him; with them he made himself a child, that in them he might form the mind and perfect man according to Jesus Christ."[1]

Experience shows that chairs are not very suitable for a catechism; they take up more room than children generally require; they easily get out of order; they make it difficult to watch over the children when they are kneeling, and they cannot be arranged in the form of an amphitheatre. All these inconveniences are avoided by using forms; but they must be comfortable for the children to sit on, for, otherwise, they might soon get too tired to profit by the catechism. Still, it is not desirable for all the forms to have backs;[2] these backs are in the children's way when they have to kneel, and force them into a most uncomfortable posture, unless the forms are very wide apart, which would be against the good order of the catechism. The height of the benches should be in proportion to the size of the children; that is to say, not so low that the children would have to stretch their legs out under their neighbours' bench, and not so high that their feet would hang when they sit down; for this would be an endless cause of restlessness, and would distract themselves and their neighbours.

The forms ought to be placed parallel with each other, not too far off nor too close, but so that every child could move out from the middle of his form without much inconvenience to the children he has

---

[1] *Vie de S. François de Sales*, by Père de la Rivière, p. 362.

[2] It is a good thing that the chief dignitaries should have seats with backs, so that they may be distinguished from the rest.

OF THE PLACE FOR THE CATECHISM

to pass, and without obliging them to leave their places to let him pass. Whatever may be the form of the chapel, good order demands that the catechism should be divided into certain *quarters*; this is the name given to a certain number of forms arranged parallel with each other. If a chapel is oblong in form, two quarters can be formed, separated from each other by a passage, and one may be called the *Epistle* quarter, and the other the *Gospel* quarter, according to the side of the altar which it is opposite to. If a chapel is in the form of a quarter of a circle, it is necessary to divide it into at least three quarters; if only in two, in a chapel of a certain size, the forms which are farthest off from the centre will be found too long, and the children who are in the middle of them could not leave their places without causing a good deal of disturbance. Moreover, the watching over these quarters would be very difficult, and the dignitaries could not execute their functions with any convenience.

It is desirable that there should be a passage on either side of these quarters, so that the children and the catechists may be able to move freely, and that the discipline of the catechism may be maintained. The end of each form should be numbered, so that the children, recognising the form on which they are to sit, will always occupy the same place.[1] The catechisms where the forms rise up gradually

[1] It is best to put the first numbers on the forms which are at the end of the chapel; it is a sort of compensation to the children who have to sit there.

in an amphitheatre have immense advantages over all others; the children, however far off they may be, can easily make themselves heard; they see everything which is done in the catechism, and are more attentive to it; and the catechists have all the children in sight, and can keep watch over them without trouble.

CHAPTER II

CONCERNING THE CHILDREN WHO ARE TO BE COMPRISED IN THE CATECHISM, AND THE WAY OF ARRANGING THEM

EXPERIENCE only shows too clearly the serious disadvantages inseparable from having boys and girls in one catechism. It is true that many catechists justify this practice, trusting to the simplicity and innocence of life in their parishes. Nevertheless this mixture, which obliges them to be extremely careful of what they say, is full of danger to many a child; and whoever has had experience of the catechism should never allow it, unless from unavoidable circumstances it is a necessity; and then, to prevent abuses, he will have to be most severely watchful.

After having separated the boys and girls, they must be each divided into different classes or catechisms according to their age, so that the instruction given may be in proportion to their capacity. It is evident that the instruction suited for little children will not be suitable for those who have already some knowledge of religion, nor for those who are being prepared for their first

Communion, or who have already made it. If the same explanations are given to all, it must follow, of necessity, that one set will be wearied by useless repetitions, and the other by explanations beyond their understanding. It is in view of this that many diocesan catechisms are divided into three parts, each containing the explanation of the same truths, but with more or less development, according to the age and capacity of the children forming each part.

After having thus divided the children into several catechisms, the next thing is to assign to each child the place he or she is to occupy. It is impossible to be too careful in the arrangement of this placing; experience showing that on this one part of the work depends, in great measure, the maintenance of good order in each catechism. Before explaining in detail how this placement is done, we will notice some practices founded on long observation, and which have passed into rules in the catechisms of S. Sulpice. The children who belong to the same boarding-school are put together; the inattentive ones are put near those who are the most attentive and quiet; taking care, however, that the bad ones do not spoil the good; and, in view of this, the inattentive ones are brought more forward, so that they may be more under the eye of the catechist. Although no respect of persons is used in the assignment of places, still, to spare the feelings of the parents or of the masters of the schools, it is thought better not to put a very poorly-clothed child next to a well-dressed one. Next to the poorest, children of a middle class are placed; and then, next to these latter, the more distinguished ones, so that the contrast between the two is not so evident. But the poor children would not be shocked by seeing the first place given to others, if these are steady and earnest, and thus being both an example and an ornament to the catechism. But they are mixed up in such a way that it cannot be said one quarter is set apart for the poor and another quarter for the rich; any such distinction would be odious to the catechists, and humiliating for the poorer children, who, moreover, are all equal to the others in the house of God.

In catechisms which contain both children from schools and free children, it does not seem possible to settle the places at the first nor even at the second meeting; it will be announced at the third, after having received the lists from the heads of schools.

The chief of the catechism, a fortnight before the first meeting, writes to the masters of schools to let them know the day the catechism will open, the hour at which it will begin and close, and begs them to send him, a week before the opening, the list of their children who are to attend the catechism. He advises them to separate the children who have made their first Communion from those who have not; and he adds that, if the list is only sent to him on the very day of the opening, it will be difficult for him to give the children of his school the same places which they have generally occupied.

Although the definite arrangement of places cannot be made on the first Sunday, yet the children are not to be left on that day to go where they will. This first meeting would of necessity be disorderly, and so the children would begin the habit of being disorderly at the catechism. The means employed to keep them in order, although not giving them fixed places, are as follows:—

The children belonging to the boarding or other schools are first brought into the chapel, and afterwards the free children. Each school comes in separately; it is brought in by the catechist who has the charge of the placing. As he enters the chapel, he gives out in a loud voice the name of the school which is following him: *Pension de M. N——*. Then the chief, who ought to have the plan of the forms (gummed on to a piece of cardboard) in his hand, with their numbers and the places marked out which each school generally occupies, receives this one and leads it to its place. While he is doing this, the catechist goes out of the chapel to look up another school. If one school is absent, or does not come in time for the placing, some forms would be left empty for them.

It is necessary that there should be another catechist in the chapel who by his presence would keep order there, and also be at the disposal of the chief; another at the door to prevent the free children from coming in, and finally, one in the church, to keep silence there.

But within the chapel the chief and the catechist who brings in the children ought solely to be concerned in the placing. A third catechist would only be a hindrance. It must be the chief who assigns the places, for experience has frequently shown that another catechist has not the same knowledge of the schools and their places, and the numbers of the forms, neither has he the same authority in having all the different movements promptly carried out.

When all the schools are in the chapel, the free children are brought in, and made to fill the vacant places, without any effort to separate those who are well or poorly clothed; it is a slight inconvenience, which will only last for three times.

At the close of this first meeting, the chief of the catechism, after having charged all the children to take the same places on the following Sunday, announces to them that the list of the schools is about to be read out, and the *free children* to have their names written down. (Those who do not belong to any school which takes part in the catechism are called *free children*.) The chief, speaking in a decided and commanding tone, tells the children that all, when they hear their names called, are to go out immediately, without waiting for their companions, and if any should take the liberty of going out before their names are called, will be sent away from the catechism; he demands perfect silence, and reads out in a loud voice the lists sent by the masters of schools.[1] As each child hears his name called, he gets up, and as he goes out, at the door of the chapel he is given a printed

[1] The chief should have read these lists beforehand, particularly those which may not be written very legibly, so that he may be able to read them out fluently, without hesitating or making mistakes in the names.

ticket, of this sort: *I am called* ... *I was born the* ... *of the year* ... *I live at* ... The child is to bring back this ticket on the following Sunday, after having filled it in.

While this is going on, the chief remains in his place in the sanctuary, another catechist stands in the middle of the chapel to keep order, the rest are distributed here and there to prevent any children slipping away before they have been called and entered; and finally another is at the door to prevent children running into the church. Two well-disposed children are appointed to give out the printed tickets of which we have spoken; they are practised in it beforehand. They are stationed at the door, or in whatever place is thought most convenient for this distribution.

When the schools have left, we proceed to enter the names of the *free children*. All the catechists take part in this. They ought each to be provided with a writing-case, and a card after the following pattern, not a piece of paper.

When a child presents himself to be registered, all the questions marked on the card should be put to him. The children come forward in the order in which they are sitting on the forms. After a child has been registered, he is given the ticket,[1] which he is to bring back on the following Sunday, and he is desired to go out at once, for otherwise he might be registered by another catechist.

We have already said that, to spare the feelings

[1] These tickets may be given out by two children stationed at the doors of the chapel, as has been said with regard to the schools.

OF THE CHILDREN 31

of parents and the heads of schools, we avoid placing a poorly-clothed child next to one of much higher rank, and that, without putting one grade into one quarter, and the rest into another, we so mix them that those in quite easy circumstances shall be next to those of a middle class, and these

\	CARD FOR REGISTERING THE CHILDREN.				
Day, Month, and Year of Entering.	1. What is your Family Name?	1. Your Baptismal Name?	From what School?	In what parish do you live?	Dismissal. (Here is your printed ticket. Go out at once.)
....	....	....	....	....	
....	....	....	....	....	
....	2. How is it written?	2. Have you not any other?		Have you made your first Communion?	
	....	....		....	
	....	....		....	
	3. Is it written like this?				
	....				
	....				

again next to the poorest. The knowledge of these three classes is absolutely necessary for a satisfactory placing. *Jam vero ultima columna ultima tabellæ inscriptionis inservit ad designandum ad quamnam harum trium classium pertineat unusquisque puerorum. Ideo, dum scribit nomina pueri, caute expendat catechista ipsius externum cultum, et utrum ad primam classem pertineat vel ad secundam vel ad tertiam, notabit signo de quo inter catechistas conventum fuit.*

That this registering may be done in an orderly way, the children must be dispersed in the chapel, and divided into as many small groups as there are catechists engaged in registering. It is good for them to be a little apart one from another, that the catechists may be more at liberty. The free children must be again warned not to leave the chapel before they have been registered, and if anyone is seen to leave his place, or to stand up or be restless, the chief should speak to him publicly, and beg the catechist of his group to register him after all the rest.

When all the lists sent by the masters or mistresses of schools are entered, and the list of the names on the registration cards, then the great dignitaries are chosen, and the children who are to occupy places of honour; and then we begin to draw out the plan of the placing. The number of forms which the chapel contains should be known beforehand, the number belonging to each form and the number of children it will hold, and finally the place which each school has usually the right to occupy. For making out this plan, several large sheets of paper are used, so that if a name has to be erased, or an entire form changed, there need not be a constant turning over of small leaves, but at a glance the empty places would be seen and those already filled up. As a child's name is entered on the plan, it is taken off the lists, to avoid the risk of giving him two places, but only a pencil-mark is drawn through it, so that the lists can be referred to again, if need be. In distributing the places it is well to show some favour to the old members, particularly in choosing the heads of forms, if they are known to be steady and regular.

It is not generally possible to make out the plan at once. Before it is perfect, much has to be erased, and much written. When quite completed, two copies are made; one for the chief of the catechism, the other for the catechist who superintends the placing. But as some changes have always to be made in response to entreaties, the cards for the heads of forms are not made out till the week after the plan has been announced.

Finally, on the third Sunday, the list of places is read out. As this operation always causes a certain excitement, it is kept for the end of the catechism; it is not even mentioned to the children beforehand; it would be quite enough to upset them. The chief should have provided for everything, and be in concert with the other catechists. If he should be in the least embarrassed, if the catechists should fail in firmness and vigilance, if silence should not be kept, the arrangement of places would become a scene of frightful disorder, and this would affect many meetings, for the children would get the habit of looking on the catechism as a scene of disorder and confusion. They will receive quite a different impression, and will take their places in an orderly manner, quietly and quickly, if the chief seems to know thoroughly what he is about, if he is never at all puzzled, but assigns the places with a tone of authority; and above all, if silence reigns in the catechism.

The new arrangement of places is given out as follows:—

The catechists are placed here and there in the chapel, to keep order and silence, and to exercise very strict watchfulness. The chief calls out about thirty or forty of the children seated on the forms farthest back from the altar, and lets them stand aside in the passages, or sit on any empty forms there may be. Then holding in his hand the plan of arrangement, he calls out first the number of the most distant form, then the *head of the form*, and finally the children, who come in succession to take their places as they hear their names called. The catechist who has for the year the charge of the placing holds in his hand a copy of the plan, and makes sure that the children are placed in the order indicated by the chief; then they pass on to another form, and so throughout.

If there is no place fit to receive the children who have had to leave their forms, they might be taken into the church adjoining the chapel, and they would be told to wait there till they are called to go into the chapel. A catechist would be with them to keep silence; another, who would have in his hand a second copy of the plan, would stand at the door and call them one by one; as they entered, the chief would call out their names, and the catechist superintending would put each one in his place.

When the children are all in their places, they are charged to remember the number of their form, and their own place, so that they can take the same the next Sunday ; and to make them more careful, they are warned that those who go anywhere else will be marked as absent by the *heads of the forms*, who will all have their cards the next day.

However perfect the arrangement may be, there must from time to time be some changes made ; for some of the children will leave, and new ones will come. The one catechist whose business it is to receive and register those who present themselves during the year, ought to have a memorandum book containing the arrangement, and mark in it the actual condition of the forms, and the vacant places, so that he may be able to fill them up with the new-comers. In this book he would write the names rather far apart, that he may be able to insert other names in case of need. But this is not done on the cards of the *heads of forms* ; they would soon be full of erasures, and would need to be continually renewed. A plan has been devised for making the necessary changes without having to erase anything; this is done by writing the names on separate tickets, which are fastened to the card by twine, as in the specimen we give. These tickets are of paper or very thin cardboard ; their place can be changed at will or new ones put in without being obliged to write out new cards. In this way the cards can go on from one year to another; they may last a very long time, provided that the *heads of forms* take care not to soil them.

In conclusion, we must observe that special places are appointed for the dignitaries. Every catechism being divided into several quarters, and each quarter into several forms, a dignitary called *head of the form* is placed at the head of each form; he watches over the children of his form, but his chief business is to make note of those who are absent, and those who come late; at the head of each quarter is an assistant, who keeps watch over the *heads of forms* in his quarter, and marks those who are absent from the catechism. Finally, over the whole catechism is placed an intendent, who keeps watch on assistants, and who should be alive to everything which may conduce to the good of the catechism. Concerning the dignitaries, we shall have to speak more in detail later on. In this way, all the children are under each other's *surveillance*, and the responsibility of the catechists is greatly lessened.

A rather large catechism ought to be conducted, if possible, by several catechists. At S. Sulpice, a catechism of from 200 to 400 children has usually five catechists; they ought always to appear at the catechism in their surplices;[1] one of these is the chief of the catechism. The chief is always stationed in the sanctuary; he stands, and in front of him is a chair on which he rests the portfolio which holds the children's analyses and the pictures. It is he who gives out the notices, who rebukes the children publicly, who gives the signals for their rising or sitting; and lastly, he never takes his eyes off the children: he is, as it were, the general movement of the catechism, the centre to which

[1] Catechista amictus superpelliceo. *Decretal. synodal. diocesis Augustanæ*, anno 1610.

everything converges. The other catechists are stationed at the different points of the catechism; their seats are rather high, so that from them they can command the quarter assigned to them by the chief. They do not speak publicly in the catechism except when they are in the pulpit.

CHAPTER III

GENERAL EXERCISES OF THE CATECHISM

ARTICLE I

Of Hymns to be sung

EXPERIENCE teaches us that to keep children attentive, there must be a great deal of variety in the catechism. With this view a whole series of different exercises has been devised, which succeed each other without interruption, only separated by hymns. Singing, when conducted in this way, contributes very much to the success of the catechism. "We must consider that children's brains are weak, that because of their age they are only alive to pleasure, and yet a correctness and seriousness is often expected of them by those who would themselves be incapable of it."[1] Besides, what is more likely to disgust and weary the children than this constant repetition of the same things, which must always be in the exercise of the catechism? To remedy this difficulty, the venerable César de Bus introduced the singing of hymns; S. François de

[1] Fénelon, *Education des Filles*, ch. v.

Sales did the same, and from time to time, to rejoice with a holy joy the hearts of the children he was catechising, he had the hymns sung to the accompaniment of the organ. In the Life of this holy bishop written by Auguste de Sales, he says, with reference to this: "The holy bishop generally took turns with his canons in the work of catechising. An hour having passed, some devout hymn was sung, sometimes with the voices alone, sometimes with the accompaniment of the organ; this hymn was composed by the blessed man himself, or some other: certain it is that as a kind of recreation, he sometimes gave his mind to this sort of poetry, or else he would choose one of David's psalms, and hand it to the musician to put a tune to it."[1]

Another advantage of singing hymns is that it teaches and edifies the children in a pleasant way. "It was by the pleasure of verse and music," says Fénélon,[2] "that the chief sciences, maxims of virtue, and politeness of manners were introduced among the Hebrews, the Egyptians, and the Greeks. People who are not well-read will hardly believe it, it is so different from our ways; still, it needs but a slight knowledge of history to be quite certain that this was the common practice for several centuries." It is certain at least that the Church in adopting this custom desired to provide for the faithful, and specially for the children, a way of instruction which would be easy, and at the same

[1] *Histoire de S. François de Sales*, by Charles Auguste de Sales, his nephew, in 4to, 1634, p. 283.
[2] *Education des Filles*, ch. v.

time excite in their hearts ardent and high thoughts towards goodness. S. Francis Xavier composed hymns for the use of catechumens, and set to music the Lord's Prayer, the angelic salutation, and the Apostles' Creed. The author of his Life says that by this means he not only banished all the bad songs which these new Christians had known before their baptism, but also provided his flock with a new means of edification. "For the hymns of the holy missionary so delighted men, women, and children that they sang them day and night in their houses and in the fields."[1] S. Carlo Borromeo produced similar effects at Milan, by the hymns which he had sung in his catechisms. M. Alain de Solminiaque, Bishop of Cahors, put the divine commandments into verse, and also the Apostles' Creed and the *Exercice du Chrétien*, for the use of the people whom he catechised. Finally, singing hymns helps to keep order and silence under certain circumstances, where otherwise there would inevitably be restlessness and confusion, such as in the change from one exercise to another, or in going away. Those who are accustomed to the catechism know that when an exercise has come to an end, the children make a confused sort of noise, such as one hears in churches after the first point of the sermon; they take their books, they look out their hymns, they sometimes ask questions of their neighbours or even of the catechists, as if, satisfied with their previous attention, they were now trying to make up for it. A similar thing must happen when they are going

[1] *Vie de S. François Xavier*, by Père Bonhours.

away from the catechism, because they get up together, form by form, and defile into the passages while other children are leaving their forms to follow them, and others again are behind them. At such times hymns are always sung by the children; the singing covers the noise, it hardly lets them be aware of the inevitable confusion, and by this pious device they are led to believe that the catechism is always calm and collected.

Article II

The Entry into the Chapel

Experience proves that the way the children come into the chapel often gives the character to the whole meeting, and that if the children come to the catechism in a disorderly manner, it is almost impossible to bring them back to quietness and attention. It is therefore a good plan to have a certain place assigned in the church, where the children may gather, and wait in silence for the signal for the general entry. At the given signal they all get up together, and, walking quietly two and two, they come into their chapel, and go each to their place, never taking the liberty of climbing over the forms. During this entry, the catechists ought to be extremely vigilant, keeping their eyes on the children, that they may maintain order and prevent any frivolity.

During the entry, the catechist who superintends the singing gives to the chief of the catechism a piece of paper on which is clearly written the order and page of every hymn which is to be sung that day; he himself keeping a duplicate to direct the choir.[1] This memorandum varies according to the exercises; it is generally made out in the following way:—

```
       LIST OF HYMNS FOR THE......SUNDAY OF......

   After the prayer       .    .    .    .   . Page......
   Before the instruction .    .    .    .   . Page......
   After the instruction  .    .    .    .   . Page......
   After the homily       .    .    .    .   . Page......
   At the departure       .    .    .    .   . Page......
```

As soon as the children have taken their places, the chief says a few words to them, reminding them of the reverence with which they should join in the prayer, which begins the exercises; then he strikes three times with a wooden book, called a *claquoir*;[2] at the first the children stand, at the second they bow to the altar, at the third they kneel down. Then a catechist, kneeling on the altar step, says the prayer, clearly and solemnly. Meanwhile the other catechists keep special watch over the children, to

---

[1] This piece of paper the chief fastens with a pin to the covering of his chair; without this precaution, he would run the risk of mislaying it, and of not being able immediately to give out the hymns.

[2] This book, which is about 8 or 9 inches broad, and about $3\frac{1}{2}$ or 4 inches long, opens by means of a hinge at the back, the two parts of the book ought to be of equal thickness.

prevent any of them from lounging on the forms, or disturbing their neighbours. When the prayer is ended the chief again strikes three times on the *claquoir*; at the first the children stand up, at the second they bow to the altar, and at the third they sit down; and as soon as they are seated, he gives out clearly the page of the hymn, of which they are to sing two or three verses.

Article III

Questioning

After the children have sung three or four verses, and immediately on the conclusion of the last, the chief makes several claps with the *claquoir*, which is the signal agreed on for stopping the singing, and then begins either the *questioning* or the repetition of the diocesan catechism. This recitation, which is uninteresting to the catechist, and wearisome to the children, if done in a dry and monotonous manner, can become interesting and even amusing if it is conducted by a catechist who has a bright and cheerful manner, and who knows when and where to give praise or blame, and how to awake the emulation of the children.

The questioning is done as follows in the catechisms of S. Sulpice:—

While the hymn which follows the prayer is being sung, the catechist whose business it is to conduct the questioning goes into the pulpit, prepares the book in which is the lesson the children have learnt, and also the catalogue in which the children's names are written according to the order of the forms.[1] As soon as the hymn is finished, he names a child, always calling him by his baptismal name as well as his surname. The child immediately stands up, makes the sign of the cross, saying the words aloud, and answers the questions of the catechism.[2]

It is important to study the names in the catalogue and to know by heart the places they occupy, so as to be able to pronounce them correctly and to find them at once. If the catechist mispronounces the name, his audience will of course begin to titter, and the children themselves for no fault will feel mortified, and sometimes it will even inspire them with a secret dislike for the catechism. If a child has a ridiculous name, it should not be said openly; better to put a question on purpose to his neighbour, or to the two next to him, and when they have both answered, then simply to say "*the next.*"

When a child does not answer, the catechist ought generally to pass on to another without repeating the question, making in the catalogue a bad mark for the child who did not answer. If it became a habit to repeat the questions, the children would very soon take advantage of this indulgence, and the questioning would take up an endless time. If

[1] This catalogue ought to be of cardboard, and folded into parts, like the large altar-cards.

[2] "Formato signo crucis et prolatis alta voce verbis, eam catechismi partem quæ assignate fuerit recitabunt" (S. François de Sales, *Mod. Catechismi Opuscules*, vol ii. p. 29).

REPETITION OF THE CATECHISM

the children do not know their lessons, they must never be allowed to excuse themselves aloud, or to answer in any way whatsoever. Such a liberty would very soon degenerate into bad temper and impertinence. It is for the catechist who is nearest the child to listen to his whispered excuse, and to repeat it aloud if he thinks proper.

The children should not be questioned in alphabetical order, nor in the order of the forms, lest the other children should be less attentive, thinking themselves far removed. But the questions should be put sometimes in one quarter, sometimes in another, pass suddenly from one form to another, and thus keep all the children on the alert. Therefore the questioning must be quick, lively, and animated; the catechist, while he is questioning one child, must be prepared with the name of the next he means to question; there must always be someone speaking, either the catechist questioning, or the children answering. To keep the questioning animated, it is absolutely necessary to have the questions ready. And it was for this reason that the ancient rules of S. Sulpice exacted that the catechists should learn them by heart, and never make use of a book.

In large catechisms two or three questions are asked of each child, if the answers are short; but if they are long, such as those which contain the *acts*, only one question is asked, so that a greater number of children may be asked. The same children should not be questioned too often; still, particularly in the little catechisms, a child who has not answered well may be questioned a second time, to see if he remembers the answer which another has given. And a child may be asked again if it is a difficult question, such as only the most advanced could answer. This privilege granted to the most forward and the steadiest may lead the others to be more attentive, so that they in their turn may deserve to be questioned oftener.

If idle or rude children are questioned, or conceited children, whom it is necessary to humble, and they should answer badly, it is well to reprove them severely, to make them feel the necessity of being steady, well-behaved, and attentive; if they give good answers, they should be immediately given a question which they cannot answer, and then tell them there are many things they do not yet know, but that they can learn, if they listen attentively, and are very constant at the catechism. If, on the other hand, shy children are being questioned, they should not be discouraged by being blamed too sharply. Sometimes it is a good thing to help them, giving them the first word of the answer, and even saying a few words of encouragement: "I am satisfied with you. You know it very well; you are only too shy to say it well." "Give a little praise and encouragement to those who are naturally timid," says M. de la Chétardie; "never let them get confused, so that they should be laughed at.[1] When you want to begin to make a little child speak and answer, and you want to give him a little courage, first put the question you are going to ask him to two or three

[1] *Catéchisme de Bourges*, vol. i. Avis, pt. ii. No. 7.

WAYS OF EXCITING EMULATION 47

others who are more advanced, and after they have answered well, then put it to the child to whom you want to give confidence, praise his answer a little, give him some little prize, then let another child speak who does not answer so well, and then again return to the first."

Another way of encouraging a timid child, is to give him a very simple question, one to which he has only to answer yes or no, and then immediately give him a word of praise.

In the catechisms of S. Sulpice three ways are employed to excite the emulation of the children during the questioning, and to make the exercise interesting—praise, good numbers, and the game of good points *(jeu de bons points)*. An intelligent catechist, and perhaps even slightly humorous, can make the questioning very pleasant, praising and blaming at the right moment, criticising the children's way of reciting, whether too low or too high; setting up a sort of rivalry or opposition between the children of different quarters, or different schools, between the attentive and inattentive; in throwing out a sort of challenge as to the one who will answer the best. For example: "This is a child who is a credit to his school.—This child apparently is afraid of irritating his chest; his mother has forbidden him to speak loud.—This child does not want to make his first Communion.—A little louder; remember you are speaking for the whole catechism to hear.—If this child does not speak louder, I must go on to another.—I am not surprised that this child knows nothing; he does not know (or has forgotten) how to make the sign of the cross." These remarks from time to time, which by the tone and manner of the questioner may be made exceedingly lively, wonderfully excite the emulation of the children, and stir them up to do well. By these means, childish as they are in themselves, almost incredible results may be obtained; sometimes you may see three or four hundred children keeping the most profound silence, sitting as if in suspense, each holding himself ready to answer immediately, if he is questioned; and when they have answered, they look joyful and radiant, resolving to do better still the following Sunday.

The announcing the number which each child has gained by his recitation, which is immediately written opposite his name on the list, contributes also to make the questioning bright and interesting; No. 5 is given to one who has recited very well; No. 4 to one who has done well, but not so well as the first; No. 3 to him who only repeated pretty well; No. 2 to one who recites badly; and No. 1 to him who recites very badly. No. 5 is very rarely given; it is always spoken of as of great value; the child must know his lesson perfectly well, and the answers must be the longest and most difficult. When it has been given, it is often referred to as of importance. It is a triumph to have gained it, and this is a case where a successful rivalry can be set up between two schools. But still, with a child that one has to be careful about, or is anxious to win over, one may sometimes be very indulgent, and only give him very short and very easy questions;

Article IV

The Game of "Le bon point"

The game of *le bon point*, one of the pleasantest exercises of the catechism, and one that is of the greatest profit to the children, gives great interest to the questioning. By the game of *le bon point* the secret has been found of constantly repeating to them the truths which we desire to engrave in their memory, and yet without wearying them by this repetition. It consists in proposing to one of the children, who has won No. 4 or No. 5,[1] a series of short, clear, and definite questions upon a mystery, or a proof, or some fundamental truth of religion. The questions are put one after another to the child, according to his capacity, and in a lively, animated way, as if a kind of challenge. There results from this a sort of combat, in which sometimes a clever child is pressed almost further than he can go; and when the chief knows how to keep up the interest, all the audience may be seen taking part, their attention redoubled, and they almost

---

[1] "Prior consignabit responsuros et disputatores, eligetque semper perspicaciores et magis idoneos" (S. François de Sales, *Mod. Catechismi Opuscules*, vol. ii. p. 27).

holding their breath in the uncertainty of the victory. Sometimes the chief is unwilling to grant the good point; then the catechist who is conducting the questioning intercedes for the child; the chief seems to resist, and the catechist persists, but always deferentially; and finally, as may be supposed, the child, to the great joy of the catechism, wins the day, and receives *le bon point*. This is the name given to a small card, on which is engraved the monogram of Mary. The children who have won three of them, or the dignitaries two, can change them for a print. If the child answers badly, he loses the *bon point*, and he is advised to redouble his attention, so that he may be more fortunate when next he is questioned.

The chief of the catechism plays the game of *le bon point* between himself and a child; but sometimes, for the sake of variety, he sets up a sort of battle between several champions. He begins by putting a question to one of the children he can depend on, and as soon as he has answered his question rightly, he calls the name of a child who is far behind the first, and changes his tone a little, giving the impression that the first child has answered wrongly. In the little catechisms the second child will almost always give just the contrary answer to the first. In the greater catechisms he puts the question to an ignorant child, who, he feels sure, will give a wrong answer. Then he calls for a third child, one of the most forward, and tells him to say which of the two has answered best. If he says the first child, the chief puts a new question to him and then to the first child, and then another question, till at last one of the two answers wrongly; and then he gives the good point to the one who remains the victor. In general, if the children give different answers, the catechist should not be in a hurry to resolve the difficulty himself. So M. de la Chétardie recommends, and he adds: "It will keep them still in suspense. . . . You will be better listened to when after a little time you tell them what they ought to believe; so it is better to hold back your decision."

For the success of the game of *le bon point* it is important to prepare beforehand and to write down the questions which are to be put to the children, even the commonest ones. Without this precaution, which the most experienced catechists do not dispense with, the questions would not be clear enough for the child to understand them immediately, nor definite enough for him to answer correctly. It is related of the venerable César de Bus, that he carefully prepared the questions which he meant to ask in his catechisms. "As he was humble and prudent," says the author of his Life, "he took nothing with him for public use but what he had prepared in his closet and meditated on in his oratory, and above all for those sort of instructions in which great exactness is necessary.[1] He was not only careful to prepare himself, his foresight led him also to prepare specially the children who would have to answer his questions in public."

[1] *Vie de César de Bus*, p. 85.

It is also necessary that the catechist during the game of *le bon point* should be completely master of himself, have a perfect freedom of mind and great cheerfulness of heart, in order to keep up the interest of this exercise; for the success of the game of the good point demands that the catechist shall not hurry, shall not say too much, that he shall be glad when the child answers well, that he shall be skilful in taking advantage of right and clear answers, enhancing their value by repeating them word for word, distinctly and intelligibly, giving a somewhat higher meaning to them; he should also cleverly fill in any small thing lacking, so that the children will be quite surprised that they answered so well. Also he should be able to say his questions, and give them in a lively, striking manner, if the child's answers should give occasion for it. And all this demands in the catechist a great freedom of mind and heart; and it is necessary for him also, so that he may have his eye on the whole catechism while he is speaking, and keep order.

The way to gain this freedom is to accustom oneself to have nothing in view but the will of God, and to be above being troubled by any failures which may arise. If the catechist is annoyed after some blunder which may have been remarked upon, if he is vexed when the children are inattentive or answer badly, he will never be in a condition to do much good in a catechism. "This is of extreme importance, for," as we read in the old regulations of S. Sulpice, "the devil never fails to disturb and discourage a catechist; he distracts the children with all sorts of other things, and at the same time tempts the catechist so strongly to annoyance and impatience, particularly when he has something very important to say, that unless he is on his guard against snares, he is in danger of doing no good at all, but of leaving the victory to his enemy."

The game of *le bon point* is then most perfect when the child says much and the catechist says little. "If you make long speeches," says M. de la Chétardie, "the children will be wearied, they will be tired, they will go to sleep, they will behave badly, and they will learn nothing." Inexperienced catechists fancy that if they are to be of use to the children they must tell them every good thing they know. But they will soon find out that the children, being incapable of remembering these long speeches or of understanding them, will, while this sort of talking is going on, only try how they can amuse themselves and distract each other. "A good catechist is not one who speaks the best and the oftenest, but one who can question well."

It is important always to repeat the same things to the children, to give them the same definitions, the same proofs, and almost always in the same words. "By this means they will answer boldly, easily, quickly, and even enjoy it. They will become accustomed to doctrinal language, and as they grow older, their knowledge will increase, and will be further expanded by sermons, by reading and reflection; they will find the echo in themselves of what they hear or read. For instance, suppose you should ask them, *What is the Decalogue?* and they would answer, *It is the abridgement of the law of God, contained in ten commandments,* never let them vary, always make them answer in the same terms. It would seem that it would be better to vary the questions every day, to use different words, to go out of one's ordinary groove, because, it is said, otherwise the children will only speak like parrots, and if they go to another catechism they will know nothing. But experience shows that this is a mistake, and constrains us to see that by this changing and frequent alteration we put out of the child's mind one day what on a former day we put into it; we build up and we destroy; their memory gets confused, their ideas run into each other, they no longer know what to hold by, what to believe or what to say; in short, they no longer remember anything, their knowledge is all confusion and uncertainty, and they are vexed to seem not to know or to understand what they are questioned about."

Moreover, by this means, the catechists maintain uniformity in the various catechisms; and the children, passing from a little catechism to a higher, will not be altogether new to the questions they hear put in their new catechism. Finally, by constantly hearing these questions, the children have them impressed on their memory without effort and almost without knowing it; and it is surprising at the end of the year, to find a great number calmly explaining proofs and somewhat difficult mysteries, which, without any effort, they have got stored in their memories.

When the questioning is finished, the lesson which is to be recited on the following Sunday is given out; and, so that no one can pretend ignorance, one child and then another is asked what is the lesson which has just been given, and they are made to speak out, so that every one can hear them.

Article V

Recitation of the Gospel

After the questioning the exercise called the Recitation of the Gospel follows. From the time that the children begin to attend the catechisms, if they know how to read, they are encouraged to learn the Gospels by heart. S. Jerome says that at seven years old they should be brought to this: that they should constantly have the book in their hands, and let it be their constant nourishment and the treasure of their hearts.[1] At S. Sulpice they are very zealous in learning the Gospel; indeed there are boys who recite it every Sunday in French, Latin, and Greek.

---

[1] *S. Hieronym ad Gaudentium de Pacatulæ infantulæ educatione.* Quum septimus annus exceperit, et cæperit erubescere, discat memoriter evangelia, sui cordis thesaurum faciat.

The children who have learned the Gospel must give to the head of their form a small piece of paper called Notice for the Gospel, as below :—

> CHARLES GOSSIN knows the Gospel for the second Sunday after the Epiphany.

> JULES ÉMERIC knows the Gospel for the first Sunday in Advent, *in Latin and in Greek*.

The catechist who superintends the Recitation of the Gospels keeps these notices in his hand and calls out one and another of the children, each reciting a few lines of the Gospel, the next taking it up at the place where the first leaves off. Then the little *Catéchisme historique* is recited by those who have sent in their notices for this recitation.

As the recitation of the Gospel is not compulsory, it is well to encourage the children who send in notices of reciting. One good number is given to those who have learnt it in French, two good numbers to those who have learnt it in Latin, and three to those who repeated it in Greek. All these numbers are marked on the great register, and at the end of the year prizes for the Gospel are distributed to the children who have shown the greatest zeal in this exercise. If it is discovered that a child has given in a notice without having learnt the Gospel, the notice is publicly torn up, and all the good numbers he may have won from

ON THE ANALYSES

the beginning of the year are taken away from him. If a child comes late, or is inattentive, or does not speak loud enough, he is punished by not being allowed to recite the Gospel.

Article VI

Report of the Analyses (Diligences)

After the recitation the chief gives the report of the analyses of the instruction, which the children have brought written out. A great deal of interest should be shown about these, and the great seal and the lesser seals spoken of as of importance. Sometimes he may begin by the lower seals, so that the interest will increase as he goes on. Various things will provide him with occasions for praising the industry of the children, or of reproving them, or of lamenting the small number of analyses. He can also take up and explain in few words any questions which have not been well treated of in the analyses. We may observe in passing that the analyses will be all the better just in proportion as the division of the instruction has been methodical, the manner simple, the reasoning clear, the speaking not hurried, and repetitions frequent. All children are not capable of making analyses, but they all profit by them if the chief of the catechism takes care to read out some of the most striking passages, and to remark on what is best without naming the children.[1] See chap. v. art. ii.

Article VII

Of the Instruction

When the chief of the catechism has finished the report of the analyses, he gives out a hymn for the children, and the choir immediately starts it. While this hymn is being sung, the catechist who is to give the instruction goes into the pulpit, and begins to speak when the chief gives the signal. If he sees any confusion in the catechism, he waits a few moments and says: "I cannot begin till all the children are attending."

This instruction is simply the explanation of the lesson in the diocesan catechism, which the children have learnt by heart. It is the principal and fundamental exercise of all catechisms. The other exercises may have their use, but this is indispensable and essential; it is also very difficult. In fact it is a difficult thing to hold the attention of a number of giddy, volatile children for half an hour, and to keep them to so serious a subject as morals or religion. It is difficult to adapt the most abstract

[1] In the little catechisms the name of a child may be sometimes given, as an encouragement to him; and if it is thought fitting, the same may be done in the catechisms of first Communion. But if a prayer or a resolution is read out, no name is given, and it is well for the children to know this.

truths and the most sublime mysteries to the capacity of children, to impress them on their mind, and to make them so dear to their heart that they will be persuaded to make them the rule of their conduct. Thus it is easier to find a good preacher than a good catechist.

As this matter is of extreme importance, we find it necessary to treat of it separately in the following chapter. We will merely now say in passing, that the greater part of the instruction should be suited to the larger part of the audience; and for attaining this object one thing is quite necessary—that the tone used for familiar conversation should be adopted in the instruction. "We naturally," says Fleury, "speak in short sentences, and children much more so than others. They cannot take in many ideas at once, nor grasp the relations between them; they do not speak continuously, but in short sentences. And in speaking to them we should imitate this, and speak in short and clear sentences."[1] Nevertheless, though simple, the instruction must be given in a way which will interest the children. The great art is to be at ease oneself, to look frank and pleasant, though dignified and quiet; the tones and gestures should be natural, varied from time to time to arouse attention. Thus the children will themselves be at their ease, and their mind and heart gladly open to receive. Questions should be frequent, and the form in which the questions are put varied, but always clear, bright, and pleasant. Sometimes their curiosity must be excited by certain original ways of

[1] *Catéchisme Historique*, Preliminary Discourse.

putting things, which will keep them, so to speak, in suspense. The catechist can surprise and refresh them pleasantly with unexpected sallies and repartees, not being afraid sometimes to provoke a smile, though with all his brightness still preserving a quiet and becoming manner. Sometimes he can propose little cases of conscience, giving a wrong decision sometimes on purpose, that he may be set right by the children. In short, what we have said about the game of the good point may be applied equally to the instruction, and the catechist should remember that the judgment which children form on religion depends in great measure on the way they are taught it. Here, as in many other things, *the form carries with it the fundamental thing* (*la forme emporte le fond*).

If the method we have shown is followed, the children will be delighted to come to the catechism. At S. Sulpice, far from not liking to be questioned, their emulation is greatly excited, and they ask for it eagerly, and many complain and feel much hurt that they are only so rarely questioned.

Article VIII

Notices and the Homily

After the instruction, which should always end with a practical resolution, the catechist leaves the pulpit and the children sing a hymn. The chief then gives his notices, unless he has done so before the instruction.

The notices are of great importance; one may even say that all the success of the catechism depends on the way in which the chief gives them out. This is his time for speaking of the progress of the children, of the pleasure they are giving to their catechists, of their diligence, their absences, etc. Then he reminds them of certain points of rule which they have neglected; he announces the festivals which will occur in the week, and the days of fasting or abstinence; he commends the sick children to the prayers of the catechism, and also such persons as the children ask to be prayed for. In every catechism there should be a collection of notices ready prepared; and further, the chief should note down in a little book those he means to give, so that nothing essential may be omitted.

When the chief has finished his notices, he gives out a hymn, which will prepare the children for the homily.

The catechist who has to give the homily then kneels down on the altar step, and afterwards goes into the pulpit. In his hand is the book of the Gospels in French, his finger at the place which is to be the subject of the homily, and which he will read first of all. When the chief has stopped the singing of the hymn by two or three little strokes of the *claquoir*, he strikes one loud blow, which is the signal for the children (if they are sitting) to stand up. The catechist who is in the pulpit, standing, reads aloud the Gospel for the day. The reading ended, the children sit down ; the catechist puts his book on the pulpit desk, and, still standing, gives them a clear, forcible, urgent and moving address. It should not last more than half a quarter of an hour. We will speak of this more fully in another special chapter.

Article IX

Good Marks and Departure of the Catechism

After the homily, each catechist gives the names of two children who have been specially remarkable for their attention and quietness throughout; the chief names three, and each one receives a good point. Children who have gained three good points, and the dignitaries who have gained two, may then exchange them for a small engraving.

In general, the chief then calls out three children who have been chosen on the preceding Sunday to recite the Acts of the theological virtues. They immediately leave their forms, and having done so, the signal is given for the children to kneel down. The appointed children each recite one Act, and the catechist who said the *prayer before the catechism* also says the concluding prayer. M. de la Chétardie speaks thus of the importance and the advantage of this custom : " Take care that your children learn by heart acts of faith, of hope, of charity, of contrition, of adoration, etc., and make them recite

DEPARTURE OF THE CHILDREN

them aloud every Sunday. The smallest children can do this. For besides that all the faithful are bound in conscience often to make these acts, the children will be thinking about them all the week in their anxiety to say them well the following Sunday; the parents will like to listen to them at home, their family are edified and come to hear them in the church, and this is a great encouragement."

After the prayer the chief signs to the children to sit, and gives out the hymn which is to be sung while they are going out. They go out form by form; the signal is given to two or three forms at once, more or less, according to the width of the passages and the size of the entrance door. While this goes on the chief speaks to no one. If anyone comes to interrupt him, he simply asks him to wait till every one is gone out, and he goes on giving the signals with the *claquoir* without keeping the children waiting, and without allowing the least gap in the lines formed by the departing children. During the departure a catechist must stand at the door, to keep the children in proper order and quietness.

CHAPTER IV

ON THE INSTRUCTION OF THE CHILDREN

FAITH is necessary to salvation; and yet can we hide from ourselves the fact that there are a very great number of Christians in whom faith does not exist? How many are there, forty or fifty years old, who, all their lives, have repeated mechanically forms of prayer, acts of faith, hope, and charity, without understanding anything about them? who neither know what faith is, nor what they ought to believe, nor why they must believe! . . . A pastor who knows his duties and seeks the salvation of his flock does not confine himself to making the children learn the letter of the catechism; he deems himself strictly obliged to give them a definite knowledge of the mysteries of the faith, and of eternal life; and to instruct them in the full meaning of the creed, the sacraments, the commandments, etc. However clear and simple a catechism may be, its style, its expressions are all quite different from the language the children speak. They will hardly find in it any words which are familiar to them, or, if they do find them, they will not have the same meaning to them. How, then, can they

ON INSTRUCTION OF THE CHILDREN 65

understand, unless they are given clear explanations suited to their capacity? and what use will it be to them to know the catechism by heart, if its explanation is not made clear to them?

A child who knows his catechism by heart, but yet would not understand the things he has learned if they were put to him in other terms, could not be considered to know his religion. But efforts are not always crowned with success; and then one is discouraged, and tempted to think that it is not possible to get ideas of spiritual things into minds so limited and so material; never suspecting that it is perhaps less the fault of the audience than of the catechist, and that there are very few children or ignorant people who are not capable of being solidly instructed, if the instruction is adapted to their capacity. "Experience shows," says Bossuet, "that if anyone sets himself to it in earnest, and, while exciting in his hearers a desire to learn, shows that he is always ready to teach them, he may bring them on greatly in the knowledge of God. There are certain villages which, simply through having had some good curés who have devoted themselves to their instruction, have made most surprising progress in Christian doctrine; so that, when so much is said about the people being incapable, it is to be feared that this is a mere pretext for excusing oneself from the trouble of teaching them. It is true that it does demand taking a great deal of trouble."[1]

The catechist who would really instruct his

[1] *Catéchisme de Meaux*, Avertissement.

audience should, in the exercise called *instruction*, which is nothing else than the explanation of one or more lessons of the catechism, observe three principal things, namely, brevity, clearness, and decisive proofs.

Article I

The Qualities necessary for the Instruction; Brevity and Clearness

Lengthiness in instruction, a common fault, comes generally from lack of preparation. If the catechist has not given a fitting preparation to his instruction, he easily falls into vagueness, he says nothing definite, he continually repeats himself, and goes over again what he has said; it is generally this which makes the instructions so long. This fault was common among preachers in the time of S. François de Sales, and this holy bishop complained of it as one of the greatest hindrances to the effects of preaching. "When the vine makes much wood," he said, "then it bears less fruit."[1] He said also, when a discourse is too long, the end puts out of your mind the middle, and the middle the beginning. It must be added that brevity is, above all things, necessary in instructions given to children; their mind is like a vessel with a very narrow opening, which can only be filled drop by

[1] *Le Guide de ceux qui annoncent la parole de Dieu*, p. 81.

drop. If the instruction is to be of any use, they must be told very little at a time. "Believe me," the same saint says to the Bishop of Belley, "that it is from experience—and from long experience—that I tell you this: The more you tell them, the less they will retain; the less you tell them, the more they will profit by it: if the memory of the audience is too heavily loaded, it breaks down, just as too much oil extinguishes lamps, and over-watering chokes plants. . . . Quite ordinary preachers will be acceptable, if they are short; while excellent ones are a burden if they are too long." The same must be said of catechists; and, for this reason, the Council of Trent, in the decree which imposes on all pastors the duty of instructing their people on Sundays and festivals, recommends brevity and clearness in the instructions.[1]

Clearness is another quality essential to a good instruction. Clearness results from simplicity in the thoughts, in their natural and distinct expression, and in the preciseness of the method. If the thoughts are obscure to the hearer, if the expressions only give him a vague or dark idea, if there is confusion in the order of the thoughts, it is impossible for the instruction to be clear.

To make sure of the clearness of his thoughts, the catechist needs not only himself to grasp what he

[1] Concil. Trident, sess. v. cap. ii.: "Quicunque parochiales, vel alias curam animarum habentes Ecclesias . . . per se vel alios idoneos . . . diebus saltem Dominicis et festis solemnibus plebes sibi commissas pro sua et earum capacitate pascant salutaribus verbis, docendo quæ scire omnibus necessarium est ad salutem, annuntiandoque eis *cum brevitate* et facilitate sermonis vitia . . . virtutes," etc.

wishes to say, and be able to give an account of it to himself; in order to express himself clearly, he must also put himself in the place of the hearer; he must get rid of his own ideas, and adopt those which, according to his age, his education, and his instruction, his hearer is likely to have, and then calmly examine if it is likely that he will grasp what he means to make him understand. This should be done even when the truth is so clearly explained that it would seem impossible not to understand it.[1]

It would be useless to set before children thoughts which are clear and suitable to their age, if difficult words are used to express them; for instance, if one were to use figurative expressions, which are not in common use, because the greater number of young children do not know the relation which exists between the reality and the figure.[2] All grand words should equally be avoided; children do not understand them. Moreover, the catechism is a familiar instruction; the catechist should, therefore, speak quite simply, without assumption, without exaggeration.

[1] *Quintil.* lib. viii. c. ii.: "Non ut intelligere possit, sed ne omnino non intelligere, curandum."

[2] One should avoid, therefore, this way of speaking: *the intoxication of the passions, the light of faith, the edifice of perfection, the tribunal of penitence.* Not that in making things intelligible to children, we may not use similitudes; we may compare the passions to intoxication, faith to a light, perfection to an edifice, penitence to a tribunal; but we are speaking now of figurative expressions, which must not be confounded with comparisons. Figurative expressions presuppose a knowledge in the hearer; while comparisons often give that knowledge.

He also should be equally careful to avoid technical expressions which are in use among the learned, but which ordinary people do not understand; he should confine himself to explaining to the children any words of this kind which occur in the diocesan catechism, but he should not teach them any new ones. Thus, if he is speaking of the different kinds of grace, after having divided grace into *actual* and *habitual*, according to the method of the catechism, let him not go on to subdivide actual grace into *prevenient*, *concomitant*, and *subsequent*, but let him express the same ideas without using words which want explaining; let him rather say: " Grace, or the help of God, is necessary for us, not only while we are performing our actions, so that we may do them piously; but without this help of God we could not even begin or finish them with any profit for our salvation. For this reason, good Christians make the sign of the cross at the beginging and end of their chief actions." For the same reason, such terms as *principle, consequence, essence*, should be avoided; and generally all abstract terms, which convey no idea to the children, excepting always such as occur in the diocesan catechism, which they have to learn by heart. In short, the general rule for the teacher is to avoid all words which convey nothing to the hearers. He ought to be all the more careful to say nothing which is not quite clear, because those who are listening are not at liberty to interrupt him and ask for an explanation; for, in public instruction, it is not the custom to interrupt, neither would it be fitting to interrupt the catechist by asking him questions.

The catechist, therefore, who desires thoroughly to instruct his children, will not confine himself to forming a clear and precise idea of what he wishes to teach them. He will seek for the best and easiest ways of imparting the knowledge to them, for what is clear in itself is not always so for minds which are still unformed and uncultured. Children, and people whose minds are limited, have their own way of seeing and hearing. If a teacher does not study their mind and their character with the view of discovering their ideas; if he does not set himself to see how they use words, what meaning they give to them, examining even if certain expressions convey any idea to their minds, he will run the risk of not being understood, even when he is speaking quite clearly. Still, to be understood by children, "it is not necessary," says Fleury, "to speak in bad grammar as they do, nor to use their jokes or their proverbs; the majesty of religion and respect for the word of God must always be preserved." The catechist ought to be simple; but he can be so without speaking in low and vulgar language. Let him avoid grand words, and long and confused sentences; let him speak in a natural tone; let him show evidently that he feels what he is trying to inspire the children with, and he will certainly be listened to and understood. But yet, if he sees that certain essential words are not known by the children, he can take those which they have themselves employed, or which he knows to be in use

METHOD IMPORTANT IN INSTRUCTION

among them, if there is nothing offensive in them; he can say them after he has used the right words; they will then serve as definitions, and the children will understand without any more being said.

We must further remark that there are many words, so necessary and so familiar, that it never occurs to us that the children do not understand them, while in reality they attach no meaning to them at all, or else a wrong meaning. Such, for example, are the words, *attention, distraction, intention, thought, desires:* and such expressions as these, *to do everything for God, to give one's heart to God,* and a thousand similar ones. A catechist therefore should be well on his guard not to use them without being sure they will be understood; otherwise, it would be better to use a paraphrase which would express clearly what they mean. Those whose business it is to instruct ignorant people cannot pay too much attention to this. Their instructions are often useless, because they employ these terms, very clear and full of meaning to educated people, but which awake no ideas in those of whom we are speaking, or only wrong ideas.

There is nothing which so helps the preacher, nothing which makes him more useful, or gives more pleasure to the hearers, than *method*.

Method demands, in the first place, that the subject be precisely divided. For this, it must be grasped in all its extent, it must be thoroughly gone into, and its nature clearly apprehended. Then the division will be complete and distinct; it will be complete, because it is all taken in and no essential part left out; it will be distinct in its parts, not divided where there is no distinction; merely divided where there is a real separation of subject. Too detailed a division should be avoided. A combination of fragments and morsels would be the result, rather than of parts and members.

"To help you in this," says S. François de Sales, "I may tell you that every mystery may be considered under these three points: *Who? For what? How? Who rose again?* Our Lord. *Why?* For His glory and for our good. *How?* Glorious and immortal. *Who was born?* The Saviour? *Why?* To save us. *How?* Poor, naked, cold, in a stable, a little infant."

It is not enough for the instruction to be methodical in itself, the children also must perceive the method, and follow the catechist by the help of the division. "I quite approve of the method being clear and evident," says again S. François de Sales, "and I blame those who think they do a clever thing in concealing their method. What, I ask you, is the use of a method, if it is not evident, and if the hearer knows nothing of it?"

In order that the hearer may easily understand the division, it must be given out clearly and briefly, that is to say, with only necessary words, and without any circumlocutions. In the catechisms of S. Sulpice, after the division of the instruction has been given out, one or two children are made to repeat it, and in this way it is found whether or no they have grasped it. If they have not understood, the children are so completely upset that they think it a useless trouble to go on taking notes. A catechist who one day forgot to announce the division of his instruction, so distressed the children who were taking notes, that one of them began to cry aloud. The chief, who saw what was the cause of this sorrow, gave out the division of the instruction, and immediately joy lighted up every face. Another time a child of nine, belonging to the little catechism for girls, seeing that the catechist had forgotten to give out the division of the instruction, had the boldness to stand up and interrupt him by reminding him of his omission; but, and this is equally worthy of remark, on the following Sunday she fell on her knees before the catechist, and asked his pardon for the liberty, accusing herself as for a fault.

After having divided the instruction into several parts, the catechist will find it necessary to put a certain order in the arrangement of thoughts and proofs. Otherwise he will often be making repetitions or omissions, or circumlocutions which tend to nothing, and can only by chance do any good. A comparison or an example brought in too soon will hardly make any impression.

Article II

Of Proofs to be employed in the Instruction

Proofs are necessary to convince children as much as grown-up people, the only difference is in the choice of them. It is not well to give a great many proofs, it would confuse the children's mind; one or two, three at the most. But for those hearers whom we desire to convince, they must be clear and indisputable. If they are drawn from reason, they must be in conformity with the rules of logic. A good catechist ought to be a good logician; without the help of logic he will neither know how to define precisely, how to divide rightly, nor how to reason and discourse in a thorough manner. Instead of proofs he will explain in other words what he wants to prove, and from sound principles he will frequently draw quite wrong consequences.

The most indisputable proofs are those which are drawn from Holy Scripture. When we use the sacred writings, it is God Himself who speaks. Fruit is most wholesome when taken from the tree, water most pure at its source. All that the catechist teaches comes with very special force when it is confirmed by Scripture. But yet it must not be quoted too often; it would lose its effect on the hearers if the catechist used it very frequently in proof. Neither must it be quoted in a different sense from the true meaning. S. François de Sales would not allow the mystical sense to be spoken of, without having first explained the literal sense. "Otherwise," he said, "it is building the roof of a house before laying the foundations. Holy Scripture is not stuff we may cut as we will and make garments according to our own fashion." When the true meaning of the letter was explained, then he would allow moral explanations to be made, but this to be done with great judgment. He said that forced figures were spoilt figures, and forced morals like the carillon in bells, which could be made to say anything we like.

After proofs drawn from Holy Scripture, the catechist may employ those furnished by the words and sayings of the holy fathers; but he should only choose those which are short, definite, and forcible, and again, only use them very rarely. Short and forcible sentences are such as these from S. Augustine: *He who made you without yourself, will not save you without yourself. God promises you pardon, but no one has promised you to-morrow.*

There are other proofs which the catechist should make use of: those which are drawn from natural reason. One who has not been affected by authority will sometimes be convinced by a simple but strong proof from reason. Proofs of reason are such as the human mind can draw either from metaphysical truths, or from physical or moral things.

Those that can be drawn from metaphysical things are generally of no use at all for children, because, as Fénélon says,[1] "Childhood is not fitted for reasoning." Children feel things more than they understand them, therefore one must speak to the feelings, to the imagination, to the heart, rather than to the intellect. A simple but striking exposition of facts which establish the truths of religion convinces them more solidly and more lastingly than the most satisfactory metaphysical demonstrations, or the most subtle reasonings. Children must

[1] Fénélon, *Education des Filles*, ch. vii.

be convinced by the things which they see, and from those which they know by the light of their senses, such as animals, plants, the stars, the earth, they must be led on to those which by the light of their intellect they cannot easily penetrate. This style of proof, which consists in bringing together two objects different, but analogous in some respects, and on this analogy founding a conclusion in respect to the one which is best known, and then applying it to the other which is less known, is called *comparison*.

"The restlessness and frivolity of children are the greatest hindrances to their instruction. Their brain is like a lighted taper in a place exposed to the wind: the light is never steady. A child asks you a question, but before you have answered, his eyes are up at the ceiling, counting the figures painted on it, or the pieces of glass in the windows; if you try to bring him back to his first subject, you weary him as if you were keeping him in prison." Happily, children are as curious as they are volatile; they are continually asking, because everything is still new to them; there are some who ask questions without end about everything they see, the surprise of novelty fills them with wonder at everything they come across; and thus in children *curiosity is a natural impulse which leads on half-way to instruction*. Now what is there more fit to excite their curiosity and to quiet the restlessness of their mind than a comparison taken from sensible things which are all round them, and which come to them through their senses? It speaks to their imagination, and it

ILLUSTRATIONS OR COMPARISONS

always interests them, provided that the thing is described to them with animation, and that the comparison is well put before them. As the catechist talks to them, the picture he is drawing excites their attention, and keeps their curiosity awake; and when the application comes, their faces glow with surprise and the secret delight of their hearts.

This is the reason why those who have given themselves to the instruction of the ignorant have always made frequent use of comparisons which appeal to the senses. The Son of God, sent to *preach the Gospel to the poor*, scarcely said anything without employing a comparison. The commonest things provided Him with so many subjects of instruction; a father of a family, a son, a servant; less than this even, a meal, a measure, a little flower, a light, a field, a tree, a flower, a sparrow; which made S. Vincent de Paul say, in speaking to the priests of his community: "The community must devote themselves to explaining the truths of the Gospel by familiar comparisons when they are working in missions." Let us study then to train our minds to this method, herein following our Lord, who, as the holy Gospel says, *sine parabolis non loquebatur ad eos*.[1] All the men who have been raised up by God in these latter times to give more distinction to the important work of the catechism, have made frequent use of comparisons. Père de la Rivière says of S. François de Sales:[2] "It was the greatest delight to hear how familiarly he explained the rudi-

[1] *Vie de S. Vincent de Paul*, by Abelly, vol. ii.
[2] *Vie de S. François de Sales*, p. 362.

ments of our faith to the children; on each subject a wealth of comparisons fell from his lips in explanation."

To bring a truth home to the children, a comparison should have three qualities—brevity, fitness, and clearness. Without brevity it would degenerate into description, and the children, who are incapable of continuous attention, would soon be tired, or else would not grasp the point of analogy. Still too great conciseness should be avoided; the comparison would be obscure, and the analogy would not be perceived. It would only be like a picture passed before the eyes of the spectator.

But the charm of a comparison consists in its fitness. There should be some ingenuity in it, the listener should find in it something he had not observed himself, but which strikes him and pleases him at the same time. This takes place when the likeness between the two objects is clear and unmistakable. S. François de Sales, wishing to explain why Jesus Christ prayed only for S. Peter, though the whole Church was in peril, uses the comparison of a gardener who wishes to keep a young plant from perishing by dryness. This gardener, he says, does not waste his time in watering each branch or each flower; he gives all the water to the bottom of the plant, so that it may get to the root, believing then that all the rest will be safe. "Thus our Lord prayed for the chief; He watered this root, so that through the chief the faith should always be preserved in the Church."[1]

[1] S. François de Sales, *Discours de Controverses*, Discours xxxiv.

Finally, the comparison must be clear. It will be so if it is drawn from things well known to the listeners. If, to give them an idea of sin, it should be compared to a (poisonous) plant, which only grows in the other hemisphere, and which they have never heard talked about, it would be difficult to make them imagine the evil and mischief of it. Thus, in using comparisons, the very simplest things ought to be chosen; there is nothing which is too low or too common. It is true one may use trivial comparisons, which might offend delicate ears, though they would not surprise the people; but this defect does not arise from the object of the comparison in itself; it comes simply from the way in which it is used, and the occasion on which it is used. What is there more low or common than a shepherd's crook, a bridle, a stick, a rudder? And yet, in the most stately discourses, similitudes drawn from these objects find their place. Art and good taste gives an interest to the commonest things, just as lapidaries give sparkling brilliancy to diamonds.

Three sources may be pointed out for comparisons: natural and artificial things which affect the senses, Holy Scripture, and in reading other chosen works. "The book of nature," says S. François de Sales, "is good for similitudes, for comparisons between the less and the greater, and for a thousand other things. The ancient fathers are full of it, Holy Scripture too, in a thousand places: *Vade ad formicam; sicut gallina congregat pullos suos; quemadmodum cervus; quasi struthio in deserto; con-*

siderate lilia agri, and a hundred thousand similar." This holy bishop, whose writings are a treasure-house of the most fitting and the most pleasing comparisons, gives us an excellent rule for finding them out in the Holy Scriptures. "The words must be considered," he says, "to see if they are not metaphorical; for if they are, then there is a comparison directly for anyone who knows how to look for it. For example, in these words: *Viam mandatorum tuorum cucurri, cum dilatasti cor meum;* consider the words *dilatasti* and *cucurri*, for they are both parts of one metaphor. Now you must think of things which go quicker when they are filled out; and you will find some, such as ships when the wind fill their sails. Ships lying becalmed in port, as soon as a favourable wind catches the sails, filling them and expanding them, go on fast; so when the favourable wind or breath of the Holy Spirit enters into our heart, our soul hastens in full sail into the sea of the commandments.[1]

"David, speaking of things of the world, says: *Periit memoria eorum cum sonitu* (Ps. ix. 7 Vulg.). I draw two comparisons from two things which make a sound when they come to an end. If a glass is broken, it sounds as it breaks; thus when the wicked perish, there is some little sound; in death they are talked of. But as the glass is for ever useless, so these poor wretches, without hope of salvation, remain for ever lost. And again, when a great or a rich man dies, the bells are tolled, he has a grand funeral;

[1] *Lettre è M. André Frémiot*, Archbishop of Bourges, *Opuscules*, tome ii. pp. 173, 174.

ILLUSTRATIONS OR COMPARISONS

but the bell ceases, and who calls for a blessing on him? Who speaks of him? No one.

"S. Paul, speaking of a man who does some good works, but has no charity, says of him: *Factus est velut æs sonans et cymbalum tinniens.* We get a comparison from the bell which calls others to the church, but never enters it; and just so, a man who does good works but without charity, may edify others, and help them into Paradise, while he himself enters not. . . . .

"And certainly he who takes note of all this will be fruitful in beautiful comparisons; but all must be done decently, nothing said which is low or unfit or abject."

As it is not given to everyone to invent short and right and clear comparisons, it is quite well that those who have less fertile minds should avail themselves of comparisons made by others. There are many collections of comparisons which may be a great help. A work has been published which contains many and very beautiful ones. It is entitled, *Jeunesse instruite d'après la Méthode de Fénélon.*[1] Authors who are the most rich in comparisons should also be used, such as S. Basil, S. John Chrysostom, S. Gregory of Nazianzus, S. Cyprian; and among moderns, S. François de Sales, Grenade, etc.

We must not omit two important considerations. The first is, not to have too many comparisons; they should be so skilfully bound up with the foundation of things that the listener, all his attention being taken up with understanding what he is

[1] One volume in 12. Paris and Besançon. 1808.

being taught, will not be aware of the art employed. The second is, to take care in an instruction that the comparisons do not all take one form, as if they were all cast in the same mould. This uniformity can be avoided by turning them differently, and by beginning them in different ways, sometimes with these words: *as, in the same way, so also;* at other times in this way: *figure to yourselves, picture to yourselves, imagine; see, consider; we see this also in . . . . . , there is nothing more evident;* or even also in the way of interrogation: *Who does not know? who does not see? does not nature show us continually in the course of the stars? . . . . in the habits of animals?*

Examples are no less useful to the catechist than comparisons in gaining the attention of the children, and helping their understanding. A story is a sort of painting which speaks to the imagination, and it has a great charm, when, according to S. Augustine's expression, the thing seems to pass before us. Examples combine all the advantages we have spoken of as to comparison; but they have, moreover, what comparison has not, the power easily to touch and move, specially at that tender age, because they appeal more to the heart than to the mind. "You may constantly see the children in an ecstasy of delight, or shedding tears as they listen to a story. Never fail," says Fénélon, "to take advantage of this tendency."[1] In short, examples fix themselves strongly in the memory, and the recollection will last for a long time, which is not the case

[1] *Education des Filles*, ch. vi.

with comparisons,—at least, unless they are very striking.

The examples of which we are speaking may be classed in two divisions—some are historical, the others, pure fiction. Historic examples, such as we find in the lives of men, are more striking than others, because of their truth, of which the listener has no sort of doubt. They may be taken from Holy Scripture, from the lives of saints, or from profane history. "We must try," says Fénélon, "to give the children a greater liking for sacred stories than for others, not by telling them they are more beautiful, which perhaps they would not believe, but by making them feel it without saying anything. Let them see how important they are, how uncommon, how wonderful, how full of natural pictures, how noble and vigorous." There is, moreover, a great advantage in using Bible stories, for they teach the children religion without their suspecting it. With regard to stories taken from the lives of saints, S. François de Sales speaks thus in his letter to the Archbishop of Bourges: "And stories of the saints, may we use them? Why, can there be anything so profitable, anything so beautiful? And, moreover, the life of saints, is it anything but the Gospel put into practice? There is no more difference between the written Gospel and the life of saints than there is between music noted down and music sung. And profane stories, what use can be made of them? They are good; but we must use them as we do mushrooms, very little, only to excite the appetite; and even then they must be well prepared; and, as S. Jerome says, "we must treat them as the Israelites treated the captive women when they wished to marry them; we must pare their nails and cut their hair, that is to say, we must make them entirely subservient to the Gospel and true Christian virtue, by taking away from them anything which in their heathen and profane manners may be reprehensible"; as the Holy Scripture says, "we must *separare pretiosum a vili.*"

An example taken from history should be true, should have something important or remarkable in it, and should be told quite simply. A story from history should never be told unless it comes from good authority; in the times in which we live, we should be even very reserved with regard to visions and ecstasies, however well-founded they may be. The object of examples should be to interest, or to instruct, or to touch, but never only to create a smile; the church is not a place of amusement. Moreover, it would infallibly cause distraction among the children; their reverence for the word of God would be lessened, and also for the minister who preaches it to them. We say also that an example from history should have something remarkable about it, because without this it would make no impression on the hearers. It may be remarkable as to the events themselves, or because of the country in which they happened, or because of the people who took part in them. "Examples of ancient and illustrious people of our own country, or of the saints of the particular province in which we are preaching, have generally the greatest effect, and leave the strongest impression on the mind. It is the same with examples of vigour and fortitude which we may find among weak or common people; as of a woman, or a child, or a servant, or a helpless and forlorn person."[1] The example even of a heathen may have this special point of interest, and one may set it with advantage against the cowardice of Christians of our time.

However striking an example drawn from history may be, it will make little impression on the hearers if it is not given with freshness and animation. "You must take care," says S. François de Sales, "not to give useless descriptions, as many scholars do; instead of giving the story of Abraham simply, and drawing from it a good moral, they set themselves to describe the beauty of Isaac, the sharpness of Abraham's sword, the surroundings of the place of sacrifice, and similar useless things. You should not be too brief, lest the example should leave no impression, nor too long, lest it should be wearisome. . . . Examples have a wonderful power, only they must be well set forth, and well applied. See how the holy fathers set before us the example of Abraham sacrificing his son, to show us how we should spare nothing when it is a question of doing the will of God. They remark on everything which can enhance the obedience of Abraham. *Abraham,* they say, *old Abraham, who had but this son, so handsome, so good, so virtuous and so lovable; yet without a word, without a murmur, without hesitation, he*

---

[1] *Rhétorique de Grenade,* vol. ii. p. 223; *Le Guide de ceux qui annoncent la parole de Dieu,* p. 46.

brings him to the mountain, and, with his own hands, prepares to sacrifice him. And certainly, the way in which they apply it is still stronger; and yet thou, a Christian, canst not make up thy mind to sacrifice, I do not say thy son, thy daughter, all thy goods, or a large part of them, but one single crown-piece to help the poor who ask alms of thee in the name of God!"

It may be asked if it is justifiable to imagine dialogues between the persons of the story. S. François de Sales shall answer this question. "Care must be taken," he says, "in introducing dialogues between the persons of the story, unless they are in the words of Scripture, or unless they are quite probable. It does not do to imitate certain preachers who bring in Isaac as lamenting on the altar, imploring his father's compassion that he may escape from death, and Abraham arguing with himself and bemoaning himself. . . . Therefore, in dialogues, two rules should be observed: one, to be sure they are founded on evident probability; the other, not to make them very long, for that would cool the interest both in the preacher and the hearer."[1] If they have these two qualities, they may be confidently introduced, particularly in speaking to children. "Make your stories animated and familiar," says Fénélon; "make your people speak; children have a lively imagination, and will think they see and hear them. For instance, tell the story of Joseph: make his brothers speak like brutes, and Jacob like a tender and afflicted father; let Joseph speak him-

[1] *Guide de ceux qui annoncent la parole de Dieu*, p. 46.

self, let him, being master of Egypt, be evidently pleased at concealing himself from his brothers, at making them afraid, and then revealing himself. This lively description, added to the real wonder of the story, will charm a child, provided he is not given too much of it, but is rather left to wish for it."[1]

It remains for us to speak of fictitious examples, known by the name of parables, which are used for want of any true stories adapted to the subject. The object of the parable is to bring home a truth of morals or of religion; it should be drawn from what happens in the ordinary life of men. It is composed of two essential parts, and in some sort may be said to be composed of a body and a soul—the body, that is to say, the story as everyone hears it; the soul, that is, the moral meaning which is hidden under the words of the story. Though the parable must not be taken for more than it is, namely, a fiction, yet the children should not be told of this till after the moral application has been given; it would take off all their interest. For the parable, being taken from things of ordinary life, has not generally the element of the wonderful which is found in an allegory, which of itself excites the curiosity of the children.

Let us see how, for want of a true story, one may use a parable, to bring home to the children a truth, so that they can understand it. Supposing that we wish to make them understand the difference there is between perfect contrition, imperfect contrition,

[1] *Education des Filles.*

and merely servile fear, we can use the following parable:—

"A father had three children whom he sent out every day into the fields to watch three little lambs which he had given into their charge. It happened one day that the children went to sleep, and while they were asleep, some wolves from the neighbouring forest fell upon the lambs and carried them away. The children, wakened by the piteous bleating of their lambs, and seeing the wolves in the distance who were carrying them away, began to weep and to fill the whole place with their cries of distress. They were all three inconsolable; but from different reasons.

"The eldest said, as he came home, I am crying because my father will beat me and punish me for having let my lamb be carried away; if it were not for that I shouldn't cry. The second said, I am crying because of the punishment I shall have, and also because my father will be so grieved when he knows that the wolves have eaten my lamb. The youngest, who was crying more bitterly than the others, said, bursting into tears again, My good father will be so very sorry, I had rather be punished all my life than cause him so much sorrow."

Then when you come to apply this parable to the subject of contrition, the children will understand it easily; and to make them remember it the better, when you speak again of contrition, you can give them a sort of challenge to repeat it to you.

The work entitled *Paraboles du Père Bonaventure*,

and also the *Catéchisme de Constance*, which contains many parables, may be used with advantage.

Article III

On the Manner of Giving Instruction

Hitherto we have been speaking of the qualities of a good instruction: it should be short, clear, and convincing; it now remains to explain the best way of giving it to the children. It can be done either in a continuous discourse, or by way of questions.

The first course is not used in the catechisms of S. Sulpice. An inexperienced catechist ought not to make use of it; because he will not be able to keep up the children's attention for half-an-hour, unless he has already been broken in to the ministry of catechisms, or unless it is very easy to him to fit his ideas to the capacity of children. Besides, when a catechist is in the habit of speaking uninterruptedly, the children are not afraid of being questioned and taken by surprise; and many do not listen to what he says, nor make any effort to follow him; and others make no analysis, being discouraged by the difficulty they find in taking notes.

The other method is not subject to these inconveniences. Generally, we can see even that catechists who follow it interest their hearers, though they are not accustomed to the work of catechisms, and though their powers are only ordinary. It is not always carried out in the same way. In the great catechisms, where many children take notes for their analyses, the subject and the division of the instruction is given out first, and made to be repeated by one of the children. Then the catechist gives the first part of the instruction with its proofs, and when he has finished, he calls upon a few children to repeat the proofs; after which he passes on to the second and third part, which also he is careful to have repeated. This is a useful plan, for it makes the children attentive, and it makes them hear the instruction twice over without their suspecting it; but they must be made to repeat it brightly and in an interesting way, for if it should become monotonous, the catechism would suffer. In the little catechisms the proofs are embodied in short, clear, and precise questions. Instead of giving the proofs himself, the catechist, so to speak, obliges the children to give them, and to this end he propounds to them questions which he knows they will be able to answer.

Thus, for instance, if the instruction is on this article of the catechism: *What is God ? God is the Creator of heaven and earth,*—in speaking to a little child, questions can be put like this :—

"My child, who is it that makes pictures? A. *The painters.* And those who make watches and clocks? A. *The clockmakers.* And those who make houses? A. *The masons.* But do you not suppose that the houses build themselves? A. *No, sir.* What! have you then never seen stones going through the streets without anyone needing to carry them, and arranging themselves to make a nice house? A. *No, sir.*

"Among all you children, is there not one who has seen stones going along the street in a sort of procession?

"Then who is it that carried the stones and arranged them as we see them. A. *The masons.*

"Yes, my children, the masons; and if you have seen any of them at work, you will have observed that when the cartloads of stone were brought to them, they divided them with a saw, or chipped them with iron hammers, and then placed and arranged them with their hands.

"But if the houses cannot make themselves, what of the mountains, which are so great, and the rivers, and the stars, and the sun,—did they make themselves? A. *No, sir.* Then did the masons build the mountains? did they make the rivers? did they make the stars, and fasten them up in the high heavens? A. *No, sir; it was God Who did all that.*

"Yes, my children, God. You see that He is much stronger, much greater, much more skilful than all men put together; men cannot stay in the sun when it is hot, they cannot even fix their eyes on it; and God could make it, and even fasten it in the heavens like a lighted lamp hung in the middle of a room. The thunder, which frightens you so, it is He who makes it rumble; it is He too who makes the stars shine with such dazzling brightness."

"It is well to accustom children to speak of God,

of the mysteries, and generally of all holy things, with a great deal of reverence. Thus, for example, after having given them the idea of God, they may be asked what is His Name who has made all things; and as they will of course answer that it is God, you could repeat that answer, saying in a very reverent tone: *Yes, my children, it is God; you have not known about Him before, and that is why you spoke with so little reverence. But now you will never mention His Name, never speak of Him without great respect; you, N——, will never again say, It is God* [here imitate the children's manner]. *How shall you say it?* He must be taught to pronounce the holy Name very reverently, and several children must be made to repeat it."[1]

In order that the questions or instructions may be profitable, certain things are necessary—

1. Questions should not be asked which are vague, obscure, or confused, neither should they be too long.

2. Avoid useless, too subtle questions, and, above all, avoid such as would awake in the children's mind any dangerous answers or thoughts, such as doubts on the faith, a misplaced curiosity about religion, or anything tending to any impropriety.

3. Vary the style of propounding the questions; this variety takes away the monotony, and amuses and interests. It is even well to say now and then a few words which will cause a smile and amusement; the catechism does not demand the seriousness of the pulpit. Still it would not allow of any

[1] *Miroir du Clergé*, vol. ii. pp. 28 and 46.

ridiculous anecdotes, any stories which would excite bursts of laughter, or any low and unbecoming jokes.

4. Put the question so that the children can answer it. It is often the fault of the catechist if they are silent; either the question is beyond them, or it is badly put; and then the children get discouraged, they make no further effort to find answers, but leave everything to the catechist. On the other hand, if the children answer well, their little successes encourage them, and gradually they get accustomed to use their understanding. A catechist who is really interested in the progress of those whom he instructs, knows how to appreciate this advantage, and leaves nothing undone to gain it. He asks easy questions, he tells them and shows them that they know what he asks, he puts them in the way, or suggests the answer in the question, he praises them when they answer fairly well, and thus uses all sorts of little devices to open their mind, and make them use their judgment, and to accustom them to try to understand what is said to them. But sometimes it is a good thing to put questions which you know they will not be able to answer; for instance, when you are wanting to get their attention to something of importance which has to be explained, and which it is somewhat difficult to grasp.

5. In questions and explanations, you must, as a rule, adapt them to the average capacity of the children. There are some children who are very intelligent, and some who are very dull—it would

be a bad plan to regulate your pace according to either of these classes. The more advanced can be made use of to help the others to understand. But even this must not be done without discretion, for if it was always had recourse to, the dull ones would be discouraged, and would make no effort to find the answers for themselves. Again, it is well sometimes that the answers should not be given all at once; for instance, when there are certain necessary preliminaries, or when you want to prepare their minds to understand some truth which is difficult to grasp; if the answer should come too soon, the result would be that, not having been brought to this truth step by step, either they will not rightly grasp it, or it will be less striking to them.

6. Although in general it is not well to speak much and to question little, yet there are circumstances which make it necessary. Thus, if you are relating a fact, or if you wish to excite admiration, the effect would depend on the whole thing together, and you would not succeed if you followed the ordinary course; in this case, the questions should be less frequent, and simply with a view of exciting attention, and employed, too, with such skill that the picture or story is not broken in upon. When afterwards you call on the children to repeat them, you must not dwell on details; but while they are speaking, bring them into connection with the whole thing.

7. The catechist should be very careful, when questioning on some incident of history which he

has related, to fix the mind of the children on the principal point. He is mistaken if he thinks it is enough to tell them, in the course of his narration, that such or such a thing is what they must chiefly remember. If he asks them what has struck them, he will often find that, in spite of constant warning, their attention has fixed itself on some accessory, or some expression, and that they have forgotten the real object. It is necessary, then, to bring them back to the one idea he has in view, to imprint it on their memory, and to get rid of all other ideas, which may have been useful in leading them up to it, however good they may be otherwise, and though in other circumstances he would have dwelt upon them. If he does not take pains to blot out these ideas, they will divide their attention, and distract them from the principal object.

8. It often happens that, when the children answer, or repeat what has been said to them, the way in which they do weakens the impression which was produced when they were spoken to, because they cannot present the truths in the same light and with the same power. The catechist can supplement this by taking up the answer, and adding a few words of interest which will keep up or revive the first feeling.

9. If the subject should be difficult, the catechist should warn the children to listen well, so that they may be able to repeat what he will tell them; if it should be very difficult for the children, he ought rather to exaggerate the difficulty, so, as it were, to provoke their attention. Then he will put the

questions to himself, he will answer them clearly, and make his answers plainer by comparisons and examples; and afterwards he will put the same questions to the children, and make them repeat the same answers he has given.[1]

10. If we desire that the knowledge we try to give the children should influence their conduct, too much care cannot be taken to explain things practically to them. Thus, if you are speaking of their faults, describe them quite naturally, and show the children what they must do to correct them. If you want to persuade them to fulfil their duties regularly and properly, give them a model of how they should set about it; in a word, show them yourself how to put their knowledge into practice: just as a master is not satisfied with giving rules and principles to the apprentice he is training, but he shows him, by doing the thing before his eyes, how he must set about putting his rules into practice. It is not therefore enough to tell the children that, before they confess, they must ask God for grace to know their sins, must examine themselves well, must excite themselves to contrition, must try to remember all the motives which should urge them to it. If the catechist, for in-

---

[1] *Statut Episcopi Yprensis*, ann. 1630, p. 532: "Lectionem recitatam paulo fusius explicet, proponendo sibi ipsi brevissimas quæstiunculas ad illius clariorem intelligentiam, ac illis respondendo, exemplisque ac similitudinibus illustrando: deinde easdem quæstiunculas proponat capacioribus pueris, ut ad eas respondeant, timidos et verecundos adjuvando, verbumque unum aut alterum quandoque suggerendo, quibus responsionem ostendat; quam si puer compleverit, vel aliquot verbis insinuet se aliquo modo intelligere, illum laudabit, et responsionem prosequetur, curando illum vel alterum aliquoties repetere."

stance, is going to teach them how to prepare for the sacrament of penitence, he will say to a child: "In order to confess well, N——, what must be done? ... *Examine oneself* ... Good; but how are you to set about making this examination? Is it not a very difficult thing? Let us see. Suppose now you were going to examine your conscience; show me how you would do it, ... or, if you like it better, I will show you how I should do it, and you shall tell me if I do it the right way. First, I should go into a room, or some place where I could be by myself, so that I should be quite quiet; I should kneel down before a crucifix or an image, and I should say with all my heart: My God, I greatly desire to know my sins. (*This should be said before the children with the reverent feeling and manner which they ought to have.*) Thou knowest that often I do not remember in the evening what I have done in the morning; my God, help me, I pray Thee, I entreat Thee, to know what evil I have done. Well, N——, am I doing it rightly; may I hope that the good God will help me to know my sins? A. *Yes, sir.* Then I should begin my examination, etc."

If the catechist goes on thus to the end of the preparation, putting himself in the place of a child who confesses properly, then saying how he should behave as he goes to the church, and while he is waiting for the time to confess, with what feeling he should go to the tribunal and make known his sins, and finally, how he should behave himself after confession, and till he was out of the church, the children would know much better what to do and how to confess than if he only said: *You must do such-and-such a thing, you must do so-and-so.*

"When the catechist is speaking, or when the children are answering, he should watch them, to see if they understand, and if what he is saying is making any impression on them. He will easily see it by their tone, their manner, their attitude, their changes of countenance. But this watchfulness must be done quite naturally, without the children being aware of it."[1] When the catechist concludes that they understand, he ought to go on to another subject, so as not to weary and tire them. For children, though they are very eager to learn what they do not know, are also very impatient if you try to keep them to something which they have learnt already. If the catechist thinks that they have not understood, he should go back over his proof, give it to them in some new form, and as simply as he can.

For this he must be master of his subject, he must be so full of it that he will not be burdened by the fear of losing the chain of his ideas, otherwise he will not venture to take a flight, he will be cold, and so will the children be. For the same reason, he ought so to prepare himself both as to the ground-work of his subject and his manner of treating it, that he shall not be a

[1] *Miroir du Clergé*, vol. ii. p. 39.

INSTRUCTION BY QUESTIONS

slave to the line he has planned for himself. If he is not master of his subject, he will be liable— (1) To find himself embarrassed by answers or questions which he had not expected; (2) Not to be able to take advantage of the opportunity the children sometimes give him of saying very good things, and which connect themselves very well with the subject; (3) Not to dare to go another road, though he sees that the one he is on will not lead to the end he has in view, and that he shall not be able to explain to the children what he desires.

S. Augustine says that a catechist who learns his instruction by heart will not be free to go back in this way over his words.[1] For this reason, although it may be of great advantage to write out not only the questions we propose to put to the children, but also the whole instruction, it is not equally good to learn it by heart.

"It is profitable, particularly when a catechist is young at his work, to think over, after the catechism, how he has acquitted himself in this function, what mistakes he has made, what success he has had, how far the children seemed, by their answers, to have grasped what he had told them. By this means he will be training

---

[1] S. Augustine, *de Doctrina Christiana*, lib. iv. cap. 10. "Solit nutu suo significare avida multitudo cognoscendi, utrum intellexerit. Quod donec significet versandum est quod agitur multimodo varietate dicendi; quod in potestate non habent, qui præparata, et ad verbum memoriter retenta pronuntiant."

himself in the great art of instruction. He would attain his end much more surely if, added to this, he could be warned by some of his colleagues of any failures which he might not himself perceive."[1]

[1] *Miroir du Clergé*, vol. ii. p. 43.

CHAPTER V

ON THE SANCTIFICATION OF THE CHILDREN

THE catechist who should confine himself to informing the mind of the children, without striving to sanctify them, to preserve the innocence of those who are pure, to convert the hearts of those who are far from God, to bring them all to contract good habits, would be neglecting the most essential part of his mission.

"Their tender age, their teachableness, the easiness of their nature, make them susceptible of all the good impressions we wish to give them. . . . Nothing is easier than to inspire these young hearts with sentiments of piety, . . . the fear of God, the horror of sin, the love of virtue."[1] While the character of children is still unformed, and while, like soft wax, it can take all impressions with equal ease, we must then be practising them in all sorts of good things; so that when reason begins to appear, and the habit of looking into things is formed, they will only follow the bent of the early impressions they have received, reason suggesting to them what is useful, and habit

[1] *Pensées du P. Neveu*, vol. iv. p. 259.

giving them the power of doing easily what is right.

Since the object of the catechism is not instruction only, but embraces also the sanctification of the children, it is one of the most important and most difficult parts of the pastoral ministry, which itself is *the art of arts*, according to S. Gregory's expression: *Ars artium regimen animarum*. The catechism then is the work of God, a supernatural work, and all natural means either of knowledge or of virtue are absolutely disproportionate, a work, in a word, which can only succeed by the help of grace and blessings from heaven. God, in honouring us with the holy and difficult functions of catechists, makes us mediators between Himself and His dear children, and imposes on us the obligation of attracting to them that dew of light and love which alone can fertilise the dry and light soil of childhood, and make it bring forth fruits of life and salvation. More than this, God only is capable of doing His own work. He is too jealous of His glory to yield it to anyone; we then can only co-operate in so far as we are docile instruments in His hands, directed and animated by His Holy Spirit, and emptied of all that is our own.

Article I

On the Virtues which Catechists should acquire in order that they may labour with profit at the Sanctification of Children

Gentleness and Love for the Children

Catechists should set themselves to know the children and to win their hearts; it is the surest way to lead them to God. Indeed, it is also the great principle in the conversion and direction of souls, developed with such care and practised with such success by S. François de Sales, and after him Fénélon; and it is, so to speak, the summary of all the maxims and the reason of all the customs in the catechisms of S. Sulpice.

But as no one can win love unless he himself loves, the catechist should have a real love for his children; not that false love which shows itself in a weak yielding to passions, flattering them and not venturing to combat them, but that wise and, if it need be, firm love, which knows how to vary its measures for attaining its object with equal power and gentleness. It must not be supposed that to make children love you, it needs only to be very pleasant with them, to show them attention and kindness, never to blame them for their faults, to talk to them only of amusements and games, to give them all they ask for, to be blind to their small failings, and allow them to be quite familiar with you, lavishing on them flattery, gifts, and caresses. Catechists who treat them in this way are not those who make themselves beloved; on the contrary, it more often happens that the children, though they seem to love them, have no regard or respect for them, and very soon feel that contempt for them which familiarity breeds.

But this defect, which proceeds from a weak and indolent character or an excess of self-conceit, is far less dangerous than its opposite—harshness, particularly when added to an irritable temper. Young catechists sometimes fall into this snare; you find them ordering authoritatively, answering sharply, being constantly angry. Their desire is to make themselves feared and respected. They are quite mistaken; the harsh tone only repels the children, and makes the catechist odious and ridiculous. If you believe that you must be imposing to the children, it should be by the ascendency which your ministry gives you, the sacred dress which you wear, and by wise firmness when it is necessary. Do not seek to command respect by a severe tone, by a very serious manner, or by rough and abrupt ways; all these are so many ways of making the children dislike the catechist.

No doubt you must make use of authority and fear, but rarely, always with discretion, and only as a means of attaining to love, never as an end in themselves. In order to be loved you must find an entrance into the child's heart, you must have the key to it, you must stir up its powers, you must persuade it to desire goodness in such a way that the child shall desire it freely and independently of all servile fear. Can men be persuaded by force? Can force make them desire what they do not desire? Do we not see that even the lowest of the people neither believe nor always wish just at the desire of the most powerful princes? Thus Jesus Christ, whose kingdom is within men, because he desires to have our love, does nothing by violence, but everything by persuasion. *Nihil agit vi, sed omnia suadendo.*[1]

"It is easier to reprove than to persuade; it is more consistent with human haughtiness and impatience to strike those who resist than to improve them, or than to humble oneself, or than to pray, or than to die to self. Directly anything wrong appears in the hearts of others everyone is tempted to say to Jesus Christ: *Wilt Thou that we command fire to come down from heaven to consume them?* But Jesus Christ answers: *Ye know not what spirit ye are of.* He reproves this indiscreet zeal. . . ."

"You blame me for speaking to the children kindly and pleasantly," Gerson replies to certain criticisers of his behaviour towards the children he catechised, "you blame me for interesting myself in their innocent games, for sharing their joys, for always receiving them with expressions of pleasure and satisfaction; . . . but I want the children to listen willingly to what I say, and to do what I tell them. Without that, I should never attain to doing them any good; to attain to this, I must be master

[1] *De vera Relig. christ.*, cap. xvi. 2°, 21.

of their hearts, and it is only kindness and gentleness which will gain their hearts, for, as a poet has said: *Non benè conveniunt, nec eâdem sede morantur majestas et amor.* Seneca remarks that it is in the nature of man to kick against a command, but to let himself be led by persuasion. We see it even in animals, who can be trained much more easily by gentle caresses than by the fear of threats. I have read in S. Paul that fathers should treat their children kindly, lest they be discouraged, *ne pusillo animo fiant.* He himself was to the faithful as a nurse cherishing her children, and it is my wish to be the same to the children. He recommends us, if we wish to help a neighbour who has fallen into sin, to admonish him with great gentleness; he does not except children; why, then, should I treat them with harshness? And Jesus Christ, after having invited all those who are in trouble to come to Him, does He not add that He will receive them with great kindness and with the tenderest compassion? Ah! it was because He knew that nothing was so sure to attract people as the certainty of being lovingly received. My divine Master, I will imitate Thee, and, whatever may be said, I will never give up being kind and gentle to children.

"And men of God, what means have they used to gain a victory over souls? How, for instance, did S. Ambrose win S. Augustine? Did he exclaim, *Go from me, you who are plunged in infamous vices, and have added to them the wicked heresy of the Manicheans?* On the contrary, he received him kindly, and it was by that very means that he converted him. *I began to love him*, says S. Augustine,[1] *not because of the truth he taught me, but because he showed me kindness and affection.*

"I will only bring forward one reason, but that one is irresistible. The actions of Jesus Christ are of great weight; in them are found hidden all the treasures of wisdom and knowledge. Therefore it was not without a special dispensation of His ineffable providence that Jesus Christ rebuked His disciples severely when they prevented the children from coming to Him, and that, calling the little ones, He took them in His arms, laid His hands on them, and blessed them: *Amplexabatur, imponens eis manus, et benedicebat eos.* O good Jesus! When I see Thee open Thine arms to press these little children so tenderly to Thy bosom, my inmost heart is moved. Oh! I will love those whom Thou so greatly lovest, I will imitate Thy kindness; like Thee, I will have the yearnings of a mother for them.

"Dear children, come to me, then; listen to the voice of the tenderest father, the dearest friend, when he calls you; have no fear, no timidity; I am come in the name of the Lord, to bring you words of salvation. Come to me with confidence; you will find nothing in me to repel you, you will see by my face what pleasure I have in being with you. We will mutually exchange spiritual gifts; I will give you the milk of Christian doctrine, and you will open heaven to me by your prayers; you will interest your good angels in my favour, the angels who always see the face of the Heavenly Father.

[1] S. Aug. *Confession*, lib. 5.

You will win for me the heart of Jesus Christ, who so greatly loves the little ones and those who take care of them. Thus we shall all reach the heavenly reward, I by instructing you, you by practising my instructions. In this life the tender bonds of love will unite us in Jesus Christ, and will lead us on to that ineffable union which is reserved for us in heaven, where we shall never cease from loving each other, from blessing God, the tender Father of children and little ones, and from celebrating for ever those loving words which fell from the adorable lips of our good Saviour: *Suffer the children to come unto Me, for of such is the kingdom of heaven.*"

The event showed that Gerson's conduct, far from being blamable, was, on the contrary, worthy of serving as a model for all pastors of souls. The fatherly tenderness which he showed towards the children was repaid on their part by their love to him, and by boundless confidence in him. He very soon became confessor to all the children in Lyon. The greater number, touched by his extreme kindness to them, opened to him all the wounds which the devil had made in their souls, and several owned to him that they would never have confessed their sins to another priest, not so gentle with them, not even if they were at the point of death, and feeling certain of damnation.[1]

---

[1] Gerson, *Opuscul. de parvulis ad Christum trahendis*, p. 287. "Ecce coram Deo, quia non mentior plures audivi a triennio confitentes parvulos . . . qui patebantur se nunquam peccata sua fuisse dicturos alteri non sic eis condescendenti . . . instante etiam mortis articulo, quantum libet damnari debuissent."

Zeal for the Salvation of the Children

The most indispensable quality in a catechist, and one which nothing else will make up for, and which, to a certain extent, can make up for all the rest, is zeal, that love for children which is pure and supernatural, and which leads us to devote ourselves to their instruction and salvation. S. Bernard draws out admirably the qualities of that love of God which is the model of a true zeal for souls. According to this father, we ought to love God with wisdom, with sweetness, and with strength. Let knowledge, he says, inform your love, let charity kindle it, and let constancy maintain it. Let it be circumspect, let it be ardent, let it be unconquerable.[1]

True zeal should be wise, enlightened, and circumspect in the choice of means; it would avoid haste, moderate natural activity, know how to reflect, pray and consult before deciding; it would never act on a first impulse or in a moment of emotion, but always calmly, and with self-control. It is wisdom which would teach us how to make ourselves all things to all men to win them all to Jesus Christ, to have patience with certain characters, to urge on others, to use sometimes severity and sometimes gentleness, suiting our remedies to the evils we desire to cure.

---

[1] *In Cant. serm.* xx. No. 4. "Zelum tuum inflammet caritas, informet scientia, firmet constantia. Sit circumspectus, sit fervidus, sit invictus."

"The true pastor does not tie himself down to any special line of conduct; he is gentle, he is severe, he threatens, he encourages, he hopes, he fears, he corrects, he consoles. *With the weak he becomes weak; he makes himself all things to all men, that he may gain all.* O blessed weakness of the pastor, who in pure condescension makes himself as weak on purpose, that he may adapt himself to those souls who have little strength!"[1]

It is impossible to describe all the ill effects which may be produced by an impetuous, hard, and obstinate zeal on the part of a catechist who lets himself be guided by his imagination, and looks on his own ideas as the decrees of heaven. One single burst of this false zeal is enough sometimes to alienate the children hopelessly, or at least to close their hearts; and their confidence once gone, what can one hope for? We will not stop here to draw out the maxims of discretion and prudence which are necessary in the conduct of catechisms; they will come out more and more as we go on; and sometimes a wise mind only is needful to find them out. Everyone is sufficiently aware that there should be a difference in the government of catechisms for girls and those for boys. For the boys there needs great firmness and decision when you speak to them all together, but great kindness when you speak to any one of them alone. But, on the other hand, with the girls you have to speak very kindly and gently to them when they are

[1] Fénélon, *Discours pour le sacre de l'Electeur de Cologne*, 2nd part.

together, but with great reserve when you speak to them separately.

The love which kindles true zeal is a supernatural love, and the Holy Spirit is the source of it. Catechists should be on their guard against a certain natural love which one is too often apt to feel for some children. It is founded on flesh and blood, the causes of it to be found in the external appearance, or the rank, or the fortune, or a sympathy of character and temper,—in short, it is founded on the mean and selfish views of vanity and self-love. It is generally the cause of excessive attentions and odious partialities, quite incompatible with that spirit of holiness and inviolable justice so necessary in a catechist. The children, however young they may be, can see quickly enough any weakness in those who are over them, and they are irritated by this respect of persons. Then they will look on their catechists as capricious and unjust; they will lose the respect they had for them. They will tell their parents that they are neglected and despised because they are poor and poorly dressed, and that the children of the rich are favoured. The parents will feel themselves despised through their children; they will perhaps lose all confidence in the catechists, and give way to spite and anger. We find some counsels on this subject in an ancient *Coutumier des catéchismes de Saint-Sulpice*. " It is quite certain that in a catechism everything is observed; it will be easily seen if you show more affection to a well-dressed than to a poor child; if you speak to him oftener, if you praise and reward him oftener, though he may not always deserve it. Therefore, when you have reasons for so doing, it is well, for fear of offending those weak ones who do not know the motives of your conduct, and also that you may cheer the poor parents and edify all, to reward also some poor child who deserves it, after you have rewarded the rich ones; after you have been speaking to a rich one, to speak to a poor child; after you have praised one, to praise the other. In short, you must take care not to despise or neglect the poor children, but pay attention to both with prudence and charity, so that neither will have cause to complain.

For this purpose, it is well to observe the following rules:—

The first, not to imitate those who, seeking only themselves and not God nor the salvation of souls, neglect the poor children and devote themselves exclusively to cultivating the rich, because they respond more, and generally have more intelligence than the poor.

The second rule to be observed is, not to neglect the rich under the pretext of devoting yourself to the poor; this happens sometimes with young catechists who have much zeal and little experience; they think that by so doing they are performing a great act of virtue, because they have heard it said that we must love the poor, prefer them to the rich, etc. But not having enough discretion to judge when and under what circumstances such conduct is to be commended, they do it without any consideration, and easily offend the children and their parents.

The third rule to be observed is to hold the poor in great estimation and to labour most carefully for their instruction, without, however, neglecting the rich. There are even certain rules of politeness which charity does not only not forbid us to use towards these last, but, on the contrary, commands us to follow, so that we may draw them to God. Since charity and Christian prudence command us to use the best means for winning souls, it is necessary to be careful in certain things with the rich which need not be observed with the poor.

Finally, catechists need great constancy of mind, to bear much that is repugnant in their ministry; never to be cast down by difficulties and contradictions, nor discouraged by the small success of their labours. Though the work of the catechism may be generally both interesting and pleasant, and the catechists may sometimes have much comfort in it, yet there are cloudy days, days of difficulties and trials, when it is necessary to be armed with courage and patience. Moreover, we feel how difficult it is to instruct and convert these poor children, many of whom, in the unhappy times in which we live, have lived in the most profound ignorance of religion, and in habits of vice which they have imbibed, so to speak, with their mother's milk. Many of these children, surrounded by immoral or irreligious parents, only see wickedness, only hear blasphemies or mockery of religion, and often lose, in one moment at home, the little they have gained during several months of catechism. Yes, in these days, it needs almost miracles of grace and of zeal, in so short a time to form in these children habits of faith, of piety, and of innocence, which may henceforth protect them against evil influences.

"Poor children," exclaims Gerson, "how I am touched by your fate! What snares surround you on all sides! At an age when one is susceptible of all sorts of impressions, and above all those which gratify our corrupt nature, what do you meet with all around you? Often bad companions, children who are already corrupted, and who infect you with their poison. What do you see, what do you hear among grown men, who should be your guide? How many bad examples! how many false maxims! Alas, what will become of you? There is pressing need for someone to nourish you with the divine Word, to build a dyke against the torrent of iniquity which is about to engulph you; and yet people are amazed that I hasten to fly to your help!

"If an ox, if an ass, fall into a pit, someone will hasten to draw it out, and yet people are surprised that I hasten to give you a helping hand when I see you on the brink of a precipice! If a house takes fire, and the flames threaten to spread to the whole town, and a brave man mounts the roofs, stops the progress of the fire, extinguishes the flames, every one cries out that he has done a grand thing, that he has saved a town. And yet, what has he done? He has saved a few houses of wood and stone. But the souls of children,—they are the temples of the living God, the sanctuaries of the Holy Spirit, the city of God,—I am to see them

THE SALVATION OF THE CHILDREN 115

a prey to the fire of passions and the flames of hell;
the devils hastening from every side to kindle this
fire, and I, a minister of Jesus Christ, if I strive to
extinguish it, am to be told that it is not a grand
enough work for me, not worthy enough!

"God forbid that I should listen to such language!
Not thus has my divine Master spoken. The
lessons of His gospel and the ever-powerful voice of
His example call me to the help of the children.
From Him I learn to behave towards them as a hen
towards her chickens: see with what constant
solicitude she watches over them, how tenderly she
is always calling them, how she gathers them round
her, how she guards them from their enemies, how
she forgets to feed herself in her sole care for their
needs! This is the model which Jesus Christ has
set before me, and I am only to feel towards them
with coolness and indifference!

"I am told that I waste my time and my trouble
with the children, that they tell lies, that they are
frivolous, and inconstant, and do not profit by the
instruction given them. I own that there are some
who answer to this character; but it is a gross
calumny to assert it of all. There are some among
the children who have not yet lost their innocence.
Oh, how important it is to keep them in this happy
condition! How God loves to be served by these
pure souls! The Holy Spirit loves to dwell in these
temples; what happiness to preserve them for Him!
With what joy does God receive the first fruits of
their affections, the offering of a heart not yet
sullied by the contagious breath of the world!

How important it is that these good feelings in them should be strengthened to persevere, to grow and fructify, that the wickedness of the times should not stifle their budding virtues!

"A great number of children, I grant, are not in this happy condition. Seduced by the temptations of the devil, drawn on by bad companions, they have not preserved their innocence; it has suffered a sad shipwreck; sometimes even they have contracted very bad habits. But however they may be corrupted, it is certain that it will always be easier to amend them now than if we wait till their passions are developed in all their strength, and the roots of their evil habits grown deeply into their hearts. Just as trees, while they are still young, can more easily be made to stand upright, and can be bent and trained by the gardener; so also it is much easier to correct the habits of children generally, than those of older people. If I could only attain to being of use to one, if I could only save one single soul in the course of a month or a year, would you say the time was wasted? But, by God's mercy, there are a good many who do profit by my care; and what a comfort to me, to see them walking in the way of salvation!

"I know there are children who continue in a hardened state; that others, after having done well for some time, leave the holy road in which they had begun to walk; still I do not look on my labour as lost, even with them; for besides the reward which I shall receive from the sovereign Master, I hope that the word of God which I have sown in their hearts will produce its fruit some other time. Do we not see men, when advanced in years, and particularly when they find themselves exposed to much adversity,—do we not find that they remember the lessons they received in their childhood, that they regret that they have not profited by them better, and then that they return to God in all sincerity? I will not then be weary of planting and watering. God will give the increase when and how He pleases."[1]

Moreover, God does not demand of us success, and our crown will be all the more beautiful and glorious in proportion to the hardness of our combats. Ah! when we are tempted to sink under the weight of the ministry, let us look to heaven or to Calvary, let us go to our Lord dwelling in the sacrament of His love, and soon our wearied soul will feel its calm, its courage, and its love renewed. After Gerson's example, let us arm ourselves with invincible courage: a merely natural love would soon be exhausted. When one thinks that the glory of God and the salvation of so many souls is involved, can any labour seem too hard, any toils too manifold or too humiliating? Can we look on any time as lost in which we are trying to make God loved by souls who are so dear to Him? "In vain do I look all around," says Gerson again; "I do not find that there is anything grander than to snatch children from the wickedness and evil influences with which the enemy of the human race seeks to infect their hearts at the most tender

[1] Gerson, *de Parvulis ad Christum trahendis*.

age. What a noble undertaking is it, to ruin the work of the devil, to drag these young souls from the gates of hell, to plant these little saplings, who are the delight of Jesus Christ, in the garden of the Church, to water them, to cultivate them, that they may adorn the garden of the bridegroom!"

The Spirit of Piety and of Prayer

This zeal, in spite of all trials of which we have just spoken, can only be attained by the catechist by fervour, union with God, and entire dependence on grace; in a word, by the spirit of piety and of prayer. Saints are fit for all things. Nothing but a sound, enlightened, generous, and constant piety can touch and convert the children, or supply those holy and zealous addresses which are necessary for forming them in virtue. We must be touched and penetrated ourselves before we can touch and persuade others. With a saintly catechist, everything speaks, everything moves. The unction which touches, the heavenly fire which enlightens, kindles, and converts souls, is gained at the foot of the crucifix, and in fervent prayer. The week spent with fervour and regularity is the best preparation for the success of the Sunday catechism. And, indeed, how can burning words come from a frozen heart?

It is sometimes asked why, in certain catechisms, everything languishes, in spite of the cleverness and care of the catechists, while in others everything succeeds and everything prospers? A host of strange causes are suggested; the real reason is generally a lack of piety. How many catechists there are who have said a great deal throughout the year, have given themselves a great deal of trouble, but yet have not once succeeded in producing in their children the least movement of compunction or of the love of God! Why do our words touch the children so little, while saints would convert them easily? Ah! it is because our own heart is not sufficiently touched; it is because we do not know how, in fervent prayer and at the foot of the crucifix, to draw out those words of fire which move and change souls. Let us kindle in ourselves the love of God, and very soon we shall extend it to others. Let us worry ourselves a little less, but pray more; let us become saints, and nothing will be able to resist us.

As a proof of what we have just said, and also because it is a model worthy of being set before all catechists, we are glad to bring forward the example of M. d'Argenteuil, whose name is held in blessed memory in the catechisms of S. Sulpice. He was not gifted with extraordinary talents, nor had he a pleasing exterior, but the grace of God was with him at every step. Never, perhaps, have children had more love for the catechism, nor more zeal for piety, than they showed in his time. His least words, his impressive voice, went straight to the heart. It is difficult to form an idea of the effect which he produced on the children, and even on the parents who heard him. In one retreat, every one spontaneously fell on their knees and wept, seeing the tears he shed at the small success of a talented preacher. No one could refuse him anything : never was known such abundance of alms, such great perseverance on the part of the children in attending the catechisms, or more cordiality amongst themselves ; every one was charmed by his frankness, his simplicity, his gentleness, and his invariable cheerfulness. His inventive charity suggested to him all sorts of little devices for winning hearts ; such, for instance, as a new seal for the *diligences*, giving to all a new picture, some small pious practice, or a new hymn. His instructions were so clear, so interesting, so well divided, that they could remember the whole of them. He prepared them in prayer, often on his knees, and with severe mortifications ; and God gave a blessing to all his words.[1]

After all we have just said, the importance of the following counsels for catechists will be appreciated ; they are taken from an ancient *coutumier* of S. Sulpice, and are attributed, with good reason, to M. Olier :—

"1. A catechist should strive to live as holily as is possible to him, so as to deserve to receive from God the grace necessary for a catechist.

"2. He ought to ask of God this grace for his prayers, his communions, and his other good works, and also grace to fulfil his charge in the way God demands of him, to the full extent of His designs both for himself and for those who will come under him in the catechism.

[1] *Histoire des Catéchismes de Saint-Sulpice*, p. 173.

"3. He ought to pray God earnestly for those whom he catechises, that He will give them docile hearts and minds, and dispose them to profit by instruction. He ought even to ask the earnest prayers of others in order to supplement the imperfections of his own.

"4. Before starting, he should ask the blessing of our Lord and of His holy Mother, in the private chapel, putting his mind, his heart, and what he means to say to the children into the hands of the blessed Virgin, beseeching her to obtain for him the grace to be moved and guided entirely by her beloved Son, to seek only His glory, and to omit nothing which may promote it.

"5. Arrived at the church, he will kneel before the blessed Sacrament, and he will not fail there to make an act of faith as to his inability of himself to teach anything good or profitable for the salvation of souls, and as to the uselessness of his plans, his care, and his instructions, if God does not deign to bless them. He will beseech God not to suffer his sins to be a hindrance to His holy grace; he will give himself up to His Holy Spirit; he will renounce himself and his own views wholly, placing himself in the hands of God as an instrument, that he may say nothing and do nothing but as He moves and guides him. He will implore the help of the blessed Virgin, and of the patron saints and guardian angels of the children.

"6. Arrived at the place where the catechism is held, he will again invoke the Spirit of our Lord, saying with heart and lips: *Veni, sancte Spiritus*, etc.; he will place himself in the hands of the blessed Virgin, and after having again greeted the holy guardian angels and patron saints of the children, he will begin his work cheerfully, thinking himself happy to have so delightful and lovable a charge. As he draws near to the children, he will greet their guardian angels, and beseech them to help him to keep them good.

"7. During the catechism, he must look upon the children, *tanquam Christum membratim divisum*, according to S. Augustine's idea; and often lift up his heart to God. Catechists could even say to each other: *Sarsum corda*.

"8. After the catechism, he should say a short prayer, thanking God for His favours, asking of Him pardon for any faults he has committed, and renouncing all thoughts of vanity, say: *Tibi gloria nobis confusio*; then, leaving everything to our Lord, forgetting all that may cause him anxiety, he can depart in peace and in union with God."

Catechists should do everything with great purity of intention, if their labours are to be pleasing to God, and profitable to the children. If they only set before themselves the glory of God, the salvation of souls, and their own sanctification, their efforts will be crowned with success, and to themselves they will become a fount of blessings and merits; but if they seek themselves, if they have their own interests in view, God will strike their works with sterility and disaster; *Scribe virum istum sterilem*.[1] It will hardly be believed what harm vanity does to

[1] Jer. xxii. 30.

those who are charged with the guidance of others. It is a subtle poison which often insinuates itself into everything they do. They worry themselves, they are anxious about pleasing certain people among their hearers; they are always thinking of what others will say of them. Vain efforts they are, which only serve to narrow the heart and excite the imagination; they dry up all piety, and spoil and weaken every gift. And besides this, let no one deceive himself; vanity is often an object of ridicule to everyone, and by God's permission, one who seeks the praise of men only finds humiliation, while if he had sought for humiliation, he would have found esteem. Reputation, as is often said, is to virtue what the shadow is to a body; it follows him who flies from it, it flies from him who seeks it. God is pleased to crown with glory him who only takes pleasure in the ignominy of the cross.

In order to keep alive and strengthen more and more this spirit of holiness, which is so necessary for them, catechists should, from time to time, make an examination of conscience on the duties of a catechist, and even take them as a subject for their meditation, trying to realise their dignity and their importance.

In this holy exercise, they should picture to themselves their dear children on their knees at their feet, beseeching them, by the mercies of Jesus Christ, to become saints, that they may save the souls which have been purchased with the price of His blood. In short, they should always set Jesus Christ before them as the model of their own conduct, and take for their motto those touching words which He condescended to say of Himself: *Sanctifico meipsum ut sint et ipsi sanctificati in veritate.*

"But how can a man, clothed in mortal flesh, and beset with infirmities, attain to such heavenly virtues, that he may be an angel of God upon earth? I answer," says Fénélon, "that *God is rich to all who call upon Him.* He commands us to pray, so that we lose not, for want of praying, the good things He provides for us; He promises, He invites, He prays us, so to speak, to pray to Him. It is true it needs a strong love to shepherd a large flock; it needs to be almost more than man to be a leader of men; it needs that none of the weaknesses of humanity should appear in him; it is only after the question has been thrice repeated to you as to Peter: *Lovest thou me?* and that thrice the answer has been drawn from your heart: *Lord, Thou knowest that I love Thee*, that the Great Shepherd says, *Feed My sheep.* But yet He who demands so courageous and patient a love is the very same who gives it to us. *Come ye; buy it, without money.* It is bought by the simple desire for it; only he who does not wish to have it is left without it. O infinite good! We have but to will, and we possess it!

"You see then there is an order in the gifts of God; take care not to reverse it; grace alone can give love, and grace is only given to prayer. Pray then without ceasing; if each one of the flock ought thus to pray, how should it be with the shepherd? You are the mediator between heaven and earth;

help those who pray by joining your prayers to theirs; pray for all who do not pray. Speak to God on behalf of those to whom you would not venture to speak of God. When you see them hardened and irritated against good, be like Moses, the friend of God: go away from the people, and on the mountain converse familiarly with Him, face to face; then go back to the people crowned with rays of glory which this ineffable intercourse will have shed around your head; let prayer be the source of all your inspirations in this work! Oh for that spirit of prayer which has power with God Himself, and which gives the shepherd everything which he needs for the flock! O Spirit of Prayer! it is Thou who wilt form new apostles who shall change the face of the earth! O Spirit! O Love! come to quicken us, come to teach us to pray, and do Thou pray in us! Come to love us and to make us love Thee! To pray without ceasing for grace to love God and to make others love Him, this is the apostolic life. Live this hidden life with Jesus Christ in God, and you will taste how gracious the Lord is. Then you will be a pillar in the house of God; then you will be the love and the joy of the Church."

Let us conclude, then, from all that has been said that a catechist will not be able to fulfil all the obligations of his ministry unless he possesses and knows how to combine gentleness and zeal, love of the work and piety; gentleness, so that he may attract and win the souls of the children to Jesus Christ; zeal, so that he may be able to make a stand against all vice, repress all disorder, and enforce the observance of all rules; love of the work, so that he will be able carefully to prepare the spiritual food, and deliver it faithfully to the children; finally, sound and heartfelt piety, so will he draw down the blessing of heaven on all else, and while providing for the sanctification of others, will also be working out his own. The spirit which should animate a catechist therefore, and particularly the head of a catechism, is at once a spirit of kindness and gentleness, a spirit of zeal and firmness, a spirit of labour and patience, a spirit of piety and prayer.

But he will only be perfect, when, uniting all these characters in his own person, he seems in turn to be one or the other, according to various needs and circumstances. If he shows too much zeal and too little gentleness, his government will be hard, severe, and unbearable; if, on the other hand, he is too gentle and has too little zeal, he will err by weakness, and his ministrations will be ruined by an excess of kindness. If he neglects piety and devotes himself to work, his instructions may be correct, useful, and suitable to the children, but they will be without unction and without piety, and the children will not become more pious in consequence, nor more attached to the performance of their duties; if, on the contrary, he neglects the labour to give himself to prayer, he must not expect any great fruits from his ministry.

Article II

Of certain means employed in the Catechisms of S. Sulpice towards the Sanctification of the Children

The Homily [1]

As the instruction is to teach the children the duties they have to fulfil, so the homily should persuade them to the practice of them. It is in this exercise chiefly that the children are exhorted to keep from evil, to do right, and to conquer the faults and bad dispositions peculiar to their age.

To guard against the omission of any points of morality in which the children should be instructed, it is necessary in every catechism to have a plan for the homily, marking the subjects which are to be treated of in the course of the year. Otherwise a considerable time may pass, perhaps several years following, during which the children may not once have been spoken to concerning most important duties, which they always neglect; moreover, catechists will be liable to repeat subjects which have already been sufficiently dealt with in former homilies.

But the homily must not be limited to instructing children in their obligations: "Their nature must be explained to them, they must be taught that

---

[1] Certain counsels of piety may take the place of the homily, and this is done in catechisms containing few children, or where one priest only is in charge.

they can violate them not only in visible actions, but also by sins committed in heart, often not visible outwardly at all, by thoughts, desires, determinations, even though not carried out. Children are not capable of making these reflections for themselves. They are only struck by what appeals to their senses. They will accuse themselves of actions which they have been told are sins; but they will not think of what goes on in their heart; they will not perceive the wicked passions there to which they offer no resistance, nor the bad thoughts or unruly desires in which they indulge. They must therefore be warned of their error";[1] and this is done with advantage in the homily.[2]

The homily should be clear, and, above all, should express and define precisely the particular subject the catechist means to treat of. It should be strong and effective; that is to say, it should set before the children's mind a few short, clear, and striking points, expressed with vigour and force. How could a child who is living in the mire of sin, and deaf to any voice of remorse, be converted by words which only tickle his ears? The homily must also be urgent; that is to say, the catechist must not be satisfied with showing in a general way the necessity of avoiding a certain fault, or practising a certain virtue; but he must go further, he must go down to the conscience, enter the inmost heart, and carry there that lamp which lights up the most hidden

---

[1] *Miroir du Clergé*, vol. ii. p. 23.
[2] The second volume of the *Miroir du Clergé* contains very judicious remarks on the explanation of the sixth (seventh) commandment.

recesses. The moral application of the subject is like a mirror in which they see themselves as they are. It is the most essential part of a good homily, and therefore great pains must be taken with it, and all its details must be very carefully developed. A catechist read his homily once to M. Tronson, Superior of the Seminary of S. Sulpice, who said, "Your moral is too short to touch and enkindle the hard hearts of your hearers. It is over directly, like a match, or a powder-flash." The homily must be touching, as we shall say later on.

However carefully all the above rules in the composition of the homily may be observed, yet it will not have much effect, if it is not relieved by the preacher's outward action. "*If you say wonderful things, but do not say them well, you say nothing,*" says S. François de Sales; "*say little and say it well, you say much.*" The look and set of the countenance, as well as the gesture and voice, all have their part in this exterior action, which so conduces to the success of what is said. Action ought to have three qualities: it should be natural, noble, and Christian; natural, so that it may not be irritating to the hearers; noble, to interest them in what is being said; Christian, to edify and touch them.

Affectation is everywhere, and here specially, odious and contemptible. "*Our fathers of old, and all who have had any success,*" says S. François de Sales, "*spoke heart to heart, spirit to spirit, like good fathers to their children.*" But those who put on a manner will have no fruit, and it is a fault only too common among preachers. Père Aquaviva, Superior-General of the Society of Jesus, classes this abuse among the obstacles which hinder the conversion of souls. "Everyone," he says, "must draw out the best possible from what nature has given him, and not seek to walk in another path, where assuredly he will make false steps, not having the natural dispositions which are needful in following it." M. le Camus, Bishop of Belley, relates that when trying to imitate the manner of S. François de Sales, he blamed him for it, and advised him to return to his natural manner. "*You spoil yourself,*" he said, "*and you pull down a fine building to make another against all the rules of nature and art.*"

But there may be a fault on the other side, not less blamable, that of not correcting natural defects. The efforts made by a catechist to conquer them will help to make his action and his discourse more really natural. Thus he should study to have a clear enunciation; that is to say, distinct and articulate, sounding all the syllables.[1] Children do not listen long if they only hear with difficulty. He should speak in an easy manner; the charm and harmony of music results from the variety of sounds, whereas a monotonous voice wearies the hearers, makes them sleepy, and will scarcely ever persuade to anything. Monotony can be avoided and a medium found be-

---

[1] To articulate well, it needs to know the value of the consonants, the true sound of the vowels, the length or shortness of the syllables; to place the accent rightly; to aspirate where proper; to double or soften certain letters. The size of the audience must be the measure of the voice. It must be sufficient to reach the hearer who is farthest off. There is no affectation in dwelling on the last syllables.

ACTION AND MANNER OF CATECHIST

tween a declamatory and a conversational tone, and still more if the action is in harmony with the subject of the discourse. Thus, the voice should be grave when speaking of divine things; in reasoning on natural things, simply for instruction, it should be clear and calm, but if it is to display the wonders of God, and to excite admiration for His wisdom, it should be grave. If the catechist is speaking of blamable actions, his voice will take the tone of one who is indignant. In short, the voice must adapt itself to the nature and quality of the things. It is the same if persons are introduced; if someone is supposed to be speaking, the voice must be changed and adapted to the character of that person. If a person is described as debating with himself, the preacher must speak low and like a person who does not mean to be heard. In apostrophe, that is, if he is addressing God, or inanimate things, he will raise his voice more than if speaking to men. In dialogue, the voice should be changed, as if two persons were conversing; the answer will be given in a different tone from the question. In reproof or blame, the voice should be energetic and vigorous. The tone of voice should also help to show the sentiments we desire to express: in sentiments of affection, it should be gentle and pleasant; in hatred, severe; in joy, cheerful, glad, and flowing; in sadness, feeble, and sometimes interrupted by sighs. If the catechist would excite to boldness and endurance, the voice would be loud and firm; if there is fear, it will tremble and hesitate; if anger, it will be impetuous, violent, agitated, from time to time recovering breath; if he would inspire compassion, it will be sad and plaintive.

Countenance and gesture all combine in any exterior action, and what has been said of the voice may be said equally of them. The countenance, being the mirror of the soul, should be bright in pleasant things, sad in sorrowful, and calm in serious things, and so of all the rest.

"If the catechist," says M. Fleury, "speaks of the mysteries of religion dryly and coldly, as of indifferent things; if he shows any weariness or dislike, . . . if any gesture or word escape him unworthy of what he is speaking of, he must not expect any great fruit from his instruction. Children, before they can understand the language of their country, understand the natural language common to all men, which consists in the movements of the eyes, the countenance, and the whole body; in the tone and manner of voice, which, independent of any words, express every passion. Thus they see easily enough if the catechist is in earnest or is merely passing the time, if he flatters them, or if he threatens them, if he is calm or excited. They are impressed more by what they see than by what they hear. Therefore if you wish to inspire them with the fear or love of God, you must show that you are yourself inspired with these sentiments; and in order to show it, you must really be so. When they see you recounting the wonderful things of God with deep reverence, showing naturally by your manner that you are yourself impressed with admiration and fear, they will go along with you. It will be the same in speaking of hope, if you seem to them to be filled with the thought of the coming of the kingdom of Jesus Christ; if, lifting your eyes and hands to heaven, you sigh after that blessed eternity, and try to describe the glory of the risen body and the joy of heaven. It will be the same with love, if you can paint and describe the sufferings of the Saviour tenderly, if you are so moved as even to shed tears. Now, all this will come of itself if you are thoroughly impressed with the truths of religion, and this you will be if you are a man of prayer.[1]

Action should be noble; and this demands gravity, but this is lost if the catechist has always an indignant manner, or exclaims, or excites himself. It is an extremely ill-placed impulse of zeal; the Spirit of God is calm. Nobleness in action is equally spoiled by timidity. "*Action should be generous*," says S. François de Sales; "*I say this*," he adds, "*in view of those who seem by their manner to be fearful, as if they were speaking to their fathers and not to their disciples and children.*"[2] The other extreme, however, that of being too bold and outspoken, must be avoided. It would be shown in pride and haughtiness, and these are the greatest possible hindrances to any power of persuasion. Modesty will attain its end much more surely. Any appearance of annoyance must be avoided if any accident should happen during the homily which may slightly disturb the order of the cate-

[1] *Catéchisme Historique*, Preliminary Discourse.
[2] *Lettre à l'Archevêque de Bourges*, already quoted.

chism. S. François de Sales accuses himself, as a fault against gravity, that he had one day shown some annoyance at the bell ringing before he had finished his sermon. We will add that nobleness or dignity of action demands a somewhat slow delivery. Though quickness is pleasanter than slowness, it is not so fitting in the pulpit; there gravity is always most suitable. Too great rapidity fatigues the hearer. Moreover, how can you persuade or instruct people if you do not give them time to understand?

Finally, we will conclude by saying, according to S. François de Sales, "that we must speak affectionately and devoutly, simply and frankly and confidently, being ourselves full of the doctrine we are teaching, and which we desire others to believe. The highest art," adds this holy bishop, "is to have no art; our words must enkindle, not by cries or extravagant action, but by inward affection; they must come from the heart rather than from the lips. Say what you will, heart speaks to heart, and the tongue only speaks to ears."

Confession.

Of all the means we can employ for the sanctification of the children, the most efficacious, and often the most necessary, is confession. It is through confession that the children begin to know what is their chief fault, to foresee and to avoid dangerous occasions, to strengthen themselves in good, and to break away from evil; it prevents the imperfections of children turning into habits, and prevents the beginnings of vice rooting themselves in their hearts. Therefore in the catechisms of S. Sulpice certain rules are looked upon as of the very greatest importance, which oblige the children of the elder catechisms to confess once a month, and the children of the little catechisms once in two months.[1] The fulfilment of these rules should be strongly insisted on, the children ought to hear about them often,—reiterated warnings, praise and blame, rewards and punishments, all should be employed.

Experience shows that it is well to caution the children against the shame which may prevent them from sincerely owning all their sins to their confessor. The authors of the *Miroir du Clergé* add to this remark certain warnings which it would be useful to give to the children. We could say to them: "There are some children who are ashamed to accuse themselves of certain sins: the devil persuades them to believe that there is no sin in them, and that they need not speak of them. Do you know what you ought to say to yourself when you are tempted not to tell something to your confessor? Say: 'But if there is no sin in it, why should I be ashamed to tell it? If it is not wrong, my confessor will tell me so, and my conscience will be at rest; but if, on the contrary, I do not tell it, I shall always

---

[1] Although it is not the custom in the catechisms of perseverance to ask for the certificates of confession throughout the year, yet it would be well, especially among the boys, to ask for it at Easter time; it is not an uncommon thing to find children who, either from negligence or for want of a confessor, have let this season go by without coming to the sacraments at all.

be afraid it was a sin, and I shall be liable to commit it again if I have not told everything in confession.'"

After having shown how wrong it is to hide faults in confession, the catechist will say confidently that people who do such things cannot have much sense, they can only be silly people who hide their sins in this way. "For," he will add, "what do they suppose they are doing in confession if they do not tell all? They know well that their sins will not be forgiven them; they know well also that these sins, which they are ashamed to tell in a whisper to a priest, who ought to be ready to die rather than reveal the smallest circumstance, that these sins will one day be exposed before the eyes of the whole world; that at the last judgment they will be confounded to find themselves accused of them in the presence of the whole court of heaven, and of all men who have lived on earth, and that finally they will be condemned without mercy to the eternal fires of hell for those very sins which they had not the courage to tell themselves to one man. . . . Was I not quite right, my children, to say that only silly people, people who have no sense, hide their sins in confession?"[1]

The first duty of the catechist with regard to confession is to appoint confessors for children who have not yet had one. In making out the list of the children who have not brought in their certificate of confession, he will find out those who have no confessor. Immediately before the close of the

[1] *Miroir du Clergé*, vol. ii. pp. 59, 60.

catechism he will name these children, and desire them to remain in their places; he will add that all those who have no confessor must remain also, and all must keep perfectly quiet. As soon as the chapel is empty he will call them up, one after another, and put such questions to them as the following:—Then you have no confessor? Have you never had one? Which should you like me to send you to? Are you in a school? Has not this school a chaplain who generally acts as confessor to the children? According to the answers which the child makes, he will be given, or not given, a note for a confessor. The custom of the parish of S. Sulpice is that the confessors receive no child unless he brings a note from the catechists. This plan prevents the children from changing their confessor when they like, and from running from one to another. Besides, if they were left free to choose a confessor, it would happen that a great many would go to the same; a shy child would not know who to ask, and he would feel very awkward in going to find for himself a confessor whom he did not know; whereas, armed with a note, he will ask for him by his name and present himself without fear.

On this note is written the day on which it is given, so that the confessors can judge of the promptness with which the children have come to find them. Without this precaution many children, who had put it off from week to week, would not scruple to say in excuse that they had asked for a note for a long time, but that it had only been given them a few days ago.

The catechist whose business it is to provide confessors for the children ought, on no pretext whatever, to put off a child who asks for a confessor till the following Sunday. Experience shows that this delay is extremely harmful.

As there are confessors to whom it is a pleasure to hear children's confessions, the chief of the catechism should know the feeling of each with regard to this, and, as far as he can, only send them such penitents as he knows they would desire to receive. When he thinks right to give a note to a child, he will ask him his name or names, and even the right spelling of his family name, if he can spell. When he gives him the note, he will say: "*You will go to the sacristy of the parish church to ask for your confessor, and know the day and hour when he will be in his confessional; you will listen attentively to the answer; and at the day and hour named you will go and find your confessor, and you will give him this paper; then, after he has heard your confession, you will ask him for a (billet) certificate of confession, which you will bring to us next Sunday.*"

By the word *billet* is meant a certificate signed by the confessor, saying that on such a day he has heard such a child in confession. The child's word for it must not be taken as sufficient, nor that of his parents or his master. It would be impossible to guard with certainty against all abuses, if everyone without distinction were not obliged to conform to this rule. Sometimes the heads of a school make a list of the children whom they send to their con-

OF CONFESSION

fessor, and afterwards send this list to the catechists without the confessor's signature. But however trustworthy may be the sender, this list should be considered as of no value, because it is contrary to the custom. Moreover, the master of a school may believe that the confessor has heard all the children whose names are on the list, when perhaps he may not have had time to hear half of them. Even when one of these lists is signed by the confessor, it does not do to be satisfied without first examining it, or without warning the confessor, particularly if he is new, of the frauds which may be practised. It has more than once happened that someone, even a child, employed to make out this list, has added, through good nature or friendship, or some other motive, the names of several children who really had not confessed, so that, protected by the confessor's signature, they would be safe from the rebukes of their catechists. The chaplain of a school who was shown such a list signed by himself, declared that he had not heard half the children whose names were on the list, and that several of them never came to him. It would be well for the confessor to write down, before his signature, the number of children he has heard, writing, for example, *I have heard the confessions of the fifteen children whose names follow.*

Sometimes the master of a school, or the confessor, adds at the end of the list: "Such or such a child, who had not time to make his confession with the others, will confess to-morrow or next Thursday." This note *de futuro* is never considered enough;

therefore in such a case another certificate is always demanded.

At the beginning of every month, in the great catechisms, the catechist who has in charge the *billets* of confession ought to run over in his register the column of the preceding month, and take down the names of the children who have not brought in a certificate during the month. He gives this list to the chief of the catechism, who reads aloud the names of the children, if he thinks proper. If an entire school has been negligent on this point, he should tell the master or mistress of it privately. He must never weary of repeating that, to be admitted to the first Communion, they must have been constant in making their confession every month; he must even, from time to time, make an example, threatening publicly such-and-such a child, that he will be sent away the following Sunday if he does not bring a certificate of confession.

In giving out pictures, or on the prize-giving day, he should say that several children must not be surprised that their names are not called, or that they only have small rewards, for that these distributions were not intended to profit those who do not observe the rules of the catechism. If he has resolved to send away a child who has given serious cause for displeasure, he can, when he sends him away, announce quite openly his carelessness as to this subject, and declare that those who behave in the same way will be treated with the same severity. But chiefly he should try to convince the children of the advantages of frequent confession, particularly as the time for their first Communion approaches.

In general, the children who have not brought certificates of confession should be kept back after the catechism, that they may be asked the reason of their neglect, and be made to promise to be more careful in future. If the children have no other excuse to give than their carelessness, they must be exhorted to make up for it. If they answer that their confessor only wishes them to come once in two months, they need not be very severely blamed, but yet treated as though there must have been some fault of their own. It might happen that a child would say his confessor did not wish him to confess every month, when in fact he had not been able to hear him when he came, and therefore had put him off to another day or hour. But they must be given to understand that children who try to be exempt from this rule will not be admitted to first Communion; that such is the custom, and it cannot be departed from. It is necessary to be very strict with regard to schools; they would easily slip out of it if once any indulgence were shown.

If a child declares that he has confessed, but that he has forgotten to bring his certificate, he must be told to bring it the next Sunday. If he maintains that his confessor did not give him a certificate, he must not be immediately supposed to be guilty; it may happen that the confessor forgot the paper, or that he supposes the catechists will be satisfied with the certificates the child has already brought in. Generally the child, though he may be steady and truthful, should be required to go and ask for his certificate; otherwise the greater number would say that their confessors do not give them, and there would be no certainty of anything.

If a child declares that he has lost his ticket, he must be advised to go and ask for another; or, if that should not be convenient, he should be asked what day he confessed, and to whom, if there were other children there, and who those children were. Then those children can be asked if it is so. If it is found out that the child has told a lie, he must be seriously, though lovingly, rebuked; but if it is decided that he has spoken the truth, the name of the confessor and the date of the confession must be marked on the great register, and a note written in the column for "Observations": *He lost his certificate of the.* . . . If later on he said the same thing, it would be remembered that he had made that excuse before, and he would be further questioned, to find out the truth.

Confession has the great advantage for children of making them reflect on themselves, of putting them into a fit condition for receiving good advice from their confessors; and it helps them either to preserve their innocence or to correct any bad habits they may have contracted. The catechist is not to ask the children whether they have or have not received absolution; that is a secret in their own conscience, and should be respected, and no questions asked about it; but he ought often to speak of the happiness of receiving this grace, and excite them to strive after such dispositions as will allow the confessor to absolve them, particularly if they have committed mortal sins.

It is certainly a duty for children who have lost sanctifying grace by a mortal sin to prepare themselves for the sacrament of penitence; and it is equally a duty for the confessor to prepare them, without waiting for the time of first Communion, if that is some time off. The contrary practice is based on no real principle; it is condemned by the wisest writers; it has fatal consequences for the salvation of the child. Independently of the danger of death, to which the child is liable, is it not deplorable that he should be left for several years in a state of mortal sin; that the most precious time of his life should be in some sort given up to the devil; that this mortal sin should be suffered to hold sway over this poor soul, and to form habits which are so difficult to correct later on? It is no use to say that the child has not sense enough to appreciate the gift of absolution, that it will be easier and safer to let him receive it at the retreat for first Communion; these considerations will not quiet the reasonable anxieties which a priest will feel when, having neglected to prepare the children for absolution, he comes to think seriously of it in the presence of God. The practice which we are condemning can never hold its ground against divine law, and canon law, which exacts that those who after baptism have fallen into grave sins shall have recourse to the sacrament of penitence in order to be reconciled with God. When the Church ordains that confession shall be made at least once a year, she means sacramental confession, which leads to absolution, at least for all those of whom we are now speaking.

For this reason the catechists, without interfering in what is the proper business of the confessor, should often speak to the children of the right disposition in which they should approach the holy tribunal, in order to deserve the gift of sacramental absolution.

General and Particular Admonitions.

We said, in the second chapter of this work, that the success of the catechism depends in great measure on the way in which the general admonitions are given. By these admonitions, not only can the children be instructed and touched, but also anything can be filled up which has been wanting in any of the former exercises; for instance, in a sermon, in a conference, in an instruction, or a homily. The usual subjects of these admonitions are the most essential practices of the Christian life, in which the children should be trained, their morning and evening prayer, self-examination, how to confess and how to assist at Mass, faults of character, the duties of children to their parents and masters. . . .

Only the chief catechist gives the admonitions. If they are to be of use to the children, he must always speak in a way to excite their interest, and make them listen to him with great attention. With this view, he must be constantly varying his language; sometimes it will be that of exhortation, sometimes of praise, sometimes of blame, sometimes he will be gentle, at others firm and threatening. But more often he will give his counsels simply and familiarly, always quite easily and familiarly, without affectation or pretension.

It is not necessary to give these counsels at every catechism, nor to give them at any specified time. The catechist can leave them out if there is nothing particular to say, or if he does not feel disposed to speak; but, on the other hand, he must not hesitate to seize every occasion in which he can give an admonition with advantage. Thus, although the principal admonitions are not generally given till near the end, before the homily, it is sometimes well to give them at other times,—for instance, after a hymn, before or after the instruction, with reference to something unforeseen which may have occurred in the course of the catechism. A hymn may even be interrupted and stopped in order to give an admonition.

It is evident that these general counsels cannot be adapted to the personal needs of each child. Special admonitions must be given to certain children, either if they have given serious cause for displeasure, or if their parents or masters wish them to be corrected or encouraged, or if they come themselves to ask advice from their catechists.

Generally the time after the catechism is devoted to these children. Great care must be taken, then, not to repel and chill them by a cold, preoccupied manner. It needs so little to lose the fruit of long labour, and to fail at the moment of grace! If the catechist is really too occupied, he must tell them so kindly, letting them see how sorry he is, and he must appoint them for another time.

But, in order that these special counsels may be more useful to the children, the catechist should study their temperament and their intelligence, he must have regard to their age and education. Knowledge of temperament is a much more useful thing than is commonly thought, and if a catechist is ignorant of it, he will often make mistakes. Children of a sanguine temperament are pleasant, teachable, courageous, and often good-hearted; but they are restless, passionate, quarrelsome, sensual, and pleasure-seeking. It is not much trouble to teach them; the one thing is, to lead them to the love of good, and to withdraw them from the love of the creatures. Thus, in order to persuade them to avoid sin, the catechist should dwell on the shortness of life, on death, on the judgment which will follow upon death, and in which we shall render account to God of all our evil deeds, on hell, and on heaven, and on the necessity of penitence.

Children of a sluggish temperament are gentle and quiet; they are easily excited to wish to be good; but as they are cowardly, lukewarm, and fickle, they seldom do what they resolve on. They need therefore, not so much reasons to lead them to good, as continual repetitions of the same advice, which may finally conquer and get the better of their indifference. Stories are particularly useful for these sort of children, and also pleasant illustrations, lovable truths, the thought of heaven, and everything which may strengthen them in their good resolutions.

Children of a bilious temperament are generous, eager to undertake everything, bold in danger; but they spoil these fine qualities by great faults; they are hard, impatient, passionate, proud, hasty, and given to dispute. They therefore must be treated gently and with a good deal of management, being always careful not to praise them too much, because of their pride. Their enterprising spirit needs to be somewhat moderated and restrained. They must be brought to reflect, and to do nothing precipitately.

Finally, children of a melancholy temperament are attentive, self-controlled, and persevering; but unhappily they are suspicious, self-willed, holding to their own opinion. The catechist must set himself to convince them; he must show them what is the truth quite distinctly, as it were with his finger upon it, so that they may accept it in all sincerity. He must never give way to them, nor take their view, when it is not right; such acquiescence would be extremely hurtful to them.

It is also of great use to the catechist to know how children are being brought up. When good parents devote themselves to training their children in good ways, the catechist has only to perfect what their education has happily begun. But more often, the poor children have been entirely neglected; and the rich have been spoilt by foolish indulgence; both one and the other have often had, and perhaps still have, very bad examples before them, and then the catechist's task is painful and discouraging. He must find out if he can reckon on the teaching they get from their parents, and whether he can exhibit them as patterns, or else be obliged to warn his pupils against their bad examples, though without wounding the respect which is due to them.[1]

[1] "The parents must never be compromised in the eyes of the children. If they say something wrong, and then excuse themselves by saying their parents told them, they must be told that they did not understand properly, that they did not say so: if they persist, they must be stopped, and told that it is a disgraceful thing for a child to say such things about his parents." (*Miroir du Clergé*, vol. ii. p. 41.)

CHAPTER VI

ON THE NECESSITY OF MAKING THE CATECHISM PLEASANT TO THE CHILDREN, WITH SOME MEANS TOWARDS ATTAINING THIS OBJECT

As men do not become virtuous unless they have a respect and love for virtue, so the catechist who desires to labour with profit for the salvation of the children should use all ways to make the catechism pleasant to them. "If they form a sad and sombre idea of goodness," says Fénélon, "all is lost, you are labouring in vain. It is the fault of most educations; all the pleasure is on one side, all the weariness on the other; all the weariness in study, all the pleasure in amusements. What can a child do but submit impatiently to the one, and run eagerly after his games?" It is the fault also of most catechisms. But the consequences are much more fatal, for men hardly ever lose their first impressions received in childhood. Hence it happens that a great many have, throughout their life, a secret aversion to the instructions which have so vexed and wearied them; hence arises a dislike to religion, and often even a sad inclination to unbelief. "All religious discourses," says

Fleury,[1] "seem to them melancholy and wearisome. If they listen to sermons, if they read books of devotion, it is with distaste and aversion, just as they look on medicine, good for health, but disagreeable. Religion seems to them a hard law; they only follow it from fear, without any liking or affection for it; they only keep to its formalities, and take that to be religion which is not so. Others go further, and turn away from it altogether; prejudiced by the false notions of religion which were given them either by the hardness of catechists or the foolish simplicity of women who were the first to speak to them about religion, they wish to hear nothing about it, and take for granted, without finding out for themselves, that all such discourses are not even worth attention. This is what makes libertines. . . . See how far-reaching are the bad effects of disagreeable instructions."

To cut of the cause of so great an evil, the Councils recommend the catechists not to use any severity or threats towards the children, which might cause them to dislike the catechism, and not to teach them difficult things which would give them a distaste for instruction. On the contrary, they advise them to be always extremely gentle with them, and to give them simple teaching suited to their age and capacity.[1] They would have them

---

[1] *Catéchisme Historique*, Preliminary Discourse.

[2] *Concil. Bisunt.*, anno. 1571. *Conciliorum Germaniæ*, t. viii. p. 190. "Cavebit diligenter pastor, ne severitate, minis, vel difficultate doctrinæ pueros deterreat ab ea schola; sed eum mansuetudine et

treated with the same affection and the same indulgence with which fathers and mothers treat the children they dearly love. They ordain that the instruction should be made so easy and pleasant, that it shall seem to the children more like an interesting and pleasant diversion than a serious and difficult study; in short, that they should bring them to do for love what they are obliged to do as a duty; so that, looking on it as an amusement rather than as a labour, they will apply themselves to it from inclination and not from necessity. And, in fact, the way to make the children love the catechism is much more simple and easy than is supposed. A very slight occasion is enough to give great grief to a child, and to make him shed many tears, and a very slight occasion will send him into transports of joy. The catechist, then, must be skilful in availing himself of all the natural inclinations of childhood, even of its faults, and particularly of those feelings of curiosity, of friendship, of honour, of the love of pleasure, which are so strong at this age, and which may be brought into the service of good as well as of evil.

honesta gravitate curabit ea doctrinæ christianæ rudimenta in animos suorum adolescentium paulatim et simpliciter instillare, habita ratione capacitatis et ingenii ipsorum."

S. Jerome, speaking of the education of a child says: "Amet quod cogitur discere, ut non opus sit, sed delectatio: non necessitas, sed voluntas" (*Ad Gaudentium, de Pacatulæ infantulæ educatione*).

Article I

Rewards

Rewards serve to win the hearts of the children, and to excite them to do well. Only offer them prizes, and you change the task you have set them into an agreeable occupation, almost an amusement. S. François de Sales looked on this as so important an element in the success of a catechism, that he always carried rewards in his pockets, not to be taken unawares. "Whenever," says Auguste de Sales, " boys or girls repeated well, or gave pertinent answers to his questions, he gave them images, consecrated medals, chaplets, *Agnus Dei*, little books of prayers, and other things of that sort, which he always carried with him to reward them." The learned Cardinal Bellarmin also excited the children by the attraction of rewards.[1]

Another advantage of rewards is, that the answers by which the children have gained them remain deeply engraven in their memory. It is related of dom Mabillon that, in travelling, he used to like to catechise the little children he met in the hotels, and that he always gave them " some little rewards, to leave a pleasant recollection in their minds of the instruction he had given them."[2]

For this reason the Councils and the Synods which

---

[1] *Vie de Bellarmin*, by Nicholas Frizon, in 4to, p. 255. *Vita Bellarmini*, a Jacobo Fulligato, p. 293.

[2] *Vie de Mabillon*, by Dom Ruinart.

have drawn out rules for the management of catechisms have with one voice insisted on this thing as of the first importance.¹ Some suggest to the magistrates to take a certain sum from the public funds, to be employed each year in providing rewards for the children; others propose to charge this sum on the Church fabric fund, declaring that ecclesiastical revenues could not be better employed;² finally, others, in default of these resources, recommend a collection in the church every Sunday and fête-day.³

We know that the Sovereign Pontiff Clement XI., of venerable memory, used sometimes to stop in the streets of Rome to catechise children, and that in order to rouse their emulation he gave medals and chaplets to those who answered well.

Only such rewards must be given to the children as will instruct or edify them; generally they are small devotional pictures; chaplets and medals may also be given, but, best of all, books of devotion. It is important not to give any books which are not

---

¹ *Synod. Brixiens.*, ann. 1603, p. 557: "Ut autem scholæ hujusmodi . . . cum fructu frequententur, munusculis aliisque variis modis, pro temporum ratione, juventutis studia excitare nitantur."—*Constitut. synodal. diœcesis Constant.*, ann. 1609, p. 188: "Fidei rudimenta . . . adhibitis etiam munusculis tradant."—*Synod. diœces. Antwerp.*, ann. 1610: "Emantur præmia ad pueros excitandos."

² *Constitut. synodal. diœces. Constant.*, supra: "Sumptus si qui necessarii sunt, vel pro puerorum munusculis, vel alias pro cujuslibet loci commoditate, ex ærario publico, aut ex redditibus patroni, seu fabricæ ecclesiarum subministrent: nihil enim in meliores usus collocari potest, quam quod ad recte instituendam juventutem, et a teneris annis ad pietatem imbuendam, impenditur."

³ *Synod. Gandaveus.*, ann. 1650, p. 713.

perfectly trustworthy, as also not to give any pictures which may represent the saints in any laughable or unsuitable manner; experience proves that the first impressions which children receive from pictures are seldom effaced from their mind. It must be remembered besides that the parents may profit very much from their children's rewards; they value them very much, they keep them carefully, and they like to read their books. Still it is not well to give too many rewards; if they are too common, the children would no longer value them so much; they would be given sometimes to children who were not the most attentive, nor who answered the best, and so the zeal of the others would be cooled.

You must avoid also giving the rewards after the catechism is over; they would have no effect, except the crowding of a number of children round the catechist, which would make their exit very disorderly. Generally, at least unless it is a general distribution, the pictures are only given to the children when they bring the number of good points settled by the rules. The only exception is when a child has answered in a very special way; but this should be rare, otherwise the good points would lose their value.

Article II

Festivals of Catechisms

Besides several festivals common to all catechisms, such as Christmas, Easter, and Pentecost, or a prize-giving day, each catechism ought to have its own particular festival. On these days, the chapel should be decorated more or less highly, according to the solemnity. The walls or wainscots should be covered with rather bright hangings; the sanctuary filled with vases of flowers; everything of the best should be on the altar, and, above all, a great many candles; and in the chapel there should be chandeliers and girandoles, so that the children shall be delighted with the novelty of the scene.[1] All this outward show, which strikes their eyes, and satisfies so pleasantly that insatiable desire they have for everything new, makes these days to be days of rejoicing and happiness. In order yet to increase the children's joy, it is important to let them look forward to it for some time, and in every catechism, as the day draws nearer, to speak of it as a solemn day, not telling them everything about it, but giving them to understand that they have not heard all.

Usually, on festivals, *billets* are explained, or a dialogue is recited, and pictures given away; sometimes there is a conference.

---

[1] *Synod. Antwerp., supra.* "Alliciantur pueri præmio et apparatu, et parentes et magistratus invitentur."

Article III

Recitation and Explanation of Billets

By *billets* are meant short Christian reflections relating to the object of the festival. They are recited by children, and afterwards explained, and moral conclusions and practical resolutions drawn from them. The recitation of the *billets* contributes very much to the solemnity of a festival; it shows its character, its history, and its results, in a way which is at once instructive, devout, and pleasant. The children are interested in this exercise, and are much more attentive in listening to it than when they are listening to their catechists. But the *billets* must not be long; they must be quite clear, precise, simple, and suited to the capacity of the children.

The custom of reciting *billets* seems to have originated with P. Romillion. In order to attract people to his catechisms, he gave to children of some distinction *billets*, which they learned by heart, and then recited. These children were dressed as angels, according to the custom of our southern provinces, and were stationed at different points of the catechism, in an elevated position. When they had recited their *billets*, P. Romillion, in the name of all present, thanked these little angels for the instruction they had been so good as to bring them from heaven; and he took the opportunity of repeating what they had said, and showing the importance and necessity of it.

In the catechisms of S. Sulpice, the children consider it an honour to recite a *billet*; and they are taught to look on this favour as a reward. It is not enough, however, for a child to be attentive and diligent; he must, besides, have a good voice, so that he may easily be heard in every part of the chapel; he must recite in a natural tone, devout, but without affectation; and, finally, he must have sufficient assurance not to be disturbed by all the festal surroundings, nor by the clergyman who explains the *billets*; for, in order to increase the interest of the festival, a strange clergyman is invited, who hears the *billets*, and explains them in succession. It is important to choose someone for this function who understands the mode of catechisms, who pleases the children, and who has the gift of being brief. Not more than six *billets* should be given out for reciting on the same day, for fear of wearying the children.

To each of the children chosen for this exercise is given the copy of the *billet* he has to recite, gummed on to a small piece of cardboard, and he is warned not to lose it, nor to soil it. The Sunday preceding the festival, or even on the day itself, immediately before the catechism, it would be well to collect the children who have to recite the *billets*, in the chapel, and make them repeat them one or more times, if you are not quite sure you can depend on those who should have seen that they learned them, whether at school or at home. By this means, the children will know what mistakes they make, and will avoid them in the public recitation.

Besides the copies for the children's use, there should be other, larger copies, ornamented with vignettes and gilding, and these are given, in the presence of the whole catechism, to the *explicateur*, as in turn he calls for the recitation of each *billet*. These *billets* begin by a question, asked by him in a clear voice; for instance: *What festival is celebrated to-day in the Catechism?* Immediately the child who has the *billet* which contains the answer to this question stands up, and, addressing the *explicateur*, says: *Monsieur, we celebrate to-day*, etc. In the little catechisms, the children are made to stand on a platform, in order to give a little dignity to this exercise. After the recitation, a small picture is generally given to each child who has recited a *billet*; as is also done in the case of children who take part in the dialogue.

Article IV

Dialogues

The dialogue, an exercise which particularly interests the children, turns on a subject of devotion, or dogma, or morals. The difficulty is not so much to find children who can represent well the different personages who are introduced in this little drama, as to find dialogues suitable to the children, combining simplicity of thought with a natural expression of it. Still, however indifferent the dialogue may be, it cannot fail to be useful in the catechism, for the simple reason that the children never listen so attentively as when it is one of themselves who is speaking. Moreover, this exercise gives great pleasure to the spectators, particularly when it is quite natural and full of piety; the parents feel flattered as they listen to their children, and sometimes it gives them quite a peculiar affection for the catechism. In every catechism there should be a certain number of dialogues, so that the same need not be repeated too often, for then a great deal of interest is lost.

Only children who learn easily and have a good memory are chosen to recite. It is much to be desired that they should appear in public with modest confidence, that they should make it evident that what they say is really true; their tone should be natural, and such action as they use should be quite in harmony with the words they are saying.

When the children have each learnt their part in the dialogue, it is necessary to practise them in the chapel of the catechism, for sometimes the novelty of the part disconcerts them, and they are entirely thrown out. Besides, when they have been prepared in this way, they speak in public with more assurance; they put more feeling, more vivacity, more energy, and more nature into what they say. In this preliminary repetition, each child should be in the place he will occupy in the public performance, remembering to put the one who takes the part of a good and virtuous child in the most honourable place, and where he can be best seen by the whole catechism. The children are a little apart from each other, and so arranged that all the rest can see them easily, without having to look round, for this would greatly disturb the catechism. In the little catechisms, they stand on a platform, so that they may be more easily seen and heard. Finally, to prevent any risk of failure in this exercise, which is so useful and also so pleasant, each child should have a ready prompter, who should sit near him while he is going through his part of the dialogue. This is not a useless precaution; but the office should never be given to the catechists; for, while the dialogue is going on, they could not keep watch over the other children, and insensibly the catechism would get into disorder.

Article V

Conférences

The exercise called a *conférence*, or *controversy*, consists in treating a subject, either of dogma or morality, in the form of objections and answers between two or more catechists. The *conférencier* is in the pulpit, the other, called the *interlocuteur*, sits in a place where he can be easily seen by all. The *conférence* greatly interests the children; the word seems to have a magic power in it to attract them to the catechism. But it is extremely difficult to succeed in it. M. Teysseyrre, once director of the catechisms of S. Sulpice, recommends the observance of three rules, by which the abuses which are common in this exercise may be avoided. The first is never to say anything simply to create a smile, or which would be inconsistent with the importance of this ministry, or with the reverence due to the word of God; the second, never to let the questions be too subtle, nor the objections be more easy to remember than the answers to them— the *conférencier* must always maintain an undoubted superiority; and, thirdly and lastly, not to bring forward an objection against the truth itself which is affirmed, but rather as a doubtful point which needs explanation; then the hearers will not be led astray, they will feel beforehand that the *conférencier* will have a good answer to give. Without these precautions, this sort of instruction would be more hurtful than profitable; it would degenerate into a popular diversion which would degrade religion, or into dangerous discussions which would only create doubts.

Another rule, which is quite indispensably necessary, is to say nothing in the *conférence* which has not been agreed upon beforehand. The *conférencier* and the *interlocuteur* must, therefore, arrange together and write the objections and the answers, so that nothing may be said which is not quite exact and quite right, for in this exercise, in which a certain amount of gaiety and playfulness is allowable, it is so easy to go rather too far. Finally, both one and the other should constantly recall to themselves the ministry they are exercising, they should be cheerful without being buffoons, amusing without being frivolous, and they should never say anything in a catechism which they would be ashamed to say before a more severe audience.

Article VI

Processions

At S. Sulpice a certain number of the children are selected to assist in the processions of the *Fête-Dieu*. All the children are ambitious of this honour, but it is only granted to those who have shown themselves deserving of it by their diligence, their good behaviour, and modesty. They march under a banner carried in turn by those whom the chief of the catechism has appointed beforehand; other children are appointed to hold the cords.

We read of S. François de Sales, that though bishop, and burdened with a multitude of very important affairs, yet he himself led the children of his catechism in procession through the streets of Annecy. "Every year, on two Sundays," says one of his biographers,[1] "he went all about the town in solemn procession with his children, followed by his priests, and showing such great devotion, that at the mere sight of him the hearts of sinners were smitten with contrition."

[1] Auguste de Sales, p. 284.

Article VII

Chanting Vespers and the Salut

On the festivals, and on other days marked by some solemnity, in the catechisms which are held in the afternoon, vespers are chanted,[1] or the service of the *Salut* of the Blessed Sacrament is given. As children judge of things according to the idea they receive of them, they must be made to look on, chanting the psalms as a reward for their quietness and good behaviour; they must be told that to sing the praises of God is the highest occupation of the angels, and that it would not be fitting for any but good and virtuous children to be associated with these heavenly spirits.

But this exercise, instead of edifying them, will be a fruitful source of disorder, unless care is taken to put persons with the children who are able to lead the chant and keep it up; otherwise they would heed no pauses, nor the mediations, and they would hurry on one before the other. It is well to tell them not to begin to sing at *Deus in adjutorium*, but to come in at *intende*; also to let the singers go through the whole of the first verse of each psalm, so that they may know the tone in which it is to be chanted; otherwise they would be all singing in various tones, and would cause hopeless confusion throughout the whole psalm.

---

[1] They consist of three psalms, the little chapter, the *Magnificat*, and a prayer.

When the *Salut* is given in the chapel of the catechism[1] (a thing which should rarely happen), it is the custom, immediately before the blessing, and while all are still on their knees, for a child to recite, in the name of the whole catechism, an act of self-oblation or of contrition. For this a child must be chosen who is known for his good character and who will say it in a natural tone, devoutly and distinctly.

Article VIII

Stories

A good catechist ought to make for his own particular use a collection of good stories which he can use according to circumstances. Telling interesting stories, new to the children, is a sure way to make the catechism pleasant to them; it will even awaken their attention and bring them back to a right frame of mind. But if the catechist desires his stories to be attractive and natural, he must, as it were, draw a picture rather than simply relate. "To draw a picture," says Fénélon,[2] "is not simply to describe things, but to represent all the circumstances so clearly and with such anima-

---

[1] Monseigneur the Archbishop of Paris allows the *Salut* in the catechisms of S. Sulpice on the festival day of the great catechisms, and all the days of monthly communion.

[2] *Dialogues sur l'Eloquence.*

tion that the hearer almost thinks he sees them. A mere narrative has no effect. The audience must not only be put in possession of the facts, they must be made visible to them, their senses must be impressed by a perfect representation of the touching way in which these things happened." The catechist should be very careful to keep the children to the principal point, and not to let it out of sight by lingering too long over details and circumstances. He must also beware of weakening the interest of the story by stopping to put questions to the children. If he thinks it better that one of themselves should tell the stories, he should only choose the most intelligent; other children would spoil them by their monotonous manner, and by their unconnected way of speaking.

CHAPTER VII

ON DIFFERENT WAYS OF MAKING THE CATECHISM AN EXERCISE OF EMULATION

LOVE of self is a disposition quite as natural to children as to more reasonable people; in both cases it is from this that jealousy springs. This passion is even more violent with children. "They seem sometimes as if consumed and worn out by some hidden malady, simply because others are more loved and more caressed than they are. I have seen," says S. Augustine, "an infant jealous; he could not yet speak, but yet his face was pale, and he was looking with angry eyes at the infant who was being suckled with himself."[1] This passion, if skilfully guided, can be changed into a remedy against the natural indolence of children. It can make them respect very highly goodness in others, and it inspires them with courage to conquer their own faults, that they too may become equally worthy of praise, or even more so. It is thus that the love of self becomes changed to a noble emulation, when it is directed towards a good object, and animated by praiseworthy motives.

[1] Fénélon, *Education des Filles*, chs. iii. and v.

POWER OF EMULATION

It is true that when this passion is designedly excited in children it generally produces only vanity or jealousy. But there will come a time when it will be easy to remedy this evil. "As to Celse Bénigne," wrote S. François de Sales to S. Chantal, "we must plant in his young mind quite noble and brave notions as to the service of God, and keep down strongly all ideas of merely human glory; but this by little and little."[1] And, looking forward, we must run the risk of vanity in order to draw from it that necessary quality, which, when in full possession, will itself be a remedy against the evil which produced it. Through jealousy the children can be led to emulation, and through emulation to Christian habits. If the powerful motive of emulation were not brought into play, it would be impossible to arouse the mind of children from their natural indolence, or to make them surmount the first disheartening difficulties of learning.

One may say of emulation what has been said of praises. "Though, because of vanity, we may be afraid of them," says Fénélon,[2] "we must try to make use of them to excite the children without spoiling them. We see that S. Paul often uses them to encourage the weak, or to soften his rebukes. The holy fathers used them in the same way. It is true, that if they are to do good, they must be so tempered as to avoid all exaggeration or flattery, and, at the same time, all good must be

[1] *Épitres*, bk. ii. epis. i.
[2] *Education des Filles*, ch. v.

referred back to God as the source of it." But if one is to say publicly that the children have done well, one must not be afraid to give them just praises. "We should run the risk of disheartening them if they were never praised when they do well." S. Jerome, writing about the education of a little girl, advises that she should have companions who will excite her jealousy, whose successes will be like so many goads sharply pricking her: *Quarum laudibus mordeatur*.[1] It is also for this reason that the Synods, in their rules concerning the management of catechisms, exhort the catechists to use every means for exciting the emulation of the children: they would have special exercises, such as recitations and discussions;[2] they would have prizes and rewards given to the most diligent, places of honour assigned to them, etc.[3] We proceed to show what are the most usual means employed for this purpose in the catechisms of S. Sulpice.

[1] *S. Hieromyn epist. ad Lætam*, vol. iv.
[2] *Recitationes et pia æmulandi studia disponat.* Synod. Brixien., anno 1603.
[3] *Statut. synodal Archi-episcopatus Trevirensis*, anno 1678, vol. x. *Concil. German.*, p. 63. "Hortamur parochus, ut studeant in funiculis Adami, id est, seriis admonitionibus, quæ paternum animum præferant, ut munusculorum et honoris incitamentis . . . ad doctrinam catechisticam adtrahere. . . ."

Article I

Dignities of the Catechism

In every catechism there should be various dignitaries, to whom honourable privileges are granted, which excite the emulation of the children and make them ambitious of the same. The parents themselves feel greatly flattered when their children are raised to some office; often it is quite enough to attach them to the catechism, and sometimes it will even bring them back to religion. These dignities do not only serve to excite the emulation of the children; they help to make them love the catechism, to keep up the order and discipline of the catechism and to lighten the burden of the catechists, who cannot attend to many small details without neglecting their own important functions. It is important therefore to give the children a high idea of these offices, and only to appoint to them such as can do honour to the catechism, and edify their fellow-learners. If a dignitary fails in good behaviour or in attention, he must be degraded from his office. This humiliation affects the children greatly, some have been quite inconsolable at losing their places. But if the dignitaries improve again, they can be reinstated. At S. Sulpice the dignitaries are only changed once a year in the great catechisms, and twice a year in the little. Experience proves that if promotions take place too often, the children think less of the honour.

The principal dignitaries of the catechisms of S. Sulpice are the Intendents, Assistants, Secretaries, Aspirants, and the Heads of Forms.

The first dignity is that of Intendent. It is extremely honourable. The Intendent should be placed in a good situation, his seat somewhat raised, so that he or she can be seen by the whole catechism. As the Intendents are to be a pattern for other children, they must only be chosen from those who are the best behaved and the most advanced in their learning. If the catechist is speaking of good example, he must be able to point to them; if a somewhat difficult question is asked which the other children cannot answer, he puts it to them, and makes sure that they will be able to give an answer. In catechisms of boys the Intendent should be treated with affection as well as with respect; he might sometimes even be granted the honour of saying the prayer instead of the catechist.

The function of the Intendent is to receive from the Heads of the Forms the *billets* of the Gospel, *billets* of excuse and of confession; and when he goes back to his place he arranges all these *billets* into different classes. He may be helped by the Assistants if the catechism is large. Generally it is the Intendent, unless it is done by the Heads of the Forms, who gives out and receives the *cartes de présence*. The Intendents have certain privileges, they receive pictures instead of good points, and they have power to admit two children into their catechism who are under the age prescribed by the rules.

THE ASSISTANTS AND SECRETARIES

The Assistants help the Intendent in the exercise of his charge. There are two or three of them, according to the number of divisions or quarters in the catechism. In some catechisms they are given a card on which is written the names of the Heads of Forms in their quarter, from which hang little movable strings corresponding to each name: each Assistant goes along the passage where these Heads of Forms are stationed, and draws the strings corresponding to the names of those who are not in their place. These markers serve as a guide to the catechists in knowing who are absent. When the catechism is very numerous, so that the Assistants are not enough, this function is taken by a new order, called *Inspectors of the Heads of Forms*. They take rank after the Assistants and enjoy the same privileges.

The Assistants ought to be in conspicuous places, either close to the Intendent, or to the railing, or to the head of the catechism, according to the way the places are arranged. They also receive pictures only.

The office of the Secretaries is to write down in the register of honour all circumstances connected with all the changes of catechists and dignitaries. This register is intended to receive the signatures of the children who each Sunday receive the great seal for the *diligences*.

The Aspirants are the chosen body from which the dignitaries are chosen; they sit on special forms, called *forms of honour*. This dignity is very much coveted by the children; it is only given to the best behaved. The children who have already filled the offices of Intendent, Assistant, or Secretary also sit on these honour forms. The other children conceive a great idea of these offices when they see that those who have once had the honour of filling them cannot fall back again into the ordinary rank and file.

The Heads of Forms are so called from the place they occupy, each one at the top of his form. Their office is to mark the absent children, drawing the strings on their card which answer to their names. In several catechisms, there is a special string to mark half-absences. It is a very good way of getting children to be punctual. The Heads of Forms are bound, under penalty of being deposed from their office, to allow no child on their form whose name is not written on their card. The privileges of the Heads of Forms consist in being questioned more often than the other children, in having a picture instead of two good points, and in the power of being chosen Aspirants if they prove themselves worthy of the honour. The second of the form takes the place of the first in case of absence; but he does not enjoy the privileges, nor does he, of right, succeed him.

The special arrangement of each catechism will show that there are some dignities besides these.

As the time draws near for the promotion of new dignitaries, the children must be spoken to about the coming change, and they must be trained to look upon the dignities as a reward promised to such children as are trying, by their diligence, their good behaviour, and modesty to become a pattern for others. To most, the expectation of this promotion causes them to redouble their atten-

CHOICE OF DIGNITARIES

tion; for they must be told several months before, that no children can be chosen who absent themselves from the catechism, or who come late; nor those who do not know their catechism lessons, or who do not answer out clearly; nor those who are giddy or rude, who talk to those next them in the chapel or make them talk; nor, finally, all those who give any cause of complaint to their parents or their masters, because all such children would give a bad example to the others instead of edifying them.

On the day of installation, it is well to ask M. le Curé to preside at the ceremony, and to distribute the rewards. The names of the new dignitaries should be written on a large sheet, headed by this formula, or one similar, which should be solemnly read aloud:—

SOLEMN INSTALLATION

OF

DIGNITARIES

OF { THE GREAT OR THE LITTLE } CATECHISM OF { BOYS OR GIRLS }

Of the Parish of..........

Children who, by their steadiness, their zeal, their diligence, and their modesty, have deserved to be dignitaries of this Catechism :—

To the dignity of Intendent.

N......... N.........

To the dignity of First Assistant, etc.

The Intendent is first named separately; as soon as his name is given out, and he has gone to his place, the choir begins a hymn, and the catechism sings one or two stanzas in token of rejoicing. The same thing is done for the Assistants and the Secretaries.

In order to stir up the emulation of the dignitaries as well as all the catechism children, it is well two or three times a year to have special meetings for the dignitaries, to which no one else is admitted, except perhaps some who may be Heads of Forms. They might meet directly after the catechism. At this meeting things are discussed relating to the good the dignitaries may do by their example, and to their influence on the catechism; they are reminded of all that belongs to their office, and their respective privileges. A large framed list or catalogue should be placed in some part of the chapel where it is best seen, on which is written in large letters the name of each dignitary, and the office he holds.

Article II

Diligences or Analyses

In the catechisms of S. Sulpice, by *diligences* are meant the analyses of the instructions, which the children compile and write out. It is a great point with the catechists to bring on a great number of their children to make these sort of analyses, for they have innumerable advantages. The better to persuade them to it, it must not be forgotten to tell them from time to time, that the best prizes at the solemn distribution will certainly be awarded to those children who have made them carefully and perseveringly. Their emulation also may be excited by the hope of a present reward, the seal which is impressed on the first page of these analyses showing what each child has specially deserved for his work. In the catechisms of S. Sulpice, seals of *timbre sec*, *tampons*, and *roulette* are used. The seals are of different shapes, or at least different in colour, according to the different degrees of merit. The first are black or green seals; then come the blue, then the red, and finally the large seal. The large seal is the reward of a child whose *diligence* is judged to be better than all the rest. In a catechism of perseverance, the child who has won the large seal gives a copy of his *diligence* to the chief of the catechism. At the end of a certain time, all these little *chefs-d'œuvre* are bound in a handsome volume, to be shown to the children, and then deposited in the archives.[1] When the report of the analyses is made, the catechist begins with one or two simple observations on the subject of the instruction, and the general drift of it; then he speaks of the number of the analyses, the care or the negligence of the children, and the point which many have failed to catch. These observations are of use, but they should be short.

Then the chief gives out, with some solemnity, the

[1] The chief of the catechism should give the children small sheets of paper cut expressly to form the future volume.

name of the child who has gained the large seal; and afterwards, the names of the children who have won the lesser seals, giving each a word of praise or of encouragement, or even of blame, but tempered by much kindness.[1] Sometimes he begins with the lower analyses; the children who have won the inferior seals are flattered to hear their names called out first, and by this means also, as they gradually work up to the large seal, the interest and attention become greater. In any criticisms which are made or any praises given to the children, it is very important to avoid anything which would wound their feelings or which would excite their vanity. Young catechists often make one or other of these mistakes, and the effect is grievous, above all in the catechisms of first Communion or of perseverance Criticisms, unless they are tempered with a great deal of kindness, as we have just said, humiliate and disgust the children, while exaggerated praise excites the vanity of the young girls, accustoms

---

[1] NOTA.—1. Non est attendendum semper ad intrinsecum *diligentiarum* meritum in prædicta horum honoris sigillorum distributione; alioquin per totum anni decursum tres aut duo pueri, vel unus tantum, majus sigillum sibi vindicarent, quod certo et infallibiliter cæteris omnibus dejectionis atque invidiæ præberet occasionem.

2. Attamen cautione quam maxima utatur catechista in hac distributiva œconomia sigillorum, ut videlicet pueri, non animadvertant nec etiam suspicentur in bilanci catechistica non esse pro omnibus idem unumque pondus.

3. Ideo nunquam dandum est majus sigillum puero sub tali magistri ferula constituto, quando puer alius in eadem schola institutus *diligentiam* effecit certo alia meliorem.

4. Verum in solemni præmiorum distributione, appendatur unusquisque in statera, et juxta pondus suum genuinum ipse mercedem accipiat.

them to think about themselves, fills them with a great idea of their own merits, and makes them lose their early simplicity. This want of wisdom and discernment is quite enough to spoil the whole spirit of the catechism, and it hinders a great many children from being firmly grounded in good ways.

To help them in compiling their *diligences*, the generality of the children take notes while the instruction is being given. Those who are beginning to make them must be encouraged, so that they may not be disheartened by the difficulty they will find at first in doing it. It is well to praise their efforts openly, and even sometimes to give them a higher seal than they actually deserve; this rouses them to do well. But, above all, some words of encouragement must always be given to a child who brings up his first analysis, and his self-confidence can be excited by reading aloud some part which he has treated the best. If a child leaves off making analyses, the reason must be found out; he must be asked if he is ill; and then he can be told, in very kind terms, how anxious his catechists are that he should keep up his former earnestness.

All the children have to make a practical resolution at the end of their analyses, and to add a prayer, otherwise they would have no seal. These prayers and resolutions provide the catechist quite naturally with subjects for pious and persuasive reflections when he is giving an account of the analyses; and though he does not mention the names of the children when he is speaking of the sentiments they have expressed, yet what he says is extremely useful to them. They are struck by the meaning he draws from their prayers or their resolutions, deeper than they had themselves seen; and often this innocent device moves their heart, decides their will, and a real amendment begins.

If a child brings an analysis which departs widely from the instruction given at the catechism, or if any part of it has been copied from a book, his name must not be called, nor will he be awarded a seal; but, after the catechism, he must be told privately, that what he has copied from a book, or what he has added which was not in the instruction, prevents him from competing with the other children, as the subject for competition was the instruction, as given at the catechism. At the same time, he must be warned, that if the same thing is done again, it will be necessary to say publicly why no seal is given him, which would be a great disgrace. If, notwithstanding these warnings, any children persist in doing the same thing, they must be rebuked before the whole catechism, in order that, by this act of severity, the others may be inspired with a great aversion for this bad practice.

Another too frequent abuse is, that the children bring analyses which have been made by their parents or by their masters. It is natural that parents and schoolmasters or mistresses should help the children a little, particularly at first, by reminding them of the principal points in the instruction, pointing out any faults in the spelling, so that they may correct them in their copy; but it often

ANALYSES OF THE INSTRUCTION

happens that they do the whole thing or a very large part themselves, and sometimes they write even the prayer and the resolution. Some do this with the desire of training their children the better, by giving them a pattern of the work which later on they will be able to do by themselves; others from vanity, that their children may be distinguished in the catechism; and thence arises jealousy among the parents. It is the duty of the catechist to check this abuse as much as he can. When the children own it, or when, by the style of the analysis, he can see that it has been done by the parents, he will take it out of the competition, or perhaps will think it enough to place it in a lower class, never awarding it the large seal, and he will tell the child that as long as he does not do his analysis himself, he will have no right to the rewards which belong to this special work.

It would be a great advantage to correct all the analyses; for however careful the catechist may be to make his instruction clear and intelligible, there are always in a large catechism children who understand quite the contrary to what has been said, and who put the most remarkable assertions, errors, and even heresies into their analyses. These analyses might end in really doing them harm; and besides, their parents, or other people who might read them, would believe that all these errors had really been taught in the catechism. It is important, therefore, to correct them, or at least the children should be told that in many places their analyses need correction; but this does not really remedy the evil.

And the catechists who correct the analyses find it is a real advantage to themselves. When they see, for instance, that a certain explanation has not been understood, they will conclude that it had not been suited to the capacity of the children, or that it had not been made clear to them. Then they will go back upon this point which has not been understood; they will explain it again in a game of good points, they will repeat it again for the children who have not grasped it, and in this way nothing will be left out that all have not perfectly understood.

Though a child does not succeed in his analyses, he must still always be encouraged and urged to make them. Even if they are indifferent, they will be extremely profitable to him. At the catechism, being obliged to take notes, he will be silent during the instruction, and will not disturb his neighbours. He will listen attentively, and will neither go to sleep nor let himself be distracted. He will do more; the instruction will be engraved on his memory, so that, with the help of his notes, he will be able to reproduce it on paper.

Not to speak of the prizes at the general distribution, to which the analyses give a sort of right, the child who perseveringly makes them has always, outside the catechism, a set task, a real occupation, and he will be less exposed than others to the dangers of *idleness, which teaches children much evil.* Being obliged, so to speak, to appropriate the instruction to himself, and to give it in his own way, he will be teaching himself, though away from the catechism; and one may say generally that in so doing he will be nourishing the love of virtue in his heart, while the love of sin will be diminishing. And lastly, as the analyses ought to close with a practical resolution and a prayer, each analysis will of necessity give him the opportunity of thinking to himself of his faults, of knowing them and hating them more and more, all of which would perhaps never have entered his thoughts if he had not made his *diligences*, and, in any case, it must be always good for him to think of God, to tell Him his needs, and to pray to Him.

Looking at it only with regard to the literary progress of the children, what exercise would have such advantages for them? When they make their analyses, they observe the rules of orthography; if they do not know them, they learn them, so that they may not bring on themselves any humiliating remark from the catechists; they get into the habit of reasoning correctly, and expressing their thoughts clearly. As the instructions are all in divisions, they learn, without knowing it, the mechanism of a sermon, and in this way they profit more by the sermons they will hear in the future: for it is a common thing to find that persons who do not know the method cannot tell for certain what is the subject the preacher is treating of. It forms their style; it is often quite astonishing to find how right, how pure, even how noble is the way they express themselves, and also what life and animation they throw into their remarks; and it is still more astonishing when we know that most of these children have had no other opportunities for learning all this but what the catechism has provided. One boy belonging to the great catechism was distinguished above all his fellow-pupils at school by his great facility for French composition; and he was always delighted to say that he owed all his success to his *diligences*. And consequently, in many boys' schools in the parish of S. Sulpice, and in nearly every girls' school, the composition of analyses is looked on as a duty incumbent on every child.

Besides which, the children who make analyses come more regularly, so that they may have a more complete set of analyses; for generally they are bound, to be kept in their families. Many children prize their *diligences* more highly than anything they possess; it is a pleasure to them to read them again later on, and more than once this has brought up touching recollections which time seemed to have effaced, and has really produced most excellent results. And lastly, the greater number of Christian parents attach a great value to their children's analyses; some delight to read them, to lend them to their relations, or sometimes others, to read; and this is always sure to do some good.

Article III

Distribution of Pictures

On the festival days of the catechism, that is to say, five or six times a year, pictures are distributed to the best conducted of the children. For this distribution, in order to avoid disorder and distraction, the children whose names are to be called are divided into groups of twenty or thirty; and as they get up to come for their rewards, a verse of a hymn is sung, which deadens the noise they make in leaving their seats. When the children first called have received their pictures, and the hymn is near the end of a verse, the chief of the catechism stops the singing by two or three claps of the *claquoir*, and immediately calls the names of another set. The hymns selected must have cheerful tunes, and the verses should be short, otherwise the distribution would become wearisome and too long. As far as the staff of the catechism will allow, it is well that at least three persons should be employed in this distribution; there should be one to present the pictures to the children,—and generally it is a stranger of some distinction who does this; there must be another who takes the pictures from their wrapper, separates them a little one from another, and gives them in small quantities to the person who distributes them. Without these precautions, there would inevitably be a delay in the distribution, which would be quite enough to put the whole catechism in disorder. Finally, there needs a third person to call the names of the children and to stop the singing of the hymn after each distribution; this is generally the office of the chief. He also should write on a large sheet a programme of the distribution, making it more or less solemn according to the nature of the festival. For the day of the patronal festival of the catechism, he might make use of this formula :—

FESTIVAL

OF THE { GREAT OR LITTLE } CATECHISM OF { BOYS OR GIRLS.

The Parish of.........

President, the.........day of.........

MONSIEUR.........

Rewards of honour awarded to children who, from the opening of the Catechism in this present year, have distinguished themselves by their zeal, their piety, their modest behaviour, and persevering industry.

1ST NOMINATION.	3RD NOMINATION.
N.........	N.........
N.........	N.........
N......... etc.	N......... etc.
2ND NOMINATION.	4TH NOMINATION.
N.........	N.........
N.........	N.........
N......... etc.	N......... etc.

On less solemn days of distribution, it may be simply :—

DISTRIBUTION OF PICTURES.

Presided over by M.........

The.........day of.........

On these less solemn days, the words, *first, second nomination*, etc., are not used, but still the children are made to come up in small groups.

DISTRIBUTION OF PICTURES 185

Before the distribution begins, the children must be charged to roll up their pictures as soon as they are back in their places, and not to amuse themselves with looking at them or showing them to their neighbours: they must be threatened with the loss of them if they disobey this injunction, on which depends the good order of the catechism. For, in fact, the sight of these pictures makes a wonderful disturbance, not only with the children who have gained them, but also for their neighbours, who stop singing or listening to what is being said to them, that they may look at each other's pictures. It distracts still more the children who receive nothing,—they feel their disappointment more keenly and bitterly; and sometimes it gives rise to complaints and murmurs against the catechists. As the little children would not roll their pictures properly, but rumple and quite spoil them, they had better be told to keep them flat against their breast, so that other children can only see the back of them.

Good order demands that the distribution should come after everything else, for experience shows that the children hardly listen at all after they have received their rewards, or after they know for certain that they are not to have any; besides, these pictures would hinder them from taking notes; they would be in the way, and would of necessity cause restlessness and disorder. Therefore as soon as the distribution is over, the children must be sent away as soon as possible.

As the children, and even older persons who

frequent the catechism, attach a wonderful value to these pictures, having them framed and keeping them as honourable *souvenirs*, it is well to give notice to the children a long while beforehand, so as more effectually to excite their emulation; they should be asked if they wish to have any share in it, and what they propose to do to that end. Before the distribution, the chief of the catechism should examine the subjects represented in the pictures, so that he can explain them to the children, and draw moral applications from them. For instance, if he gives them a picture of our Lord on the cross, he will say to the children that this will be to them a reminder of the love which our Lord has shown to them, and a powerful motive against falling into deadly sin, for it was this that nailed Him to the cross. It is well to give pictures which have some reference to the festival or to the time of the year. Though these pictures are the reward of merit and of goodness, yet it is necessary to avoid giving them always to the same children.

Article IV

Solemn Distribution of Prizes

The distribution of prizes, which takes place every year in all the catechisms, is without doubt the way of all others to awaken the zeal of the children, and

DISTRIBUTION OF PRIZES

to excite their emulation. It must be often spoken of, particularly as the time draws near, and these prizes must come to be looked upon as the most honourable reward a Christian child can aspire to. It is necessary to surround this distribution with a good deal of pomp and circumstance; the chapel should be decorated as on festivals; and if, for the sake of the public, it is thought better to give out the prizes in the nave, everything must be done to keep up the solemnity of the thing. The prizes should be in a conspicuous place on a table draped to the ground.

The number of prizes and pictures is in proportion to the number of the children. In each catechism at S. Sulpice a *prize of honour* is given, which is the highest and the most honourable, and then prizes for *good behaviour*, for *diligences*, for *knowledge and the catechism*, and for *gospels*. The number of prizes in each of these departments is, one for the highest, several first-class prizes, several second-class prizes, and then the *accessits*. The *accessits* are pictures of various sizes, the prizes are books. These prizes, with the exception of the prize of honour and the first prize, consist of one volume, in 12mo, for prizes of the first-class; for the prizes of the second-class, one volume in 18mo, or even in 32mo. Two prizes are never given to one child. These books are tied up with narrow ribbons of different colours, according to the divisions. The seal of the catechism, gilt, is put on the cover of the books; which, in the eyes of the children, gives these volumes, however common they may be, a value beyond all price; and inside is a printed certificate, which should give the name of the child, and for what the prize has been awarded to him; this should be signed by the chief of the catechism. The chief reads aloud, and very solemnly, first the heading of the programme of prizes; then he calls the name of the child who has won the prize of honour, and immediately gives the sign for a verse of a hymn to be sung: there are special hymns for this day. He does the same after the nomination of the first prize in each department, then after the nomination of the prizes of the first-class, then after that of the second-class, and finally, after the nomination of the *accessits*. When he calls the names of children in a school, he should add the name of the school to which they belong.

On the programme of the prizes, against the name of each child should be written the title of the book which has been given him, to prevent the chance of giving him the same book at some future time. All the programmes should be kept ready to be consulted if needed. We will now give a specimen of these programmes.

DISTRIBUTION OF PRIZES

PARISH OF......

GREAT OR LITTLE } CATECHISM { OF BOYS OR OF GIRLS.

SOLEMN DISTRIBUTION OF PRIZES.

President, MONSIEUR.........

The.........day of.........

PRIZE OF HONOUR

Awarded to N.........N.........   *(belonging to............School).*

GOOD BEHAVIOUR.	ANALYSES.	KNOWLEDGE AND CATECHISM	GOSPELS.
First Prize. Awarded to N...	*First Prize.* Awarded to N...	*First Prize.* Awarded to N...	*First Prize.* Awarded to N...
Prizes of 1st Class. Awarded to N......... N......... N.........etc.	*Prizes of 1st Class.* Awarded to N......... N......... N.........etc.	*Prizes of 1st Class.* Awarded to N......... N......... N.........etc.	*Prizes of 1st Class.* Awarded to N......... N......... N.........etc.
Prizes of 2nd Class. Awarded to N......... N......... N.........etc.	*Prizes of 2nd Class.* Awarded to N......... N......... N.........etc.	*Prizes of 2nd Class.* Awarded to N......... N......... N.........etc.	*Prizes of 2nd Class.* Awarded to N......... N......... N.........etc.
Accessit. N......... N......... N.........etc.	*Accessit.* N......... N......... N......... etc.	*Accessit.* N......... N......... N.........etc.	*Accessit.* N......... N......... N.........etc.

Article V

Visits to the Catechisms

It is much to be desired that M. le Curé, if he does not himself undertake the charge of the parish catechisms, should hold a visitation of them, at least, once a year.

These visitations, when announced some time beforehand, become a source of emulation to the children. Sometimes the day is not fixed for them, so that everyone is kept on the watch. The children are told that M. le Curé will be informed which children are giddy, or rude, or idle; he will also be told who are well-behaved and industrious, and who are persevering at the catechism, so that he may know those who deserve that he should think well of them, and deserve also the rewards he hopes to give them.

The chiefs of the catechisms must arrange with M. le Curé as to the faults which need to be corrected, and as to the advice he should give them. When he comes in to the catechism, all the children stand, and receive him by chanting the psalm, *Laudate Dominum, omnes gentes*. He is accompanied by two assistants, who are on each side of him. The assistants have chairs and M. le Curé an arm-chair; these are placed on the altar-step, facing the children. After he has said his own prayer at the foot of the altar, and when the children are seated, the visitor asks the chief if he

VISITS TO THE CATECHISMS

is satisfied with the children. He puts various questions to him as to application, regularity, earnestness, modesty, knowledge, *diligences*, certificates of confession, monthly communions, etc. The follow- are the chief:—

1. Do all the children come regularly to the catechism? Are there any who absent themselves or who only come after the catechism has begun? Have those who are absent brought notes of excuse signed by their parents?
2. Do they keep silence well? Do they whisper to those next them who are questioned? Are they quiet in their manners? Are there not some who look round at the least sound? or some who shuffle their feet and disturb the whole catechism? or others who lounge on the forms when they kneel down? Are there any children who change their places without leave? Do they all sing the hymns and do they try to sing them without confusion or hurry? When the Holy Mass is said in the catechism, do they keep their eyes on their books, or do they look about them?
3. Do they learn their catechism well? Do they answer in a clear voice, and before they answer, do they make the sign of the cross devoutly and reverently?
4. Are there many children who make analyses, and does their number increase? Which are the children who distinguish themselves most

by their zeal with regard to analysis, and also those who have only lately begun to make them, but who give hope for the future? Do these children always end their analysis by a practical resolution and a prayer, so that they may be helped to correct some one fault?

5. Do they, every month, bring certifications of confession, as prescribed by the rule? Do they give in many *billets* of Gospels?

6. Do the dignitaries faithfully fulfil their charges? Are you satisfied with the intendent, with the assistants, with the secretaries? Are the heads of forms careful in marking those who are absent? When a question is put to a child whose name is on their card, but who is not in the form, do they answer, *Absent*? Are they particular in allowing no one to be on their forms whose name is not written on their cards? Which are the heads of forms who give you the greatest satisfaction?

Before leaving, M. le Curé, or the Director-General of Catechisms, gives out special prizes to those who have shown the greatest application from the beginning of the year. This distribution is arranged in the same way as we have described above. He encourages those who receive no reward, and gives such advice to all as he judges will be most useful to them. After the visitation, the chief recapitulates these counsels, and urges the children to follow them. He again speaks of them on the following Sundays, and thus these visitations come to be looked on not only as festivals, but as days for the rekindling of energy.

Article VI

Punishments

It remains for us to speak of punishments, which must be sometimes resorted to, the more effectually to correct the idleness or the giddiness of the children. But if they are to do them good, they must only be used rarely and with discretion. If used too often, the children grow hardened to them, or, at anyrate, they will only make them behave well through fear. Fénélon says[1] that "joy and confidence should be the ordinary condition of children; otherwise their intellect becomes clouded, and their courage fails them; if they are lively, they are irritated; if they are gentle, they are made stupid. Fear is like violent remedies which we employ only in extreme cases: they purge, but they damage the constitution and exhaust the organs. A soul led by fear is always weak."

We must, therefore, resort to punishments with regret; sometimes, even, we may pretend not to observe a fault, and we can wait for a more favourable moment to speak of it. Never rebuke the child at the moment, or from your own impulse; he will only think that you are sharp and ill-tempered,

[1] *Education des Filles.*

not that you are reproving him reasonably and with real friendliness; he will only see in you a passionate man; he will not recognise you as the minister of the God of peace, and you will lose your authority for ever. Besides, at the moment, his mind will not be in a condition to own his fault, to conquer his passion, or to feel the force of what you say to him; it might even make him treat you with less respect than he ought.

Do not wound his self-respect more than you can help: for instance, speak to him privately, telling him you do it to spare him the shame of a public rebuke. A child treated like this sees that it is no pleasure to you to scold him; he is touched by the indulgence and consideration you use towards him; in future he will be afraid of making himself remarkable and grieving his catechists. Or one may make use of a third person; for instance, one of his parents or masters, to warn the child, provided you are sure they will know how to do it without irritating him.

If you feel you ought to give the rebuke in public, you will tell the children that this should have been done before, but that you hoped, by waiting, to spare him the pain of it. The important thing is that the children should be convinced that we are sorry to punish them, that we only do it for their greater good, and because we dearly love them. It is well, sometimes, to say this to a child privately, after the catechism, to comfort him a little for the pain which a public rebuke or punishment has caused him. A few kind words, then, are like a

PUNISHMENTS

plaister on the wound; the child sees you are not angry with him, that you have no feeling against him, and that he has been punished only to make him better.

In spite of the necessity for so many precautions, there are times when the public good and even his own good demands that a child should be rebuked at once and severely, particularly if it is a fault which causes scandal, or if it has been often repeated, or if it might have disastrous consequences. Then the culprit must be rebuked sharply and sternly. Afterwards it is better to pass on to something else, showing that it was only an offence committed against God by one of His children which had aroused you.

If you see that a child who has been publicly rebuked, instead of behaving better, is only angry, it is no use to try and soften him while the catechism is going on; the child would resist, his pride and anger would rise, and he would set up a struggle which would be a cause of greater scandal than the fault itself, and most damaging to all authority. Two or three such scenes would be quite enough to make the children lose all confidence in their catechists. Therefore, if you see that the public correction has not succeeded, do no more; give time for this mutinous stubbornness to subside; so you save the scandal of insubordination, and the little rebel will be condemned by his own companions, for they will be touched by your moderation. But when the catechism is over,[1] take him by himself, to pour oil

---

[1] Something of this sort should always follow after any humiliating public rebuke.

on his wound: speak as a friend to him, and show him you are only seeking his own good; still, make him feel the greatness of his fault, and be silent for a few moments to see what effect your remonstrance has. If the child is confused, if he blushes, if he turns away his head and lets some tears fall, you have won him; tell him you will forget everything. You will have nothing more to fear from him than a little thoughtlessness at times. But if, on the contrary, he listens to what you say coldly and impatiently, tell him what will be the consequences of his bad behaviour; he will be sent away from the catechism, he will be expelled publicly, there will be no first Communion for him. Finally, beseech him to think seriously of the salvation of his soul; tell him that you are quite ready to believe that his fault was only something once in a way, that he will do nothing like it in future; treat him with much kindness, as if forgetting all that had happened, and be assured that all this will work in his little head; for though children are volatile and very frivolous, yet they are capable of being strongly impressed, and the method of the catechisms of S. Sulpice is most effectual in this way. If the child does not respond to this kindness at first, do not be disheartened; sometimes we must return three or four times to the charge, particularly if you have to deal with an impatient or mischievous character. Always treat him kindly, but with all these marks of affection bring in constantly the fear of God's chastisements, and the necessity of escaping them; you will often be surprised yourself at the change which will be worked in the child.

Punishments ought to be very slight in themselves, but accompanied by every circumstance which may inspire the children with shame and remorse. The catechist therefore must refrain, not only from striking the children, but even from speaking to them in an angry and indignant tone. "*Charitas,*" says S. Augustine,[1] "*aliis blanda, aliis severa, nulli inimica, omnibus mater.*" The spirit of the catechisms of S. Sulpice is a spirit of kindness and gentleness; it allows of no ways of correcting the children which would only repel them and inspire them with dislike to the catechism and the teachings; and accordingly the custom of striking them has always been reprobated, even with a little cane, or simply with the list-card.

The punishments in use in the catechisms of S. Sulpice are, bad points, the loss of a picture, being sent away from the catechism. The bad points are very useful in compelling a child to amend his faults, for he is reminded that when three such are recorded against him, his name will have to be struck off the list, and he will be sent away. One bad point marked on a register, in the presence of the whole catechism, makes more impression on the child's mind than a simple warning. Besides, the most incorrigible child is not without some passing wishes to be better, and these can more easily be taken advantage of by this method; as, for instance, when two points have been registered against him, he can

[1] *De catechizandis rudibus.*

be told that if he behaves better, one will be scratched out; and, in fact, the catechist will always be careful to keep his word with him directly he sees the least change. Bad points are hardly used at all in the girls' catechisms.

If the child does not improve, and if he is a constant cause of scandal for the catechism, he must be sent away, but this severe course should only be taken at the last extremity, as rarely as possible, only for very important reasons, and after mature reflection. The chief, before he sends away a child, arranges with the catechists as to the manner of doing it. The elder girls are never sent away publicly: it would be too humiliating a punishment for them, and might even damage them in public opinion. Neither must the reputation of a boy suffer, when he is sent away from the catechism; his parents would be offended, and he himself might nourish a secret hatred for the catechist who had pointed him out to the whole parish as one altogether bad and who would do harm to others. It should simply be said that he must be shut out from the catechism because he does not observe the rule, and he disturbs his neighbours; that he has incurred the penalty decided on in the *article des renvois*, and that this article must be strictly observed.

When a child has been sent away from the catechism, he must not be taken back again, or at least not unless his parents come to ask pardon for him, and promise to make him more obedient and teachable. But it must be made clear to them, that as he has been a source of distraction and disorder in the catechism, he cannot be placed with the other children, whom very likely he would distract again, and that all that can be done for him is to set him on a form by himself, and thus make proof of his good behaviour, and of the reality of his change; and, moreover, that taking this humble place will give him the opportunity of making up before the whole catechism for the bad example he has set before; and also that his penitence will act on the others as a strong incentive to good behaviour.

CHAPTER VIII

HOW TO SECURE GOOD ORDER AND SUCCESS IN CATECHISMS

In every catechism it is necessary to have a definite rule, fixing the number and order of the exercises, and the registers in which will be written the names of the children, with certain special observations on each. The rule should be written on large-sized paper, and well-bound. It is read out to the children at the beginning of the year, and after Easter. This is done from the pulpit, instead of the instruction.

Of all the articles of the rule, there are none more necessary to be observed than those which enjoin silence in the catechism, and punctuality in coming at the appointed time.

Article I

On Silence

Whatever may be the special rules adopted, the most perfect silence must be enjoined on the children during the whole time of the catechism.[1] The catechist will have no trouble in bringing them to this, if, when he imposes silence on the children, he does it quietly, but still very decidedly. The essential thing is, not to say much, nor to threaten much, still less to exclaim and break out in reproaches; but to speak to the point, and, above all, to speak religiously and feelingly. Suppose, for instance, that a child is talking, or is inattentive; at first the catechist need not stop in what he is saying, it will be enough to fix his eyes on him; sometimes he will stop suddenly and look at the child who is talking; another time he will say: "*I see one child who has already forgotten what I have just said.*" If the child goes on, or if he begins again almost directly, he will address him by name, and say: "*N—— N——, I thought you would be more obedient*"; or perhaps, "*Must I then let all the catechism know you are a disobedient child?*" Another time he will say suddenly to the child who is inattentive or who is talking: "*My child, what have I just said?*" And if he does not answer, or answers badly, he will say: "*I knew how it would be when I asked you; that is how a child answers who does not listen.*" By means of these little devices, used just at the right time, a catechist, without ever resorting to punishment, or even often having to find fault, will be able quite easily to keep all the children in order, however giddy they may be. Children soon

[1] "Prior aliique operarii debent esse solliciti, ut venientes pueri observent silentium" (S. François de Sales, *Mod. Catechismi. Opuscul.*, t. ii. p. 27).

find out the character of those who are over them; they will obey without question one who shows an interest in them, and is kind and yet firm.

It is found by experience that one of the best ways of preventing children from talking, particularly in the little catechisms, is to make the boys sit with their arms crossed, and the girls with closed hands. They can easily be brought to this by crossing one's own arms, or joining hands, in a sensible way. Another way is not to allow them to turn their heads. But if children are to learn the importance of keeping silence, the catechists themselves must be most careful on this point. Therefore if ever a child can be spoken to by a sign or a look, it is better not to speak; they should do the same among themselves, never break the silence unless it is absolutely necessary, and then be careful to speak so low, that no one will hear. In this way, the children will get accustomed to look on the chapel as a sacred place where no one ought to speak. Often it is better to allow a slight accidental disturbance rather than break the silence by immediately setting it right.

Article II

On Perseverance in coming to the Catechism at the exact time

The children should be charged to come punctually to the time when the catechism begins.

They are told that by coming in time they will take part in the prayer, and this will draw upon them grace to profit by the catechism, God having promised a special blessing to the children's prayer; besides which, regularity in coming exactly to the time will give them the benefit of gaining the indulgences which the Sovereign Pontiff grants to children who are punctual in coming before the prayer, and not leaving till the signal given for departure;[1] that those who are there to join in the prayer rejoice the heart of their catechists, for it is a sure mark that they really desire to hear the word of God; that these children contribute to the good order and edification of the catechism, while the idle ones who come late disturb the attention of the others, and of necessity distract and unsettle them.

Another way of persuading them to be punctual is to make them feel how much they suffer themselves when they come in after the catechism has begun. They will be told, for instance, from time to time, that those who come late are looked upon as idle, and can aspire to no rewards, or dignities, or the places of heads of forms, not even to the good points. If the catechist observes that a child who has come late is well-behaved and attentive, he will say to him: "N——, if you had come earlier, I should have given you a good point." He will say to another: "You would have had the office which we have given to ——, if you had been more careful to

[1] Our Holy Father, Pope Gregory XVI., by a letter of Sept. 13, 1831, written entirely and signed by his own hand, granted this favour to the children of the Catechisms of S. Sulpice.

come punctually." At another time the catechist who is in the pulpit will name, as if about to question him, a child who came in late, and the chief, with whom he is in concert, will say aloud: "This child must not answer to-day; he came late." But it would not do to make a general rule that children who come late are not to be questioned; for in order to get a good answer it might be necessary sometimes to have recourse to them when the rest cannot give it; and besides one must be careful not to irritate a child by this humiliation. Another way is to mark those who come late as half-absent, telling them that two half-absences count for one whole. If there are elections in the catechism, and if they are electors, they can be deprived of their vote.

But none of these methods will be of any use unless the catechists themselves set an example of that punctuality which they require in the children. They ought even to go to the church or chapel a little before the time, and so by their presence prevent all that frivolity which is so natural to children when they are not looked after; they should also begin quite punctually at the time, even if there are only a very few children present. It is a very common temptation to wait to begin the catechism because there are not enough children. If you wait only a few minutes, the children who are present will tire of it, and next time will not hurry themselves, and those who come later, finding the exercises not yet begun, will not be vexed at their own unpunctuality. It is easy to imagine the confusion which would result. Therefore every one must understand that the exercises begin exactly at the hour named, and then every one will come punctually to that hour.

Article III

On the Means of Checking Absences

Absences must be guarded against by frequent warnings, and by showing the advantages of regularity, and the sometimes irreparable loss of the most valuable instruction and grace caused by absence from even one catechism. The catechists should not tell the children they will be sent away because of their absences, but rather confine themselves to threatening them with being degraded from their offices, taking away their places; with the loss of any rewards or prizes at the solemn distribution, with exclusion from their first Communion, with being put back for another year, and finally, after three absences, with their names being erased from the chart for interrogation, and they themselves being seated apart from the rest as a disgrace. When the name of a child is erased from the list, it must not be entirely blotted out; a little cross is put against it, so that the catechist who conducts the interrogation will not call his name; but yet it remains there in case he is able to take his place again. A child loses his place if he is absent three times in the course of five weeks, unless he has brought a note of excuse. But if, after being absent once, he is present five times successively, this absence is not reckoned. From time to time the children who absent themselves and have no legitimate excuse to give, must be publicly named. The chief of the catechism will also closely examine the conduct of the heads of forms, he will make sure that they are exact in marking the absences, and he will threaten those who neglect this duty with the loss of their office.

Article IV

Keeping the Registers

In every catechism there should be, besides the *catalogue d'interrogation*, a register, in which is written, in alphabetical order, the surnames and Christian names of the children, the date of their entrance into the catechism, the name of their confessor, their dwelling-place or their schools, and their absences.[1] Keeping the registers supposes the science of details, one of the most essential qualities for catechists, and above all for the chiefs. A good catechist would delight to go into the smallest details for the good order of the catechism,—in making out lists, in keeping an exact account of absences, in marking

[1] After each set of names beginning with the same letter, particularly after those which begin with the letters B, C, D, G, L, M, a small space should be left blank, so that there may be room enough to write in the names of such children as may enter in the course of the year.

KEEPING THE REGISTERS

in the registers with the greatest precision everything which should be entered in them.

If the catechist appointed to keep the registers fulfils his duty faithfully, he may be sure that, even if he is not well seconded by the other catechists, the catechism will be flourishing; if, on the contrary, he neglects it, even in things which seem trifling, he will cause much difficulty, confusion, and disorder.

If the catechist whose duty it is to take the names of the children who come to the catechism, is not careful to write them down quite exactly, his negligence on this head may have most serious consequences.

One child who came to the great catechism for boys at S. Sulpice had his name entirely altered by a mistake in one or two letters. The next year he was entered again, according to custom, and this time his name was written rightly. But as this right name did not appear on the register of the preceding year, it was supposed that the child had only newly come to the catechism, and consequently he was not admitted to first Communion. The child declared he had been there two years; last year's register was searched, but in vain they looked it through and through, the child's name was not to be found. It was supposed that he was telling a falsehood, and he was excluded from the first Communion; and in consequence of this injustice the child was so disheartened that he never appeared again at the catechism.

On another occasion, among the *billets* of confession which the children are bound to bring every month, several were found belonging to a child of the little catechism called Louis-Henri N——. At the great catechism was another child called Louis-André N——. The catechist reckons Louis-Henri's *billets* as belonging to Louis-André. It is believed that he confesses regularly every month, and he is admitted to the first Communion. But when the confessor reads the list which is sent to him of those of his penitents who are admitted, he declares he does not know this child. He is shown the *billets* of confession, he acknowledges his own signature. "But," he says, "are Henri N—— and André N—— the same child? I know the first quite well, he belongs to the little catechism; all these *billets* are his. As to the other, I never heard his name before; I cannot receive him." And, in fact, that child never made his first Communion; he felt desperate, and gave up all religious habits. If the catechist who had charge of the register had paid more attention to the child's names, he would have discovered that André N—— had no confessor; then he would have provided him with one, and thus perhaps would have been the means of giving him the happiness of making rightly his first Communion.

In fact, the children are regular in confession just in proportion to the zeal and care which is shown by the catechist whose business it is, in entering their *billets*. If he is careful to note the *billets* he receives, and to warn the children who neglect their confession, in the end they will all confess regularly. How often one has found children who have gone on three or four months at the catechism without a

REGISTERING OF CONFESSIONS

confessor, only through the neglect of the catechist, who ought to have found them one! In consequence of this neglect many children lose the unspeakable advantage of frequent confession! And what a loss it is for them! Frequent confession would have lessened the number of their sins, it would have stopped the onward course of their bad habits, and would have better prepared their hearts to receive all the blessings of Holy Communion.

The more we dread all such results, the more should we be careful in providing against them; and the way is, to follow all the rules which are appointed for the keeping of the registers, even those which seem very minute, for they are all based on experience and reason. To make it clearer, we give the reader a specimen of the great register in use in the catechisms of S. Sulpice.

The great register contains nine columns, each for a special purpose, as their names imply. After the names of the children are entered, which should be done on the first day of the reopening, about which we shall speak later on, the catechist who has charge of the great register takes the names of all those children who come to be admitted. If every catechist could take the names, the result would be that certain children would get their names written down by all the catechists, which would lead to a great deal of trouble.

Moreover, the catechist who has charge of the great register, being in the habit of entering the children, does it much better and more exactly. We will go through in succession each column of the register.

Date of Entry.	Names, Christian and Surname.	Age and Sacraments received.	Names of Confessors.	Billets of Confession.										
				January.	February.	March.	April.	May.	June.	July.	August.	September.	October.	November.

REGISTERING OF CONFESSIONS

Abodes and Schools.	Absences.									Observations	Gospels.
	November.	December.	January.	February.	March.	April.	May.	June.	July.		

First Column

Date of Entering the Catechism

This date is very important; it serves to fix the time when the child will make his first Communion; for at S. Sulpice, before a child is admitted to that, he must have been twelve full months in the catechism, not counting holiday-time. To be done correctly, not only the day and the month must be marked, but also the year; otherwise, if the catechism is at all a large one, there would inevitably result a hopeless confusion. When the register is renewed, at the beginning of each year, this date must be carried on to the new register, and care must be taken that it corresponds exactly to the old one.

Second Column

Christian Names and Surnames

The catechist whose office it is to enter the children, should not simply ask their name; many would answer, only giving their baptismal name, as that is what they are accustomed to at home; they must also be asked their family name. Sometimes the surname is the name of a saint, and the name one supposed to be the baptismal name is really the family name. In this case the catechist

CHRISTIAN NAMES AND SURNAMES 213

would ask the child what is his father's name; and if he can write, he will add, How is your name spelt?

Unless the right spelling is correctly taken, it will happen that when the children bring their analyses, or the little note we shall presently speak of, or *billets* of the Gospel, of excuse, of confession, etc., it will not be known to whom these *billets* belong. The names will be confused with others which somewhat resemble them, and it can easily be seen what great difficulties would arise from this confusion when pictures are to be given, or admissions to first Communion, etc. Besides, in arranging places, if a child is called by a name not his own, he will not go to take the place, he will think he has not been called. He will go after the catechism and have himself entered again, as if it were not already done. And thus, he will be entered twice under two different names, and he will have two places in the catechism.

Besides the surname, all the baptismal names belonging to each child should be entered. One will not suffice, for it often happens that several children have the same surname and the same baptismal name. If two children have the same surname, and only one baptismal name, and that also the same, a new name can be added to one of them, his mother's name, for instance, so that there may be no confusion in the register. For want of attending to this rule, two children in very different stations of life, both called *Henri de la Brétonnière*, were entered as one on the register, and thus sat side by side in the catechism, or rather, had only one place between them. When a child has several baptismal names, the one by which he is called in his family should be underlined, so that he may be called by the same name in the catechism.

Third Column

Age and Sacraments Received

As it is quite a common thing for children not to know exactly their own age, it does not do quite to depend on what they say when they are questioned upon it, nor even on what their schoolmasters say. The custom of obliging all children who come to the ordinary catechisms to bring certificates of birth or baptism, is liable to a great many inconveniences.[1] The only means employed in the catechisms of S. Sulpice is to give each of the children a small note, of which we give a specimen, printed on

[1] By demanding these extracts, the parents are often put to an expense which they incur willingly before the first Communion of their children, but not before knowing whether they will be admitted to it. It requires an extraordinary amount of care not to lose four or five hundred extracts, to keep them in order and return them correctly, and all the more because often there are other names in these extracts besides those by which the children are known. Sometimes the children lose these extracts, and throw the blame of this neglect on the catechists, and the parents come to demand them. In fact, they are liable to be lost in a thousand ways, and this leads to serious consequences.

gummed paper, and to tell the children that their parents are to fill in the necessary words:—

My Name is..

I was born the.............of the Month............in the Year......

I live....................................

They are told that they will have no reward, that they will not even be admitted to the first Communion, unless they bring back this paper as soon as possible, after it has been filled in. This plan, so simple in itself, is very certain in its results; the parents, who may have some interest in deceiving the catechists, will not easily bring themselves to lie definitely and in writing, particularly as they know that a certificate of baptism will be required at the time of first Communion.

Fourth Column

Names of Confessors

In the fourth column is written the name of the confessor belonging to each child; by this means the catechists find out if any of the confessors have a great number of children on their hands, and will avoid sending them more, unless they desire it. As all the *billets* of confession are signed by the confessors, by comparing the name on the *billet* with that marked on the great register it will be known if a child has of his own accord changed his confessor; there are some who go the round of all the confessors in the parish. Besides, it is right to inform the confessors when their penitents are admitted to their first Communion; it is necessary therefore that the catechists should know who they are.

Fifth Column

Billets of Confession

At S. Sulpice, children of the great catechisms who have not yet made their first Communion are obliged to bring a *billet* of confession once a month, so that it may be known for certain that they have confessed in the course of the month. Some of the dignitaries gather up the *billets* of confession, and after this general collection the intendent puts them into a box and sorts them alphabetically. Before this collection, the catechists ought not to take any *billets*; if they took only one, all the children's hands would be up to give in theirs, and this would make great confusion; besides, the dignitaries would have nothing to collect. But after the dignitaries have been round, the catechists take any *billets* which are brought to them; but they should pass them on to the intendent; for if this rule is not observed, it might happen that the catechists would put them in their pockets, and forget or lose the *billets*. Some years ago a catechist received a *billet*, and without thinking of it, slipped it into the sleeve of his cassock. When the time came for the child who had given it to him to be admitted to the first Communion, this *billet* was not reckoned, it had not been marked on the register. It appeared that the child had not made his confession often enough, and he was rejected. His parents, who unfortunately were not religious, declared that he never should make his first Communion, and they took him away from the catechism, where he has never appeared again. Some months after, the catechist found by chance the *billet*, hid in his sleeve; and frightened at the terrible consequences of such a small neglect, he prays to God daily for the unhappy child, who perhaps would have made a good first Communion, and would have been in the way of salvation, which he is far away from now.

When the catechism is over, the catechist in charge of the register takes the *billets* which he finds in the box in which the intendent has put them, and carries them away in his portfolio without losing one. When he enters them on the register, he takes one of these *billets*, reads the name of the child and finds it out on the register; if the column for the name of the confessors is blank, he writes the name which he finds on the *billet*; then, passing on to the column of the month during which the child has made his confession, he copies the date from the *billet*.

A *billet* should not be copied into the register unless the Christian and surname of the child correspond with those on the *billet*. If there is any difference, the catechist should put it aside, and try to find out to whom it belongs.[1]

There should be a special place where the *billets* can be kept, and easily found. After they have been copied they can be burnt, so that they may not get mixed with the others.

Sixth Column

Children's Abode and School

Many circumstances oblige the catechists to write to certain children, or to send someone to them or to their parents, or to go themselves to speak to one or another. A few months passed in a catechism are enough to show what difficulties may arise from not knowing the addresses of the children. They are ascertained by means of the little printed *billet* we have spoken of above. The dwelling of a child is not the school where he is a day-scholar, nor the

---

[1] It may be easily supposed that a child might deceive his catechist by giving him *billets* of confession belonging to a younger brother, whom he would send to confess instead of himself. The catechist should also look carefully at the date of the year; for there are children sometimes who have three or four *billets* belonging to the preceding year, and fancy that by this means they are quit of everything for the current year. Some children have gone a whole year without confessing, and yet have incurred no blame from their catechists, whom they deceived by bringing them *billets* which were three or four years old.

shop where he works, but the house where he spends the night. Similarly, a child's parish is the one in which he sleeps. Thus, the members of a boarding-school belong to the parish in which the school is situated.

If a child obtains permission to make his first Communion in a parish not his own, this permission must be signed by his own curé, or by the vicar in his place. A curé can refuse permission to his parishioners to go to the catechism of another parish, but this refusal does not apply to children who have already made their first Communion.

Seventh Column

Absences

We have already mentioned the *cards* used by the *first of the forms*; their use is to show the catechist what children are absent from the catechism.[1] When the catechist in charge of the great register is going to note down the absences, he takes the cards one by one, and looks out in his register, which should be arranged alphabetically, the name of each child with an absence marked, or a half-absence. He goes to the column of absences answering to the child's name, then to the column of the month, and marks the date when the child was absent from the catechism, *e.g.*, 2, 9, 16, if the

[1] It is well from time to time to test the trustworthiness of the heads of forms, and to see for oneself that the little card answering to the name of a child one knows to have been absent has been drawn.

catechisms were held on those days. He goes in this way through all the cards. If the child has only a half-absence against him, he marks a little cross instead of the date.[1] Formerly M. le Curé of S. Sulpice used to send one of the priests of the community to the parents of an absent child, to ask if it was by their wish that the child was absent from the catechism. In the last century they merely sent them printed notices. If a child is absent from the catechism, but brings a note of excuse signed by his parents, his absence is not counted, or, at least, not unless there is reason to think that the grounds of excuse are not real, or that the parents are too easy in this respect.

It is well to give every month a general report of the absences, and the names of those children who have not brought notes of excuse.

Eighth Column

Observations

In this column care should be taken not to enter any observation which would damage the reputation of the children, neither should any notes from their school masters or mistresses be copied without consideration, if they contain anything unfavour-

[1] Some catechists mark the names of absent children first on a little slip of paper, and afterwards copy them into the great register; others mark the absences in a special register arranged to correspond with the forms and the cards. Still it is well from time to time to copy the absences into the great register, so that everything relating to the conduct of the child may be seen at one glance.

able. All the rewards given to the children should be carefully entered, the books, and the pictures; the offices they have filled, and those they are filling, as well as the *billets* and dialogues they have been given to learn. It would be useful also to mark the *good points*, so that they may not always be given to the same children.

Ninth Column

Gospels

Formerly certain dignitaries called *collectors* gathered up all the *billets* of Gospels, and took them away to be marked on special lists. At Easter and at the end of the year they presented a general report of these *billets*, so that the catechist could better judge of the assiduity and the deserts of each child.[1] In the girls' catechism of *perseverance*, the president is still charged with this function: otherwise, in general, a catechist undertakes it. He first arranges in alphabetical order all the *billets* he has received, at least, if the dignitaries have not already done so; then, turning to the names of the children in the great register, he marks in the column for Gospels the number 1 for those who have learnt the Gospel in French, 2 for those who have learnt it in Latin, and 3 for those who have learnt it in Greek. As often as they learn the Gospels, these numbers are marked.

When the catechism is very large, and the keep-

[1] *Histoire des Catéchismes de Saint-Sulpice*, p. 84.

ing the register becomes too complicated, one catechist can undertake the *billets* of Gospels, another of absences, and a third the *billets* of confession; they will then bring them from time to time to the catechist who has charge of the great register, in which he will then enter them. In parishes where there are but few catechists, a layman can have the charge of the register, or even one or more children, if intelligent and trustworthy.

There is no column in the great register for marking the *diligences*, or analyses, because the greater number of children do not write any. In every catechism there is a special register for this purpose, similar to the specimen we give here. Each class of seal has a certain number or some arbitrary sign belonging to it; and the sign, which marks what seal the child has gained, is marked in the division corresponding to the child's name.

Christian Names and Surnames.	November.				December.				January.					February	
	6	13	20	27	4	11	18	25	1	8	15	22	29	5	12
Arnaud (Denise)															
Autain (Césarine)															
Bazin (Clotilde)															
Bellot (Agatha)															
Bienassis (Rosalie)															
Blattlin (Louise)															

We will conclude this chapter and the first part of the *Méthode* by some information as to the seals which have often been mentioned in the preceding pages.

There are three kinds of seals which can be used in the catechisms; seals made by a dry stamp

SEALS OF THE CATECHISM

(*timbre sec*), seals made with a damp stamp (*timbre humide*), and seals made with an open-work stamp (*découpures*).

The first is applied by means of a hand-press, such as may be seen in the office of the bishop's secretary, or in chambers occupied by notaries or others. This stamp may be in steel or copper, it may represent a cypher, or a cross, or the monogram of the Blessed Virgin, etc., and an inscription giving the title of the catechism and the name of the parish; or it may be a saint or any other symbolic figure with the inscription surrounding it.

The wet stamps are in more common use, and are more convenient. They are much used in the different bureaus of administration for putting an official sign on papers. They are generally in copper; like the others, they may represent either a cypher or a symbolic figure or the image of a saint; but as the impressions given by these stamps do not generally come out so well as those stamped in a press, the details of the cypher or figure should not be too delicate, or they will be liable to come out very imperfectly. In using these stamps a little stamping box is necessary, containing the different colours, a brush, etc.

For the perforated stamps, a thin open-work piece of metal is used, the open-work giving a cypher and an inscription; a paint-brush dipped in the right colour is passed over it. This is the most simple plan.

The same stamp will serve for seals of different

colours, if only they are carefully cleaned for a new colour.[1]

[1] Those who wish to provide themselves with stamps, will find engravers in Paris who devote themselves to this special branch. They only need to be told the subject, and if the stamps are to be in steel or copper. A press can be had for 70 francs. Round stamps, with two letters in cypher and an inscription running round, cost from 12 to 15 francs. Oval stamps, representing a saint in the middle and an inscription round, cost from 40 to 50 francs. The price is higher for stamps in steel, and in oval form, with a saint and an inscription. The open-work plates, with small colour-glass, stick of Indian ink, and paint-brush, cost from 6 to 8 francs. The necessaries for the wet stamps, in tin boxes, cost 4, 5, or 6 francs, according to the size.

PART II

RULES AND OBSERVATIONS REFERRING TO EACH CATECHISM

In a parish there may be four sorts of catechisms: the *Little Catechisms*, the *Catechisms of first Communion*, the *Week-day Catechisms*, and those of *Perseverance*.

Most of the rules which we have described in the first part of this volume apply equally to all the catechisms, but there are certain special rules belonging to each of them, which we will now point out, together with some observations which spring out of them. It will be seen that these rules can be carried out in the majority of parishes with some quite accidental modifications as to days and hours, and as to some exercises which are not suitable or not possible in certain localities.

CHAPTER I

THE LITTLE CATECHISMS

THE little catechisms have a special claim on the fatherly attention and anxiety of the pastors, for they contain the hope of the parish. There are gathered together all the quite young children whose hearts it is so important to train, that they may keep the innocence God has there implanted, and be prepared for being in the future true Christian faithful people. In the life of M. Olier it is related that in his parish church he liked to take the catechism for little children himself, and did it with wonderful love and humility.[1]

ARTICLE I

The Children who form the Little Catechisms

The little catechisms are intended for children from six or seven to ten years of age. Younger children are admitted very reluctantly, and only

[1] *Vie de M. Olier*, vol. i.

THE LITTLE CATECHISMS

if they show such marks of intelligence that we may hope our exercises will be of some use to them, and that they will be able to behave properly. Without this precaution the number of children would be much too large, the order of the catechism would suffer, there would be no discipline.

Neither are older children admitted, and if they apply, they are sent on to the catechisms of first Communion, at least unless such children cannot read, or do not know the first rudiments of Christian doctrine. Catechists who have good, teachable, and intelligent children under them, who can do honour to the catechism by their answers, are sometimes tempted to keep them beyond the age specified; but it is for the good of these children that they should be passed on to the great catechisms when they are ten years old, so that they can make their first Communion when they are about twelve; and, moreover, they will profit more by the exercises of the great catechism.

Article II

Regulations for the Little Catechisms

I. All the children should come to the catechism exactly at the time: go into the chapel without hurry, take the place which has been assigned to them, and wait quietly and in silence for the moment of prayer. They are forbidden to stop outside or in the porch.

II. At a given signal they will kneel down, without noise, their arms crossed, their eyes lowered, their manner reverent, and they will follow the prayer with attention and devotion. Then they will wait for the signal to rise.

> During the singing of the first hymn the dignitaries will distribute the cards to the heads of forms, and collect the *billets* of the Gospel and of confession. Then they will hold themselves ready to answer any interrogation of the catechist: for this they must be so attentive that they can take it up at once, if M. the Catechist does not think well to repeat the question.

III. Every time a child answers, he must begin and end with the sign of the cross. He must be extremely careful to recite or answer to anything in a clear voice, so as to be heard at all points of the catechism.

> If a child who is called is absent, the first of the form merely replies, *Absent*. Good marks will be given to those who know their catechism quite perfectly. Those, on the contrary, who have not learnt it, or who do not know it properly, will receive a bad mark. These marks or notes will be consulted in arranging the distribution of images and prizes. For those who persevere in learning, besides the catechism, the Gospel and the Historic Catechism, there will be specially good rewards.

IV. The children sing the hymns, and should listen to the instruction with attention and quietness.

> During the instruction, all will cross their arms and fix their eyes on whoever is in the pulpit, and try not to lose one word of what is explained to them of the Word of God.
>
> When the signal is given they stand up to listen to the Holy Gospel. Then, seated, they will listen to the homily, devoutly and in perfect silence and stillness, as during the instruction, but with still more attention, if possible.

V. The catechism concludes with a prayer.

> Those who are called on to recite the Acts will do so in a clear and audible voice.
>
> The children will go out form by form, following the signal. They are never to stride over the forms, which is quite contrary to modest behaviour.

VI. The children must be sure to go home directly to their parents.

> When the children leave the catechism, they are expressly forbidden to loiter under the porch or outside.
>
> They should try to remember and put in practice the resolution which will have been given them at the end of the instruction and the homily.
>
> They must behave so well both at home and at school that everyone will see how much good they get from the lessons received

in the catechism. They must persevere in all their studies, and particularly in learning their catechism well for the following Sunday.

VII. Children who come late to the catechism must make their excuse, according to custom, to the catechist who has charge of the placing.

> Those who come a little after the prayer, will apologise, merely saying, "*Je vous salue, Marie*," and then sit down.
>
> Those who only come in about the middle o towards the end of the catechism (still more those who are not there at all), should bring a note of excuse from their parents or masters; this should be done also in the case of those who, for good reasons, have not been able to learn their catechism.
>
> If they fail to bring this note they will not be able to have any rewards on the days when images are given away, even if they have only been absent once; but if there have been three absences without excuse, they will lose, besides, a prize or an *accessit* at the end of the year.

VIII. A child must very rarely go out, never during the instruction or the homily, only during the singing of a hymn.

> Permission for this must only be asked for from the catechist who has charge of the placing.

IX. Every two months the children must bring a *billet* of confession.

THE LITTLE CATECHISMS

> A child who breaks this rule (at least unless his confessor has told him not to come so often) can aspire to no rewards.

> If the catechist in charge of the lowest or middle quarter thinks that one of the children is fit to go higher, he will point him out to the chief, who, having satisfied himself of his capacity, will formally give him a place in the higher quarter, at the same time giving him a picture.

X. At the close of the catechism each catechist gives two good points, and the chief gives three.

> This number may be added to sometimes if the children have been particularly attentive.

> Such of the children as win three good points may exchange them for a picture; the dignitaries need only have two; the intendent receives pictures only; this is a privilege dating from about 1680.

XI. At different periods images will be given away, and the catechism course each year closes with a solemn distribution of prizes.

> These prizes are gained by those children who throughout the year have been the most distinguished for their perseverance, their knowledge, and, above all, for their good behaviour and their piety.

XII. Punishments are, in the first instance, confined to bad points.

> If the catechists are anxious to reward merit, they must also inflict punishments, though with regret. They hope that the children

will take good care to spare them this pain. Bad points are given—

1. To those who talk and are restless, and particularly to those who behave badly during the prayer or the homily.
2. To those who are absent from the catechism, without good reasons.
3. To those who have not learnt their catechism.
4. To those who disobey their catechists.
5. To those who give trouble to others, particularly to those who make the reports.

XIII. A child who has been reproved several times, and still continues to deserve censure, will be sent away from the catechism.

If any child shows himself to be incorrigible, and by his bad example is doing harm to the other children, he will be liable to be sent away from the catechism for a longer or shorter time as his case may require.

All who refuse to submit to this rule will be treated in this way.

XIV. There are in the catechism one *Intendent* and four *Assistants*, who at Easter can be admitted to the form of honour ; and besides, there are *Zélateurs, Aspirants, Singers,* and the *Heads of Forms*.

The form of honour contains the Intendents and Assistants who have given place to others at the beginning or middle of the year. It is a distinction which gives them all the honours of the offices they have filled, but exempts them from all obligations attached to them, excepting that of giving a good example to the whole catechism.

1. The Intendent is the child who ranks highest in the catechism; he ought to be a model for it. His office is: (1) To give out the hymns to the singers, before the prayer; he must take them into the sanctuary, the other children being never allowed to go up the steps leading to it; (2) To collect the *diligences* during the hymn which follows the prayer; (3) To give back those of the preceding Sunday after the chief has reported on them.

In 1766 it was ordained that when the Intendent of the little catechism passed on to the great, he should be, of right, second of the form, and should have a place as first when he has made his first Communion.

It was likewise ordered, that if two should pass in the course of the same year, he who came last would, like the first, be the second of a form, but could only be first when his turn came.

2. The two first Assistants should, next to the Intendent, be models for the catechism. Their office is, each in their own quarter, (1) to collect, during the hymn which follows the prayer, the *billets* of confession and the Gospels; for this reason, we find that in 1721 they were called *Collectors*; (2) to give out the cards to the Heads of Forms during the hymn which is sung at the end of the interroga-

tion, and to collect them again during the hymn which prepares for the instruction; and (3) to mark on the cards of the heads of forms in their quarter those heads who are absent. The third and fourth Assistant take the place of the others when necessary.

3. *Zélateur* means one zealous for the glory of God and for the salvation of his neighbour; this beautiful name is given to those who have brought three children to the catechism, provided that these children are at least six years old, and that they persevere in coming to hear the word of God. Good rewards are promised also to each child they bring, when these children have been three Sundays at the catechism.

4. The dignity of Aspirant will be the reward of those children who, not having been nominated at the beginning among the higher dignitaries, have since distinguished themselves not only by their good behaviour and their diligence, but also by their answers when questioned, and above all, by good analyses. The place of Aspirant is held out for their emulation throughout the whole year, and from the form reserved for them are chiefly chosen the Intendents and the Assistants, either at Easter, if a new nomination is made at that season, or at the beginning of the following year.

5. The office of Singer is only promised to children who seem worthy to sing the praises

of God, not only tuneably, but, still more, with modesty and devotion. A great deal of zeal is expected of those who are called to fill so beautiful an office. They must be careful to hold themselves ready to begin all at once, as soon as the conductor of the singing gives the note.

6. The office of the Heads of Forms is to see that the children of their form sit in the place assigned to them, and that no new child comes to sit on the form without permission from the catechist who arranges the placing. They only should answer, *Absent*, when a child of their form is called who is not there; they must mark the absences very correctly. In 1738 their negligence on this head was found to be so great, that their cards were taken away from them, and they were deprived of them for at least ten years. Every head should be an example to the form over which he presides, particularly by his good behaviour and punctuality.

Two absences without legitimate excuse will cause him the loss of his dignity. Any dignitary who has brought on himself a bad point is simultaneously deprived of his dignity.

Note.—This rule is the same for the catechism for girls.

Article III

The Instruction of the Children in the Little Catechisms

When the year begins, the chief of the catechism, with his colleagues, endeavours to find out such of the children as do not know their prayers; he puts them together in a part of the chapel known as the *little quarter*. These children are taught to make the sign of the cross properly, to repeat the Lord's Prayer, the Angelic Salutation, the Apostles' Creed, the *I confess to God*, and the Acts of the theological virtues. Certainly one could wish that they had learnt these prayers from their cradle, but how many poor children there are who, not having really Christian parents, arrive at seven or eight years of age without even knowing how to make the Christian sign on themselves! It is for us to teach them, and we ought to do it very gently, with a real love for those souls whom God sends to us; we must do it therefore with patience, and not with dislike, making the children repeat these prayers till they know them well, and promising rewards to those who, on the following Sunday, repeat them without mistake.

When these children know the prayers, they are instructed in the principal mysteries, and as they make progress, they are transferred to forms in the *great quarter*; this is done publicly, to encourage those who are less advanced, and excite them to try their best.

The public instruction is given in the way described in the first part of the *Method*, suiting the explanations to the age of the children. That they may the better understand Christian doctrine, and that their interest may be more kept alive, two kinds of instruction are given—one on the text of the catechism itself, the other on the history of religion.

The children learn a lesson out of the little catechism, and repeat it the first thing. This done, the chief, or any other catechist, takes up the lesson, question by question, to explain it, after the manner of the game of *good points*, that is to say, by questioning the children. A continuous discourse, however simple it might be, would not be listened to, if it were too long; the attention of the children must be kept up by many questions, which excite their curiosity, hold them in suspense, and give them something to do.

Nothing can be too familiar or too simple for this explanation, in which every word of the answer can be dwelt upon, and nothing left only half-understood. Any little knowledge which the children have already, we can use to lead them on to what we desire to teach them; well-chosen illustrations help very much, and a little story comes in very well to rivet their attention. We should like to give an example of this kind of instruction; but as these details would lead us too far, we prefer to mention a very useful work, in which catechists can find all they desire of this kind; the book is the *Méthode pratique*, by Mgr. Devie, Bishop of

Belley.[1] If anyone reads attentively two or three lessons of the catechism, explained in this way, he will see how to proceed himself, modifying the method a little, according to the general capacity, the intelligence, and the education of the children he has to instruct. This explanation of the catechism ought not to last more than a quarter of an hour; it need not embrace the whole of the catechism lesson; what is left to be explained becomes the subject-matter for the instruction of the following Sunday.

The other instruction we mentioned is given from the pulpit; it can be made into a little course of sacred history on which will hang naturally, according to the order of events, the explanation of the mysteries, of the commandments of God, and of worship. The most experienced men agree in thinking that the historic method is the best suited for the instruction of the children, while at the same time it interests them; but this method requires, if the object is to be attained, the catechist to relate it in an interesting manner. If he confines himself to a dry and summary narration, if he does not bring out in relief the principal circumstances of the event, if he does not picture to the children the places, the persons, the things which happen, he will not win their attention; he will only be telling them what many of them know already from the " Abridgment of Sacred History"; while, on the other hand, if he prepares carefully, his instruction is certain to be a success.

[1] *Méthode pratique pour faire le Catéchisme*, 2 vols. in 12mo.

PLAN OF INSTRUCTION

We give here a plan of these instructions, which may easily be condensed or developed, according to the number of times for which it is wanted.

I. Instruction on the catechism.
  1. Represent Jesus Christ as a child in the temple of Jerusalem. He listens to the doctors. 2. He questions them. 3. The doctors wonder at the wisdom of His answers. Apply this example to the children.

II. Tableau or description of the world.
  1. Describe the world: the earth covered with trees and plants for the nourishment of man; the mountains; the rivers, the sea, the stars, the sun. 2. By this picture prove the existence of God.

III. Creation of the world.
  1. Relate the work of creation, as it is found in Genesis, following the order of the six days. 2. From this history give an idea of the power and the wisdom of God, who alone, by His mere word, made everything, while man could not even create a twig of a tree or a little bird.

IV. Creation of the first man and the first woman.
  1. The body of Adam formed out of a little earth: God breathes upon his countenance, and gives him life. 2. Formation of Eve. 3. Adam and Eve are created and placed in the world with a reasonable soul, that that they may know God, love Him and serve Him, and be with Him in happiness for ever.

V. Sin of our first parents.
   1. The serpent; Eve listens to the serpent; she eats of the forbidden fruit and gives it to Adam. 2. How God punished this transgression of the law which He had made; His words to the serpent, to Eve, and to Adam.
VI. Man sins greatly against God. The flood.
   1. Jealousy and spite of Cain; corruption of men in proportion to their forgetfulness of God. 2. God punishes them by the flood; description of the flood.
VII. Call of Abraham.
   1. Story of this patriarch. 2. God's promise to him concerning the Saviour, who will one day be born, in his family.
VIII. Isaac, Jacob, and the twelve sons of Jacob.
   1. Principal features in the lives of these patriarchs. 2. Faith and trust in God in Isaac and Jacob. 3. Beginning of the Jewish people, that is, the family of Abraham.
IX. Servitude of the Jewish people.
   1. The Jews in Egypt. 2. Plagues of Egypt; passage of the Red Sea. 3. The goodness of God and His power in protecting His people.
X. Mount Sinai.
   1. Description of Mount Sinai; lightnings, sound of the trumpet, trembling of the earth. 2. God pronounces the Ten Commandments. 3. We are all bound to keep the Ten Commandments of God.

PLAN OF INSTRUCTION

XI. God protects those Jews who keep His commandments.
 1. Passage of the Jordan; taking of Jericho.
 2. Entry into the promised land.

XII. Condition of the Jewish people under the judges.
 1. Constant vicissitudes of successes and defeats. 2. The people are prosperous or miserable, according as they keep or break the commandments of God.

XIII. David and Solomon.
 1. The reign of these two kings. 2. Building and dedication of the temple of Jerusalem. 3. Reverence of Solomon and the people for the temple.

XIV. Prophets.
 1. Who the prophets were, and the sort of life they led. 2. Historical events concerning some of the principal prophets, such as Isaiah and Jeremiah. 3. Their zeal for the glory of God.

XV. Birth of Jesus Christ.
 1. The Holy Virgin; the Angel Gabriel announces to her that she will be the Mother of the Saviour. 2. Jesus is born in Bethlehem.

XVI. Infancy of Jesus Christ.
 1. Jesus Christ is visited by the shepherds. 2. He receives the name of Jesus eight days after His birth. 3. The wise men come to worship Him.

XVII. Childhood of Jesus Christ.

1. Picture the home of the Holy Family. 2. Jesus works with S. Joseph, and helps His Mother. 3. He obeys Joseph and Mary and goes to the temple with them: pattern for Christian children.

XVIII. Baptism of Jesus Christ.

1. Story of it as told in the Gospel; the words of the Heavenly Father; the Dove which rests on Jesus Christ. 2. The Holy Trinity, the Father, the Son, and the Holy Spirit, manifested in this event.

XIX. Penance of Jesus Christ in the wilderness.

1. Description of wilderness; what Jesus Christ did there, and for whom He endured penance. 2. Temptations of the devil; how He repelled them.

XX. Jesus Christ preaching.

1. Jesus Christ goes through towns and villages to teach men. 2. He declares to them that He is the only Son of God, promised from the beginning of the world; is reproached by the Jews because He calls Himself God, the Son of God.

XXI. Miracles of Jesus Christ.

1. Story and description of some of the miracles, such as the curing of the man born blind, the multiplication of the loaves, the raising from the dead of the widow's son at Nain. 2. Those miracles show that Jesus Christ is God.

XXII. Choice of the Apostles.

1. How Jesus Christ called to Him Simon

PLAN OF INSTRUCTION 243

Peter, Andrew, and John. 2. He appoints S. Peter to be chief of the Apostles. 3. He promises to all to send them the Holy Spirit.

XXIII. Passion and death of Jesus Christ.
1. Jesus taken in the Garden of Olives. 2. Prison, scourging, crowning with thorns. 3. Crucifixion: Jesus Christ suffers all this for us, and because He wills it.

XXIV. Resurrection of Jesus Christ.
1. Jesus Christ is buried. 2. The third day He leaves the tomb. 3. Circumstances of the resurrection related by the Evangelists: a new and manifest proof of the omnipotence of Jesus Christ; He is truly the Son of God.

XXV. Appearances of Jesus Christ, and His ascension.
1. Relate in detail two or three of the most remarkable appearances, such as the appearing to the disciples at Emmaus, to the Apostles gathered together in a closed room, to S. Thomas. 2. Ascension in presence of all the disciples: glory of Jesus Christ.

XXVI. Descent of the Holy Spirit on the Apostles.
1. Relate the story of what happened on the day of Pentecost; tongues of fire, rushing wind; miracle of the gift of tongues. 2. The Holy Trinity evidently manifested at Pentecost.

XXVII. Conversion of Jews and idolaters.
1. Considerable number of Jews converted by

the preaching of S. Peter and the other Apostles. 2. Greeks and Romans and other people are converted also. 3. Beginnings of the Church.

XXVIII. The Pope succeeds S. Peter; bishops succeed the other Apostles.

1. The Apostles disperse themselves through the whole world to preach the Gospel. 2. S. Peter settles in Rome, where he dies, and the Pope succeeds him in his capacity as head of the Church. 3. To the other Apostles the bishops succeed.

XXIX. Persecutions against the Church.

1. Draw a little picture of the persecutions raised against the Church by Jews and idolatrous nations. 2. The number and the courage of the martyrs, among whom several young children are to be found.

XXX. Ruin of Jerusalem.

1. Relate the predictions of it by Jesus Christ. 2. Wars of the Romans against the Jews; taking of Jerusalem and destruction of the temple; all efforts to restore it have been vain.

XXXI. Peace given to the Church.

1. After three centuries of persecution, the cross appears to Constantine; the Church triumphs; the cross is lifted up as a standard in the city of Rome. 2. The Church will last to the end of time.

XXXII. Our duties towards the Church.

1. Draw a picture of the Christian life, taking some features from the *Vie des Saints* or

from the *Écoliers vertueux*, bringing out this idea from them, that a Christian child must truly believe what the Church teaches us, must faithfully keep the commandments the Church gives us, and that by this means he will be sure of true and lasting happiness.[1]

These historic instructions may last about twenty minutes; for, far from wearying the children, they interest and amuse them, if they are well prepared. It would not be well to interrupt a narrative in order to question; still a question may be put on one or two of the most important parts, by which means they will be repeated, and the children will be helped to form right conclusions on these facts.

Article IV

Means of Leading Little Children to Piety

Stories, which are so useful in instructing young children, are no less useful for their edification. If we try to reason with them on the love of virtue, or on the value of some pious practice, they will hardly listen to us; but a well-chosen example, or, for want of a story, a parable or an illustration well brought in, strikes their imagination, takes possession of their mind, and touches their heart.

---

[1] The books to be consulted for these historical instructions are *Histoire Sainte* and *Histoire de l'Église*. (The two abridgments made by Lhomond, both works well known and justly valued, may help the catechist.) Fleury's *Catéchisme historique*, revised edition.

We do not mean by this to say that we need only give them these stories and illustrations, without at an early age setting forth to the children the motives which should make us act like true Christians; but these motives, which they would not understand if presented in an abstract form, easily reach their heart if they are made comprehensible by examples. More effect is gained by this means than could ever be hoped for from the soundest and best-grounded reflections we could set before them.

We make use of these stories, parables, or illustrations to lead the children to reflect on the faults most common to their age: idleness, greediness, disobedience, anger, passion, *lying*, inattention to their prayers; and then to show them the way they must set about to correct them. The future of these dear children depends very much on the efforts they have made, at the age we are now thinking of, to correct these faults in themselves and to form good habits.

Festival days are very helpful in exciting the devotion of the children, both by remembering what they commemorate, and by the unusual *éclat* with which they are celebrated. The patronal feast of the little catechism for boys may well be that of S. Joseph, foster-father and guardian of the Infant Jesus; the little catechism for girls can celebrate a festival in honour of the holy childhood of Mary.

We will not here speak of other means of edification, because they have already been sufficiently treated of in the first part of this work.

CHAPTER II

CATECHISMS OF FIRST COMMUNION

CHILDREN are not admitted to the catechism of first Communion till they are ten years old, or, at least, they must be ten years old before the 1st of January. It is important not to deviate from this rule unless for very good reasons, otherwise the catechism would be overflowing with too young children, who would distract the others and would not themselves profit. It is no less necessary to draw to the catechism all who are of this age, particularly the children of workmen and the poor; for if they only came in the following year, it would be very difficult to keep them two years in the catechism, the parents being very anxious to get them apprenticed out. In order to bring them, the parish priests give notice from the pulpit, and exhort all the parents as to the necessity of bringing their children to the catechism; the masters and mistresses of schools are also reminded of it, and notices are posted on the walls of the church.

Article I

Rule of the Catechisms of First Communion

We give here the elements of a rule; it is to be modified according to circumstances; every catechist should adapt it to his own parish, according to the advice of M. le Curé.

1. "To be admitted to the great catechism, a child must be at least ten years old, and must promise to keep the rule of the catechism."

Children are not received from other parishes; at least, not unless the consent of their own clergy is certain.

Children who present themselves for the great catechism are sent back to the little one if they do not know by heart their prayers—that is to say, *Our Father; Hail, Mary; I believe in God; I confess to God; the Acts of faith, of hope, of contrition, of charity; the commandments of God and of the Church*, or who are ignorant of the principal mysteries of religion. Children who can read ought at least to possess the Diocesan Catechism and the book of hymns used in the parish. They are advised also to have a book of Gospels and the Historical Catechism.

2. "The children must come every Sunday at the appointed hour."

As they arrive, they will go to the places which have been assigned to them. There, having knelt down and worshipped God for a few moments, they can sit down and study their catechism in a whisper, keeping always quite silent and still, thus edifying the other children and showing a profound reverence for the holy place. When they are given notice to go into the catechism chapel, they will only leave their places when called upon by one of the catechists. They will walk two and two, without hurry or disorder, and not taking each other's arm; and without striding over the forms, they will go to their own places.

3. "Every child who arrives more than a quarter of an hour after the general entry will not take his place till he has given the chief of the catechism a note of excuse signed by his masters or his parents."

4. "They will take their part in the catechism with attention, modesty, and religion."

They must not turn round, nor even speak in a whisper, though it may be to ask what the catechists have said. Everyone will sit with his arms crossed or his hands joined, at least, unless he is taking notes during the instruction, or is holding a book during the time he is allowed to have one in his hands. Great attention must be paid to the signal given for rising or sitting, for kneeling or bowing the head.

The hymns are to be sung reverently, no shouting, and never beginning or ending a line before the person whose business it is to lead.

No child can go out during the catechism without very express permission, which will be given with great reluctance; only then while a hymn is being sung, and never two children at once.

THE METHOD OF S. SULPICE

5. "After the prayer, a hymn will be sung, during which the dignitaries who are charged with this office will distribute the cards of presence; after the hymn the interrogation begins."

Each child, directly his name is called, will stand up, make the sign of the cross, answer without hurry, and so that he can be heard.

After the diocesan catechism has been repeated, the names of children who have brought *billets* of the Gospel and of the Historical Catechism will be called out. These children will rise, and remain standing till the catechists have finished hearing them repeat. One good number will be given for the Historical Catechism, one for the Gospel in French, two for the Gospel in Latin, three for the Gospel in Greek.

Then good numbers will be marked in a register, and the children who have gained the most, will, at the end of the year, receive the prize for the Gospel and the Historical Catechism.

A child who gives in a *billet*, but does not know his Gospel, will lose all the good numbers he has hitherto gained.

A child who does not know his catechism lesson at all, and who has not brought a note of excuse, will incur a bad point.

Before, during, or after the interrogation, two children who have behaved well and set a good example will have the privilege of a "game of good points" with the chief of the catechism.

At the end of the interrogation, the chief, having marked the lessons and announced the list of

CATECHISMS OF FIRST COMMUNION

analyses, will, in preparation for the instruction, give out a hymn, during which the analyses will be given back.

6. "The children are exhorted strongly to take notes during the instruction, so that they may be able to bring in good analyses the following Sunday."

The analyses are given back after eight days, with a seal varying in colour, according as they are more or less well done. Notes are taken on the instruction in perfect silence; if a child has not heard anything, he must not ask the others.

7. "During the homily, which follows the reading of the Gospel, the children must keep perfectly quiet and attentive, so that the pious sentiments with which it ought to be full may touch their heart. The homily over, they begin to go out."

While this is going on, the children remain in their places till a signal is given them.

Any children who wish to speak to the chief, or to one of the catechists, will remain in their places and wait in silence till all are gone out. (The parents also are asked to be kind enough to come at this time, if they have anything to say about their children.) Those children who do not want to speak to anyone should leave the church and go home quickly, without stopping to talk to other children.

When, for some indispensable reason, a child has not been able to come to the catechism, he must bring a note of excuse on the following Sunday.

Children who, by reason of sickness, or some other important reason, have been absent from the catechism several times following, should let the chief of the catechism know of it.

8. "Each child must bring, every month at least, a certificate of confession."

To gain admission to the week-day catechism, a child—

(1) Must be twelve years old at the time of the first Communion;

(2) He must have attended the catechisms more than twelve months;

(3) He must have brought in every month a certificate of confession;

(4) He must not have been absent more than four times;

(5) He must have faithfully kept the rule;

(6) He must have obtained express permission from his parents to follow the catechism till the end of the year, and to attend, as far as it is possible, a catechism of perseverance, at least for the year following.

For admission to the catechism for Confirmation, there must have been no absences since the first Communion, and the child's conduct must have been good in every respect.

9. "Children who seem to be incorrigible, or who dare to disobey the catechists; children who behave badly outside the catechism, playing in the streets or in public places; children who have three bad points against them, or have been absent four consecutive times without good reasons; finally,

CATECHISMS OF FIRST COMMUNION 253

children who have let four months go by without bringing one certificate of confession, will be sent away from the catechism."

Bad points are given to a child, not only for negligence in learning the catechism, but also for not having observed the rule; for instance, for having talked during the catechism, for not having his arms crossed (or hands joined), for having left his place without leave. These bad points may be annulled by gaining good ones.

Three absences or one bad point are enough to deprive the dignitaries of their office; but they may be re-elected at a future time.

10. "The rewards usually given to the children are good points, pictures, and books."

(1) Children who gain a good point during the interrogation receive it at once; and besides, each of the catechists, at the close of the catechism, will name two children who have conducted themselves best, and they will go to the chief to receive from his hand a good point, singly, as they are called. Before this distribution, children who have already gained three good points may come to him to receive a picture in exchange. The dignitaries can do this for two good points.

To deserve a picture a child must—(*a*) Have brought two certificates of confession in the course of the two months preceding the day of distribution; (*b*) He must not have been absent once during these two months, at least unless he has regularly brought notes of excuse; and (*c*) The catechists must be satisfied with the children as to their behaviour and the repetition of the catechism. If a child fails in any of these conditions, he cannot aspire to pictures.

(2) At the end of the year there will be a general distribution of prizes for children who have been remarkable for their very good behaviour and constant perseverance.

11. " The dignitaries are an Intendent, Assistants, and Secretaries."

The highest dignity is that of Intendent, whether of boys or girls. Their office is to collect the analyses and the *billets*; they are helped by their Assistants; they have the right of introducing two children under the prescribed age. According to an ancient custom in use in the catechism of S. Sulpice since the days of M. Olier, the Intendents and their Assistants receive pictures instead of good points.

The employment of the Secretaries consists in entering, in writing, all changes among the catechists and dignitaries, and all the more solemn gatherings.

The higher dignitaries must always make analyses, and behave in such a way that they may be looked upon as the example and ornament of the catechism.

There will be one or more forms of honour for the best conducted and for those who have been dignitaries.

A certain number of children will be chosen who will be called upon to do at the catechism what the angels do in heaven, that is to say, to sing the praises of God. A director for the singing will be at their head.

12. " At the head of each form will be a dignitary called the First of the Form."

Those who are First of a Form have—(1) To answer, *Absent*, when a child of their form is called who is not at the catechism; (2) Never to let any child sit on their form whose name is not on the card; (3) To be very exact in marking the absences of those children who are not on their form, even though they may be somewhere else in the catechism; (4 and last) To take great care of the cards, and give them back to the dignitaries who collect them. Those who are First of Forms should be in everything a model for the other children.

Article II

On the Instruction of the Children

The instruction of the children belonging to the catechism of first Communion demands very great care on the part of the catechist, the more so, as many of them have not belonged to the little catechisms, and if they are not thoroughly and carefully instructed at the time of first Communion, they will never know anything of religion.

In giving the necessary instruction to these children, great care is taken, even more than in the little catechisms, that the letter of the diocesan catechism is learnt and repeated quite correctly. The children are questioned as much as possible, to keep them on the alert, and in catechisms where there are too many of them, every Sunday regularly, a certain number are taken apart to repeat the lesson which all should have learnt. This does not take a great deal of time, it is done either while the interrogation is going on, taking the children into the sacristy, or when the catechism is over, keeping them back after the others. By this means, the lesson can be repeated each Sunday by sixty or eighty children.

The letter of the catechism is explained in the *instruction;* the lesson which the children have just repeated, or that which they repeated the Sunday before, being always the subject. If we make them learn one lesson, and then in the instruction explain quite another point of Christian doctrine, having no connection with what they have been studying, their mind will not take hold of it. It is the duty of the catechist to bring into his instruction all the words in the lesson which are not quite easy to understand, and all the proofs given in the text of the catechism. The instruction is simply, and should be nothing else but the explanation of the catechism, given in a lively, varied form, bringing in, if need be, illustrations or anything which may be attractive.

It is necessary to go through the whole catechism in the course of the year; for in spite of the earnest desire we have to require two years of preparation for the first Communion, it cannot but be that, from force of circumstances, there will always be many exceptions. On the other hand, it is well to avoid giving in the second year the very same instructions as in the year before; for this would take away a great deal of the interest for those children who are industrious in making analyses.

To avoid this inconvenience and make everything fit in, we explain each year—there being no fear of too frequent repetition—the most essential points, such as are the principal mysteries; for the rest, we make out a programme, according to which we dwell more on one point during the first year, and in the next year on another point. In this way we get a useful variety, and we can enter into many details which would be impossible for us if we had only one year. Thus, to give an example, the catechism of Paris has one lesson on the existence of God and another on the perfections of God. These two lessons, which immediately succeed one another, would have to be explained in one instruction: for if the whole instruction were devoted to each lesson it would be impossible to explain more than half the catechism in one year. Therefore we combine these two lessons: the first year we give and explain in detail the proofs which the catechism provides concerning the existence of God, and we dwell less on the perfections of God; the next year, on the contrary, we confine ourselves to explaining only one proof of the existence of God, and we dwell chiefly on the perfections of God and on Providence. It is the same with the other lessons of the catechism. A catechist who takes the pains to look forward and arrange the plan of his instructions, can, by following this method, explain the whole catechism thoroughly during the year, and take it up again the following year, without falling into repetitions, which would take off the interest of novelty for a certain number of children.[1]

In order still more to impress on the children's minds the explanation which has been given them of the catechism lesson, it is taken up again on the following Sunday, under the form of the *game of good points*, which gives the chief of the catechism the opportunity of drawing the attention of his audience to any points which have not been thoroughly understood.

Still, however simple may be the instructions, however careful the catechist is in questioning the children as often as possible, there will always be a certain number who will know very little, in fact hardly anything, unless in some way they can be taught separately. At S. Sulpice it is the custom, about the middle of the year, three months at least before the first Communion, to make out a list of the least intelligent children, and to give each of them into the charge of some charitable person who undertakes to teach them. The associates of the catechism discharge this ministry with much zeal; the young people belonging to the boys' catechism of perseverance also take part in this good work and with equal devotion. There are very few

---

[1] The best books to consult for the explanation of the catechism of first Communion are—the *Catéchisme de Montpellier*, the edition revised and corrected by Charancy, a very useful work; the *Catéchisme de Bourges*, explained by M. de la Chétardie; the *Catéchisme de Mans*, explained by M. le Guillois; the *Catéchisme de la foi et des mœurs chrétiennes*, by M. de Lantage, a very precious work for the spirit of piety which pervades it, and which will greatly help the catechist in impressing on himself and on the children the holy truths of the faith.

CATECHISMS OF FIRST COMMUNION

parishes where, if there are no associations, some pious and intelligent persons could not be found who would render this service to poor children.

This good work could not create any real difficulties with regard to the masters or mistresses of schools. No one suspects any want of zeal or of intelligence in these masters and mistresses towards the instruction of their children; but in many parishes there are such a number of them, that generally it would be impossible for them to give to these children of whom we are speaking the special attention they need. How could a communal schoolmistress, besides the time occupied for classes in common,—how could she find enough time to teach these backward children separately? If she wished it, she would not have the power, in spite of her goodwill. Moreover, the discipline of the schools could not suffer from this practice, for the children only go to those people who are kind enough to teach them, out of school hours; and these good people, far from turning them aside from their duties, strive to inspire them, not only with piety, but also with more respect and submission towards their masters, more zeal and application in their school work.

This work of instructing the children of the catechism has the double advantage of better preparing the children for the first Communion, and also of placing them under the patronage of some benevolent person, who will have an interest in them, and in the end may help them, by his influence and his advice, to obtain suitable employment.

CHAPTER III

WEEK-DAY CATECHISMS

A CERTAIN time before the period of first Communion a list is made out of such children as it is intended to admit to the Holy Table, and they are prepared for this blessing by more frequent exercises. This is done in every parish.[1] At S. Sulpice, these exercises, which are intended to prepare the children for the near approach of first Communion, are called *Week-day Catechisms* (*catéchismes de semaine*), because they are held during the week, and are independent of the Sunday catechisms, which the children still attend, those who are to make their first Communion in the course of the year, as well as those who will not make it till the next year.

---

[1] The *Rituel* of the diocese of Paris says: "*Parochus selectos pueros, per duos circiter menses, ante primam communionem, catechesibus particularibus doceat, bis vel ter in heddomeda*" (De sacram. Euchar., No. 63).

Article I

Conditions Necessary for Admission to the Week-day Catechisms

As a rule, only children who have attended catechisms for twelve months are admitted to the week-day catechisms; this is according to the order in the Diocesan *Rituel*, which requires that the children shall have attended the parish catechisms for a long time, *per diuturnum tempus*. If they have attended the catechisms of some school, or of another parish, they must provide themselves with a certificate from the curé of this parish, or from the catechist priest, saying for how long a time they have attended the catechism, and how they have conducted themselves there.

A second condition, no less important, is that the children have, in essential points, kept the rule of the Sunday catechism. Those who have been absent several times without just cause, or have constantly answered badly when questioned on the catechism, or who have behaved badly, in spite of repeated warnings given them, or, lastly, those who have neglected confession for a considerable part of the year, cannot, according to the ordinary rules, be admitted to the week-day catechisms.

There is, finally, a condition of age; in this matter, everyone follows the rules of his own diocese. The *Rituel* of the diocese of Paris requires the boys to be twelve years old; and if it is thought expedient to admit anyone before that age, it must be done with discretion, experience plainly showing that any indulgence on this point is generally fatal to the children, who, their first Communion once made, are neglected by their parents or their masters. Otherwise there would be less danger in consenting to it.

The most common cause for indulgence, is the necessity of apprenticing the poor children; parents of quite another class allege their anxiety to push on the studies of their children towards the special schools,—studies which they imagine must suffer more or less from week-day catechisms going on for three months in the year,—and they think to get over this difficulty if the children are admitted to the first Communion a little younger. Still, it is well to be very reluctant, and to keep to the rule if the children will not be fully twelve years old the year of their first Communion, particularly if they are being brought up in a school, or if they belong to families with little religion. The schools are tempted to take advantage of any concessions made to them for particular cases, and ask for them again; and in families with little religion, the religious education of the children is neglected. It will very seldom happen that a child loses his first Communion through being kept back till the age appointed by the rules; it happens only too often that children who are admitted too young are not sufficiently impressed by their first Communion, and having made it, they come no more to the catechisms.

The catechist should be still more firm as to the two first conditions, the time of attendance at the catechism, and the regularity of confession. If he shows himself indulgent about these things, which are very important in themselves, he will not only be acting against the real interests of the children, whom he is admitting to the first Communion in spite of their irregularity, but he will greatly damage the general discipline of the catechism. The other children will care much less about observing these rules when they see that those of their companions who have not kept them have, nevertheless, like the others, made their first Communion. No doubt there are many special considerations which oblige us sometimes to overstep the ordinary rules; there is an age when the first Communion should no longer be delayed, unless the child is quite unworthy; but all these things ought to be weighed before God. There must be no weakness, no human respect, no severity; but there must be firmness in keeping the rules, for the general interest of the children, and there must be a yielding in particular cases, when there are real reasons for relaxing the usual conditions.

Article II

Exercises of the Week-day Catechisms

The rule and exercises of the week-day catechisms differ little from those of the Sunday catechism; the following are the most important points:—

The week-day catechism is, as a rule, held on two days in the week, and for nearly three months. This time is considered sufficient for the near preparation for first Communion and for Confirmation.

The catechisms open with the usual prayer, and with singing a hymn, chosen from such as refer to the special circumstances, or to the subject about to be treated.

After the hymn, questioning on the letter of the catechism follows. Lessons are given in succession on the principal mysteries—the Holy Trinity, the Incarnation, and Redemption; on sin, on grace, on prayer, and the sacraments. The questioning is broken in upon by the "game of good points," an exercise which, if well done, is most useful in instructing a great number of children; it turns chiefly on the lesson which was explained at the last meeting of the catechism.

The report on the analyses succeeds the questioning, and then the instruction is given, which lasts half an hour. We have seen, in the catechism lessons to be repeated, what is the subject of these instructions; it is chiefly grace, prayer, and the Sacraments of Baptism, of Penitence, of the Eucharist, and of Confirmation; these, throughout the duration of the week-day catechism, we strive to make the children thoroughly understand.

The instruction over, the children are refreshed by singing a hymn, after which the chief gives his

WEEK-DAY CATECHISMS

notices and counsels. There are a certain number of notices of detail and of discipline which are very short, but which it is necessary to repeat often, in order to secure perfect regularity; some are to advise the children to get the certificate of their baptism as soon as possible, to make analyses, to sing the hymns well, and, above all, to confess regularly. Besides this, one special counsel is given, which takes the place of the Sunday homily.

The catechism ends with a distribution of good points to the children who have behaved best, and then follows the usual prayer, to which is added the *Souvenez-vous*. The children go out, at a given signal, not confusedly, all together, but form by form, singing a hymn meanwhile.

Children who have been absent must bring a note of excuse the next time the catechism meets, or the first day they come to it again. It may be settled as a rule that three absences without cause will exclude them from the week-day catechism. It is well also to require the children to confess every fortnight, and to bring a note signed by their confessor. Their negligence in this would also be a reason for exclusion, but it is the duty of the catechists to provide against this by arousing the zeal of the children, and in privately advising those who are backward about it.

Article III

Plan of Counsels and Instructions for the Week-day Catechism

It is important that the chief of the catechism should make a plan for his counsels, that in them he should enter into very practical details, and that he should give them with simplicity and piety. Counsels given promiscuously, without any connection, under the inspiration of the moment, with scarcely any preparation, will never have so much effect as may be gained by carrying out a method.

The object of the counsels given at the week-day catechism being to bring the children to a change of life so that they may be in a fit state to make a good first Communion, we ought first of all to insist on the necessity of conversion. The spiritual condition of some of these children is bad; they have committed mortal sins; their habits are deplorable. Others have faults of character which, later on, will endanger the salvation of their souls; all have something to be corrected before they can respond to the grace of God. Hence arises that necessity for conversion which, above all things, it is important that the children should be thoroughly convinced of. We ought to speak to them of it, not at the first meeting, which should be devoted to explaining the customs and rules of the catechism, but in those which immediately follow. It must then be explained to them how they should examine themselves, and how to think over their faults and bad dispositions, by which they will get to know what is that change of life which God requires of them. Therefore we have a series of counsels on the examination of conscience and on the most usual faults of children. Then, through four or five successive meetings, we set down before them what are the greatest helps towards conversion—prayer, reading on sacred subjects, frequent confession, respect towards their parents and obedience to them. Other counsels should follow, to strengthen the children against certain hindrances to conversion, such as the temptations to be disheartened, idleness, bad companions, bad examples, human respect. And lastly, the ordinary practices of Christian life are explained.

If even experience did not justify this way of proceeding, anyone can see that counsels well arranged, going on gradually to the desired end, following in a natural order, cannot but produce happy results. It need hardly be said, that the catechist, though as a rule he follows out the plan he has sketched, yet diverges from it if necessary, dwells longer on one point, goes back again to another, according to what he knows of the children. He takes care to vary the form of his counsels: one day it is an exhortation; at another time some incident of history, or again he will read some pages from the life of a pious child,[1] which will help

---

[1] The *Vie de Décalogue* may be used with great advantage in the counsels given to boys; the catechist for the girls can find many useful points in the *Vie de Fanny*, and in the *Souvenirs de la congregation de Nôtre-Dame*.

towards the counsel he is desirous to give; at other times he will take advantage of some incident or circumstance likely to arrest their attention.

The choice of instructions requires as much care as the counsels. In these catechisms, which are not large, we do not go back over all the articles of Christian doctrine, there would not be time; we simply go to the most essential points, dwelling by preference on what concerns the sacraments which the children are going to receive. The following is a plan which may be followed:—

I. Instruction. On grace.
 1. What grace is. 2. Necessity of grace for salvation. 3. Actual grace and habitual grace.

II. On prayer.
 1. Obligation we are under to pray to God. 2. What we ought to ask Him for. 3. How we must pray: attention, trust, perseverance.

III. On sin.
 1. Repeat and explain in few words the definition of sin. 2. In how many ways it is possible to commit sin: thoughts, words, actions, omissions contrary to the law of God. 3. Distinction between mortal and venial sins; when a sin is mortal, and when we may conclude that it is only venial.

IV. On the sacraments in general.
 1. What a sacrament is: take the example of baptism. 2. Effects which the sacraments produce: sanctifying grace, sacramental grace to enable us to fulfil the obligations laid

upon us by the sacrament; character. 3. How many sacraments there are.

V. On the Sacrament of Penitence.
1. Institution of the Sacrament of Penitence involved in the power conferred by Jesus Christ on His Apostles to remit and to retain sins; necessity of having recourse to this sacrament to obtain the pardon of sins committed after baptism. 2. Necessary conditions for receiving this sacrament. (These conditions are simply enumerated, without explaining them; this being done in the succeeding instructions.)

VI. On contrition.
1. What contrition is. 2. Qualities it should have: inward, supernatural, thorough (*souveraine*), and universal. Explain these conditions very carefully, particularly the second and third, which are not well known by the faithful generally.

VII. On perfect and imperfect contrition.
1. In what consists a perfect contrition; the effects it produces for sanctification. Observe that a perfect contrition does not dispense from confession, although it justifies the sinner. 2. In what consists imperfect contrition. Joined to the Sacrament of Penitence, it is sufficient to obtain from God the remission of sins. 3. The difference between these two sorts of contrition comes then from the difference between their motives: in one, it is the love of God; in the other, it is the

hope of heaven or the fear of hell, but, in both, there is a supernatural, supreme, and universal sorrow for having offended God, at least, with regard to mortal sins.

VIII. On confession.

1. Confession must be humble: we are making an avowal to God. 2. Sincere: this avowal must be made without any disguise; we must neither seek to make less of our faults nor to exaggerate them, but tell them as we know them to be. 3. Entire: we must not omit or hide any mortal sin.

IX. How to confess.

1. What we must do before confession; prayer and examination of conscience. 2. What we are to do at the time; *Confiteor* which we repeat; our sins to be told simply and carefully; listen to the advice given by the confessor with attention, respect, and submission. 3. What to do after confession.

X. On satisfaction.

1. The Sacrament of Penitence does not dispense with the necessity of satisfying (making amends to) divine justice for the sins we have committed. 2. Various works of satisfaction we may do: penance imposed by the confessor; works of piety and of mortification; patience in bearing sickness or contradictions. 3. From whom works of satisfaction derive their virtue; not from us or our personal merits, but from Jesus Christ.

XI. On indulgences.

1. What is meant by indulgence: definition in the catechism. 2. How many kinds of indulgences there are—plenary indulgence and partial indulgence: the one remits all the punishment due to sins; the other only remits a part, in a measure known to God. 3. Necessary conditions for obtaining indulgence: state of grace, works prescribed for every indulgence.

XII. On the Sacrament of the Eucharist.
1. Explain the definition of this sacrament as it is found in the catechism. 2. How Jesus Christ is present in the Eucharist: there is neither bread nor wine after the consecration: Jesus Christ, wholly, is under the species or appearances of bread, and under the species or appearances of wine. 3. Why Jesus Christ instituted this sacrament.

XIII. On the holy sacrifice of the Mass.
1. What the sacrifice of the Mass is; in what it differs from the sacrifice of the Cross, and how from that it draws all its virtue. 2. What are the effects of the holy sacrifice; glory given to God, graces which come back from it to men (propitiatory, impetratory. . . .).

XIV. On the holy sacrifice, continued.
1. To whom it is offered. Explain in what sense Masses are said in honour of the Blessed Virgin and the saints. 2. For whom the holy sacrifice is offered: the living and the dead. 3. With what dispositions must we assist at it: attention, reverence, prayer.

XV. On Communion.
 1. When ought we to communicate? Easter Communion, the viaticum. 2. Advantage of frequent Communion; rules to be observed in this respect.
XVI. On the dispositions with which we should come to Communion.
 1. Interior dispositions: state of grace; desire and confidence. 2. Outward reverence; fast. Explain concerning the Eucharistic fast and what would break it.
XVII. On sacrilegious Communion.
 1. Who are guilty of sacrilegious Communion? 2. What are the causes of sacrilegious Communions? Want of faith, hypocrisy, false shame as to owning all our sins to the confessor. 3. What are the consequences of sacrilegious communion? Hardening of the heart, weakening of the faith. (Weigh these words well, so as not to exaggerate the consequences of a sacrilegious Communion, by representing it as an unpardonable crime.)
XVIII. On the Sacrament of Confirmation.
 1. What is the Sacrament of Confirmation? Relate what is written about it in the *Acts of the Apostles*. 2. Effects of the sacrament: sanctifying grace, sacramental grace to strengthen us, as we need it, against the temptations of human respect and other temptations. 3. In what sense this sacrament makes us perfect Christians.

XIX. On Confirmation, continued.
1. Necessity of receiving the Sacrament of Confirmation: those who neglect it when they might receive it are wrong. 2. Dispositions we must bring to it: state of grace, sufficient knowledge of Christian doctrine, sincere desire to lead a Christian life.
XX. On the ceremonies of Confirmation.
1. Invocation of the Holy Spirit and imposition of hands; what this imposition of hands signifies. 2. Anointing with the holy chrism; strength, gentleness; the oil and balm of which the holy chrism is composed, serving as good examples, figuratively, of these virtues.

It is good to have one meeting set apart for the Blessed Virgin: the subject for the instruction, on that day, would be the explanation of the *Ave Maria*, or showing the reasons for the *cultus* we render to the Blessed Virgin.

Article IV

Certain extra Meetings of the week-day Catechisms

The week-day catechisms, at S. Sulpice, at certain times, diverge more or less from the order described in the preceding articles: namely, those which are devoted to the examinations, to the first act of contrition, and to the Blessed Virgin.

We will describe these, as they may be useful to other catechisms.

1. *Examination of the Children*

It is the custom in the catechisms of S. Sulpice to make the children go through two examinations before first Communion: one about the middle of the week-day catechism; the other, one week before the retreat. We do this to stimulate the zeal of the children, dividing them so as to keep each from being too full of matter.

In parishes, it is well to put a certain *éclat* into the examinations, so that the children may be more careful in their preparation; but if there are very few, it is better for them to be examined only one or two at a time, in the presence of M. le Curé and all the other examiners. But this system is impracticable in the larger parishes; many children must be questioned at the same time, and to do this, the chief of the catechism forms as many separate sections as there are examiners, giving to each the children from the schools and the few children which he can but question, and reserving to himself the more difficult, the more doubtful children, who require special attention.

The meeting for the examination opens with a short prayer, followed by a hymn. The chief gives the necessary notices; he reads out the list of children, telling each what place he is to take, and the name of the examiner; and he sees that all this is done without confusion.

WEEK-DAY CATECHISM: EXAMINATIONS

The examination turns on the Acts of the theological virtues, on the prayers which every Christian should know, and on a certain part of the diocesan catechism, chosen beforehand. The children are examined on the letter and on the meaning.

The examiner should take account of the capacity of the children, asking more from those whose powers are greater, being satisfied with only what is essential from those who are not so clever; he should be gentle or firm, keep them in suspense or encourage with kind words, according to the way in which each answers. Then on the examination chart, which he should have drawn out for himself, against the name of each child, he will put marks showing how he has answered upon each article. All the examiners employed in the same catechism take these papers and confer upon them with each other, so that at the next meeting the chief will be able to declare the result of the examination, and also any observations which have been made on the behaviour of each child. The old rules of S. Sulpice say: "All the children can be classed under five numbers. No. 1 for the children who have given entire satisfaction, as to the letter and the meaning of the catechism, and also as to their behaviour. This number should only be given to a very few. No. 2 is given to children with whom one is quite satisfied, though in a little lower degree. No. 3 is for the children who have done sufficiently well, but yet not so well as the others. No. 4 for those who may be allowed to pass, knowing what is absolutely necessary. Lastly, No. 5 is kept for the children who have answered badly. These children are at least very doubtful; their admission to the first Communion is either left uncertain, or else they are definitely sent away, according to circumstances."

Before reading out this list in public, the catechist explains the different grades; he encourages those who have gained good numbers; he holds before those who have inferior numbers the fear of not making their first Communion, if they do not take more pains. Those whose names are not on the list, he tells to wait behind till the rest are gone, to ak to him. There is a double object in this :caution: some children may have been forgotten the examination; others may have been definitely rejected, and to spare these, their names are not given in public; they are told of it privately, and given to hope that a little later they may be able to make their first Communion, if they behave better and are more attentive.

The second examination, which is held one week before the retreat, takes in all the part of the catechism which was not comprised in the first, excepting the chapter on Confirmation. Otherwise the same rules are followed; and the result is final with regard to the admission of children or the rejection of those who are judged to be unfit: namely, those who have been very negligent about their confessions; who have been absent several times without cause; who have answered very badly at the examination, though they might

WEEK-DAY CATECHISM: EXAMINATIONS

have known their catechism if they had wished it; and lastly, those whose behaviour has been bad in spite of the repeated warnings they have received.

The old book of laws remarks: "One must expect many protestations from the parents of the children who are sent away. They will say that the child has no great faults, that he is very good, that he is an expense to them and ought to be in his apprenticeship; that if he does not make his Communion this year, perhaps he never will. We must listen to these protestations; and if they are such as in any way to explain in the child's favour any circumstances with which we had not been well acquainted or to attenuate the faults for which he has been sent away, we must make a note of them and confer about them at the council, and endeavour to do what equity demands. But if these protestations are not such as to modify our decision, we must not alter it, but we must explain to the parents kindly and pleasantly the reasons for sending the child away. Everything is spoilt and nothing is gained by speaking with a hard and angry manner. The parents are disgusted, and complain still more. Perhaps, in consequence of their displeasure, they will take their children away altogether from the catechism.

It is not necessary, and often it is not expedient, to put off such children as we cannot receive to the solemn first Communion, to the following year. The author of the *Miroir du Clergé*, after having spoken of the practice of several curés who allow the children who are not ready for this, to make their first Communion separately, rightly adds: "It is much easier by this means to delay those of whose dispositions we are doubtful; the children are less disheartened, and the parents are less eager and importunate in trying to prevent the delay."[1]

This should be done in the case of children who cannot without serious inconvenience be put off to the next year. We do not, however, let these children make their Communion apart, because it is an advantage to them to be prepared by exercises which they could not go through by themselves, and also their first Communion should have something specially solemn about its surroundings which will impress them. These children are intrusted to the care of some zealous people, who prepare them carefully, and some days before the Communion take them through certain exercises which may take the place of the retreat; then a festival is chosen on which there is a Monthly Communion, or more commonly the day is chosen on which the other children come to renew their first Communion. If there are several children to be considered, they could be gathered together in a chapel, either of the parish church or of the community, where some priest would have the charity to give them some advice and a short exhortation on such days and at such time as is convenient. This plan has been employed with success.

[1] *Mirior du Clergé*. Third Obligation of the Curé: Pastoral Vigilance.

FIRST ACT OF CONTRITION

2. *First Act of Contrition*

According to a very ancient custom in the catechisms of S. Sulpice, the children, after the first examination, are assembled for an exercise known under the name of the *first act of contrition*.

The object of this exercise is to make the children reflect on the state of their conscience, and to dispose them to make their general confession well. On the day appointed, the children go to the catechism chapel; they say the prayer for the morning together; a catechist makes a short meditation according to the method shown in the *Cantiques de Saint-Sulpice*. The chief gives notices and counsels suitable to the time: they then hear Holy Mass, after which the preacher goes into the pulpit, and gives the children an exhortation tending to make them look into themselves, to feel keenly the need of doing their best to prepare for first Communion by good confessions, and without waiting for the retreat, to begin at once their general confession. Directly he has finished, the children kneel down. They get up at a given signal, sing a hymn on penitence, and go to the church, and then quietly go each to the chapel of their confessor.

It is important that at this moment the confessors shall be, or shall immediately come to, the confessional: for the children expect to find them there, according to the notices given them. The confessors are the judges of the best time for such and such children who come to them to begin their general confession: the rules of the catechism prescribe nothing on this point. But it has always been understood at S. Sulpice that at the close of the first act of contrition the children should go to their confessor, to open their heart to him and receive his advice. Among the number there are many who at that moment are disposed to do better, and are quite ready to confess sins which they have been afraid to mention before. If they are kindly received, it will be a decisive moment for them; they will be better known, and up to the time of the retreat, they will be making efforts to profit by the catechism and to correct their bad habits. If this favourable moment is let slip, they will fall back into their old state, and they will come to the retreat without having made any real effort against their faults. And the confessor himself, would he have the time then to prepare his penitent properly and to make sure of his conversion, so well as he could do, by taking him in time?

These thoughts were in the mind of the venerable priests who have handed on to us the rules of the catechisms, and experience has shown how wise they are. It is in keeping with the spirit of these rules that the author of the *Traité de la Prédication* recommends the catechist to make out a definite list of those who will make their first Communion, a month beforehand, and to make them begin their general confession without delay, after having prepared them for this very important act by touching exhortations on the necessity of owning everything to their confessor, and striving courageously at their own amendment.[1] According to the accounts given by the authors of the *Miroir du Clergé*, in many parishes in different dioceses, several public exercises of retreat were formerly given, a certain time before the first Communion, these exercises being afterwards replaced by the ordinary meetings of the catechism up to the time preceding the first Communion. The authors whom we quote recommend this practice, both in the interest of the children and in the interest also of the confessor, who will be in much less difficulty during the retreat, if many of his penitents have fully confessed to him some time previously. This is the object in view in the *first act of contrition*.

3. *Meeting consecrated to the Blessed Virgin*

In the week-day catechisms, devotion to the Blessed Virgin is frequently spoken of, besides which one entire meeting is devoted to her; this is a real festival for the children, although the ordinary exercises are not altered.

On this day, everything relates to the Blessed Virgin: the questioning, the good point, the instruction, and the counsels. Only the children who usually answer well are questioned; as the subject of the good point, we take such circumstances in the life of the Holy Virgin as may help

[1] *Traité de la Prédication*, by M. Hamon, curé of S. Sulpice, ch. x. art. 7, sec. 2.

the growth of piety in the children, and which also have some connection with the first Communion, as the Immaculate Conception, the Annunciation, the Visitation . . . The catechist who gives the instruction explains the true grounds of our devotion to the Holy Virgin. The chief, in his counsels, dwells much on the trust we ought to have in her, and on some things by which a child may be pleasing to her, and may prepare himself, in her sight, to make a good first Communion. He will particularly recommend them to say the prayer *Souvenez-vous* every day.

At the close of the meeting there is a distribution of medals or of images; they are given to all the children as they go away.

Article V

Last Meetings of the Week-Day Catechisms

In the meetings which more immediately precede the retreat, the catechist explains the rule of life to the children; he gives notices as to the dress to be worn on the day of first Communion, and he makes arrangements that the poor children shall be properly clothed.

In the book of the *Cantiques of S. Sulpice* there is a pattern rule of life, which the children should try to copy, only modifying it according to the different circumstances and different spiritual needs of each. This rule is explained simply and practically. It need not be finished before the retreat;

RULE OF LIFE

some parts can be kept for the catechisms of Confirmation; but it is well to begin to explain it early, so that the children, who write their little rule during the retreat, may understand better and be guided better as to what they should do.

Nothing is suggested to them which is not practicable at their age; they are prevented from making those exaggerated resolutions which we know will not be carried out. Very little is needed for these first years: the essential duties of a Christian child, the exercises which he ought to keep up all the rest of his life, the way to correct his faults, to profit by the education given him, and to avoid the temptations peculiar to his age.

We have always found that to read a rule of life, made by a child, is a great help to the other children of the catechism. If the catechist finds one of these rules distinguished from the rest by its simplicity, its piety, and its practical details, he should make a copy of it, and read it at the catechism without mentioning the name of the child who wrote it.

The explanation of the rule gives occasion for very useful advice; the article as to the dress to be worn on the day of first Communion, though not of equal importance, should nevertheless have the attention of the catechist, so that on this great day all the children shall present themselves at the Holy Table suitably attired.

The costume varies in different places; every parish keeps to its own uses; we only describe here those of S. Sulpice. The boys all have white trousers, and a coat or jacket; they wear a ribbon on their left arm. The rule for the girls is to have a white dress, quite high and long. It should have long sleeves, and be made of a material which is thick enough not to be in any way transparent. They wear a cap and a veil which falls over the shoulders and arms. The little girls are not allowed to have flowing hair with their veil, nor to wear a wreath on their head.

This simple and modest costume is the same for all the children, without any distinction of rich or poor. The uniformity has a good effect, and in this family festival there is no question of ranks; the children understand what they are so often told, that they are all brothers, and that they have in heaven the same one Father, who is about to give Himself equally to all. It is true that, to procure this uniformity of costume, pecuniary means are necessary. The expense is sometimes very considerable; but charity finds the means, charity helps to bear the expense, and though the catechist may have had anxieties on this point, he soon finds that they have changed into the twofold comfort of having helped poor families, and of having given a great many children the opportunity, perhaps for the first time in their life, of making some sacrifice that they may clothe their brothers and sisters who are less favoured than themselves as to worldly goods.

In the parish of S. Sulpice, every year there are children who come and place in the catechist's hands the result of little savings they have been making for one, two, or three years, to help clothe some of the poor children on the day of their first Communion. Many young girls are not satisfied with giving, with very touching generosity, all that their parents have given them for their own little pleasures; but also they ask to be allowed to make with their own hands some of the things which they mean to give to the poorest of their little companions. Is it not a happy thing that these works of charity should come to be mixed up with the pious exercises which are preparing the children for first Communion? These special gifts are supplemented by collections made at the catechisms, and in the church, on the day of Communion.

The chief of the catechism can only procure these helps, in any degree answering to the needs of the children, by speaking of them in public at the catechism. In parishes where the amount of collections would not suffice, we can only give alms, and provide some clothing for the most necessitous; the families are persuaded to make sacrifices, so that if the children cannot have new clothes and all alike, still they may all be suitably dressed.

Article VI

Retreat for First Communion

The retreat preparatory to the first Communion begins on Sunday, supposing that the first Communion is to be made on the following Thursday. This gives sufficient time; it would be difficult to make it less, and it would not do to prolong it, the exercises being a serious matter for the children, considering their age.

Sunday evening, the retreat is opened, at the time appointed. The children being assembled and placed, we begin by the usual prayer; then the chief explains the rules of discipline which are to be followed during the retreat. 1. Punctuality in coming at the exact time. This article is rigorously adhered to, and the exercises having once begun, children who come late are not admitted. 2. Silence and recollection the whole time. This is necessary all the year round, but very specially so during a retreat. 3. The hymns to be sung quietly and attentively; this helps devotion, and enables them to take in the meaning of the words they are singing. If the children scream when they sing, if they hurry on, if they beat time with their feet, this exercise, far from having any good effect on the retreat, would cause disturbance and have a very bad effect. 4. The children, on leaving the chapel, are to go home directly. In the free intervals, at those times which are not set apart for recreation, they should fill up their time with good reading, and with writing out their recollections of the retreat and their feelings about it, and also their rule of life; this should be done quite simply, and they will show it afterwards to their confessor. Children who take this little trouble reap a double benefit from it; holy thoughts suggested to them during the retreat make a deeper impression, as they are thinking about them at home; and later on, it may do them good when they read what they have written and are reminded of these precious days.

If it is possible, we should take care that the poor children and those whose parents are out all day, in workshops or elsewhere, should have a house to which they can go quietly and be looked after by some charitable person. A great number can be thus provided for, if we take the right steps beforehand. Houses belonging to benevolent societies (*maisons de patronage*), the schools of the brothers and sisters of Christian Doctrine, the presbytery in the small country parishes, are shelters for the poor children; some can be taken in by pious people, who will gladly do this act of charity, particularly if they have been engaged in preparing them for first Communion.

When these notices of discipline have been given, it is very desirable that M. le Curé of the parish should come and give the children some advice on the disposition of heart and mind with which they should follow the exercises of the retreat. The words of their own pastor will make the children feel more the importance of the retreat, and will leave useful impressions in their hearts. They sing hymns containing an invocation of the Holy Spirit, and vespers, during which a collection is made towards the clothing of those children who are poor. Vespers are followed by a discourse from the preacher, and with this the first meeting of the retreat concludes. The chief of the catechism says nothing when the preacher has finished to recall what he has just said; it is better that, as the preacher leaves the pulpit, the children should kneel down and remain two or three minutes in silence. The catechist can then, while still on his knees, suggest some pious thought, or a resolution connected with the subject of the discourse; he then gives the signal for departure, during which a hymn is sung.

On the other days, the order of the exercises is as follows:—In the morning, prayer, short meditation, Holy Mass, counsel, and discourse; in the evening, prayer, lecture or counsel, vespers sung, and the discourse. Now and then these exercises can be varied by paraphrasing some verses of a hymn.

It is desirable that the meditations, the counsels, and the discourses should all be in relation to one another, should all have the same foundation, and under different forms tend to the same end. They are much more certain then to have a real effect on the children's hearts. Some catechists think it very important to make them cry; they believe that these strong impressions, by which they are greatly affected, will the better ensure their conversion. We do not share this opinion. On this point the old rules of S. Sulpice say: "Do not try to produce violent emotions in the children, which agitate them and make them cry so that they cannot hear what is being said. These great efforts exhaust the children, and do them very little good. Something more gentle, more calm, is needed which shall reach the bottom of their heart." It is true that many

RETREAT FOR FIRST COMMUNION

do need to be strongly moved, so that they may make a true confession, and be converted; we must speak to their imagination and their heart, besides trying to explain things to their understanding. A cold and monotonous discourse, however well reasoned out, would not touch them; they would not even listen to it. Therefore we must interest them, must win their attention by illustrations, by well-chosen anecdotes, by practical applications; we must move them by warm words coming from the heart; but let us leave alone all such violent and exaggerated means as excite them beyond bounds, and yet hardly ever reach their soul.

But thus to interest and touch the children, the catechist needs to know them well and to have in his heart a great zeal for their salvation. Zeal is to be found in every pious ecclesiastic; but all do not understand children nor know what suits them. Experience sufficiently shows that many very learned preachers, while successful in the great pulpits, are not successful in this ministry to the little ones. They give the children fragments of discourses prepared for other occasions (*stations*): they are beautiful sketches, they contain good reasonings and spiritual allusions, but they are not simple; they describe nothing, they have no moral applications nor any of those special features which children need. This ought to be well considered when making choice of a preacher for retreats of first Communion.

The last day of retreat, the discourse of the morning, is intended to prepare the children for receiving the grace of absolution. Consequently the preacher explains what are the motives of contrition, and tries to awaken sorrow and confidence in their hearts. As, of all motives, the death of our Lord Jesus Christ is more powerful to touch us than any other, it is the custom of the catechisms of S. Sulpice that when the discourse is ended, either silently or singing a hymn on the Passion, they come and kneel before the altar, to kiss the crucifix as it is presented to them. Then they retire to the church in order, to the confessional of their director, unless they are to make their confession in the evening.

In the afternoon there is no retreat sermon; the meeting is entirely given up to the notices which must be given concerning the ceremony of the next day, on the parents' blessing, and on the immediate preparation for the Holy Communion.

In several parishes the custom is still kept up of going through the *communion blanche*, to show the children how they are to receive the sacred Host. This practice has advantages, no doubt, but also has great disadvantages: it is disturbing to the children, and some of the less intelligent cannot distinguish between this communion and that of the morrow. If it is thought better to give it up, it is still necessary, not only to give notices, but to make some rehearsal of the ceremony, to show the children how to come to the Holy Table, how to kneel, how to hold the cloth, how to receive the Host on their tongue. Many of the faithful do all this very badly, and cause many sad accidents.

The children must all bring certificates of confession, to obtain entrance the next day, and be admitted to the Holy Table. These certificates are shown to the catechist the evening before, and countersigned by him when there are many children and several confessors. The rule which demands a certificate of confession to be given in the day before, is very just in all respects: for it is certainly quite right to require that the children should confess on that day, and that they should give in a written proof of it, as they have done during the course of the catechisms. It is quite understood that these certificates contain nothing to show whether absolution has been given or refused; that is a secret for the confessor, a secret which he can never reveal. He merely certifies that he has heard such a child in confession. The reason why these certificates have to be looked over by the chief of the catechism is, that children who have been sent away from the catechism might confess, might obtain a certificate, and come and take their place to communicate with the others, if this precaution were not taken.

The general custom is for the children to carry a candle, and go up to give their offering at the church. The fear of accidents from fire in a large company of young girls covered with their veils, and the disturbance caused by the going to and fro with the offerings, have caused this custom to be modified in many parishes. The children give their candle, and make their offering in the catechism chapel, before going processionally to the church.

Another very estimable custom, consecrated by our traditions, is that, on the day before first Communion, the children ask pardon of their parents for all the things they may have done to displease them, and they receive from them their blessing. Some curés have had the happy idea of letting this act of filial piety be done in public, in the enclosure of the parish church. The children being in the middle and the parents standing all round, the pastor speaks a few words to both; then first he summons the children, and then makes the fathers and mothers raise their hands, and in their name he blesses the children. It is a touching ceremony, which cannot fail to have an excellent effect. If the circumstances of the place will not allow of its being done in public, the chief of the catechism makes the children promise to ask in private for this forgiveness and blessing, and he advises those whose parents are away to write to them. It is a good thing that just at the time when they are preparing for the solemn act of first Communion, they should give their father and mother an express mark of their affectionate obedience.

When the catechist has given these notices to the children, it only remains for him to tell them what should be the inward disposition of their heart this evening, and how, at the near approach of the grace God has in store for them, they should try more and more for recollection, for holy desires, and for peace of heart. If they have made a good confession, if their conscience does not reproach them with having concealed anything, nor of having committed any rather serious faults since their absolution, they may be at rest. It is well to enter into some little details on this subject, to prevent any conscientious anxieties. The confessors will be there to hear what their penitents might have to say, but these should not disturb or trouble themselves by any slight scruples which may cross their mind.

Article VII

First Communion

In the morning the sound of the bells announces a great festival: it is a day of joy to a great many families. Inside the church the decorations of the altar and the lighting are in correspondence with this holy solemnity. The children, who are assembled early in a chapel, set out in procession, and singing hymns, to the place which is reserved for them. Everything should be prepared there for their reception: forms or benches, a free passage in the middle and at the two sides, wide enough not to hinder the going to and fro. The boys arrive first, the girls follow, a little space is left between them.

During Holy Mass the children sing suitable hymns. There are times of silence, during which they follow the prayers, and a few minutes before the Communion a catechist reads the Acts from the pulpit. Generally the curé of the parish, or failing him, the celebrant, addresses a short exhortation to the children, suggesting to them sentiments of faith, of confidence, and of love, and thus prepares them for the holy action which is about to be accomplished.

While this great action is going on it is very important that nothing should happen to disturb the children, and therefore great calm and order should prevail during the ceremony. The children kneel for some minutes before going to the Holy Table; they go up then, form by form, at a given signal, in two parallel lines, and are led by the catechists. They are brought back in the same order, and the catechist is careful to see that they return to the same places they occupied before. The children have nothing to be anxious about, nothing to find out for themselves, they simply have to follow those who lead them. On returning to their place, they kneel down, and remain kneeling some time till a signal is given them to be seated. If the ceremony should be long, which happens in large parishes where the number of communicants is considerable, it is well for several catechists to be specially charged with watching over the children, and helping them to occupy the time profitably. Without this precaution what could a number of young children do, seated on forms for a whole hour or more, either before they make their Communion or afterwards, waiting till the ceremony is over?

To help the children in keeping quiet and attentive, we introduce hymns, readings, and prayers, taking care to do it so as to help their devotion without fatiguing them. Sometimes a hymn is sung accompanied by the organ, and this stirs them all up; at another time we suggest to the children that they should read their Acts over again, or perhaps recite a *dizaine de chapelet*, or perhaps read in the *Cantiques de S. Sulpice* some of the passages taken from the fourth book of the *Imitation*. Care has been taken to gather together in this book all that is wanted for the retreat time and for the day of first Communion. At intervals the children are left to themselves, only seeing that they are behaving well.

When the Communion is ended the priest again gives an exhortation to the children, to impress on them the value of the grace they have just received. Afterwards they say a prayer for their parents and benefactors, and five *Pater* and *Ave* to gain the plenary indulgence which the Holy See has granted. The prayers over, the chief of the catechism tells them the exact time for the evening gathering, and gives the signal for departure. The children then go out in order, in two files, led by the catechists; not till then are they given back to their parents.

In the evening the children come in again as in the morning. When everyone is seated, the priest who officiates begins vespers, which are sung solemnly. In the middle of the nave, opposite the pulpit, a small altar has been carefully arranged, on which are placed the symbols of baptism: water, the holy chrism, the white robe, the book of the holy Gospels, and two candles. The officiant censes this altar during the *Magnificat*.

The singing of vespers is followed by a sermon on the renewal of the baptismal promises. The preacher shows the children how much reason they have to be grateful, and to feel bound more than ever to keep faithful to God. He recalls to them baptism, Christian instruction, sacramental absolution, the blessings of the retreat, the inestimable grace of the first Communion; then, as an earnest of their faithfulness, he proposes to them that, in the presence of the holy altars, of the Holy Virgin, and their guardian angel, before the symbols of baptism, in the midst of the church, in the sight of their parents and their friends, they should make a solemn protestation that they believe in God, Father, Son, and Holy Spirit; that they renounce for ever the devil, his works and his pomps; that to their last breath they desire to belong to Jesus Christ. If the preacher has really reached the children's heart, if he has arranged his subjects clearly and precisely, this protestation is made with a holy enthusiasm and produces a great sensation. It is a remembrance for life.

Directly the preacher has left the pulpit, a hymn is sung, suitable to the occasion, such as the one which begins, *Quand l'eau sainte du baptême*, and all is arranged for the *salut* of the blessed sacrament which is about to follow. It would seem that everything should end with this, but the filial piety of our forefathers towards the Blessed Virgin did not allow them to finish so beautiful, so imposing a ceremony without again consecrating her children to her. It was M. Olier's custom to offer everything to Mary: "He loved to consecrate the children to her the day of their first Communion. Constantly, if he had anything rare or beautiful, he felt a sort of necessity to use it to her honour, and on this day he was eager to consecrate to her these young hearts whom Jesus Christ had deigned to fill with His Spirit and with His grace, persuaded that at no moment of their life would they be more worthy to be offered to her."[1]

For this pious ceremony the children are led, singing litanies, to the altar of the Holy Virgin. A catechist, in a few words, tells them what a happiness it is for them to consecrate themselves to her; then the two intendents of the boys and girls pronounce the act of consecration, while all the children sing the beautiful hymn, *Vous en êtes témoins, anges du sanctuaire*. If this procession cannot be made to Mary's altar, it would be well, immediately after the *salut*, to arrange a temporary altar in front of the Holy Table, and on it to place a statue of the Holy Virgin.

Article VIII

Catechism of Confirmation

In the greater number of parishes it is the custom for the children to receive the Sacrament of Confirmation on the same day as the first Communion, or the day after, if it is possible. In some of them an interval of eight or ten days is allowed, and we have always considered this practice to have a great advantage, for it is important that the children

[1] *Vie de M. Olier*, vol i. pt. ii. bk. iii.

should conceive a high idea of this sacrament, and not look upon it as a mere accessory, and a ceremony supplementary to the first Communion. It is good for them that their thoughts should be fixed with a very special attention on the Holy Spirit, who is so little known in the world.

It has sometimes been objected against this practice that it would result in a great deal of difficulty for the confessors, who, too often, after eight days, would find many children fallen back into bad habits, and that they would not know what to do, whether to give them absolution a second time, or to put off their Confirmation for another year, in which case they would have reason to fear that they would never receive it. But this consideration, far from making us give up the practice to which we allude, makes us value it more. If several children have fallen back, they will at least have the opportunity of seeing their confessors again, of hearing new advice and new ways of perseverance. Among the number may we not hope that some will be all the more strengthened in their resolutions?

It seems to us, therefore, that wherever it can be done, there is an advantage in separating Confirmation from first Communion. If there is only a week or fortnight's interval, it is not necessary to go through so long or so severe a retreat as that for first Communion. For this retreat it would be enough, on three successive days, to go through the exercises of the week-day catechism. The questioning, the good points, and the instruction are all on the Holy Spirit and on Confirmation. The chief advises on the proper dispositions with which they should come to the sacrament, on the need the faithful have of the Holy Spirit to lead Christian lives, and on obedience in following the inspirations of the Holy Spirit. If there are any articles in the rule of life he has not had time to explain, he speaks about them; he dwells much on human respect, which drives so many Christians away from the service of God, and which is so grievous to the Holy Spirit.

The day before the Confirmation, in the morning, prayer, meditation, Holy Mass, notices, and a discourse from the retreat preacher, preparing the children for the absolution they are about to receive; in the evening, a meeting like that on the eve of the first Communion, to keep up the thoughtful attention of the children and explain to them all they will have to do the next day. They will not make their Communion, because it is desirable that all their attention should be given to the august sacrament they are about to receive, and to which they ought to bring the same purity of heart as was required of them for the divine Eucharist. The children should write their baptismal name on a small piece of paper, and bring a linen band, with which the priest will wipe their forehead, after the bishop has anointed them with the holy chrism.

The hour for the Confirmation is settled beforehand by the bishop. If it is in the morning, everything is done nearly in the same order as on the day of first Communion. The children go first to their chapel, from whence they are led in procession to the places reserved for them in the church. They hear Holy Mass, during which hymns to the Holy Spirit are sung. After Mass the ceremony begins. We take care that all the children are present, and we tell them to kneel at the prayers and when the bishop gives the first imposition of hands. Still, if it should happen by accident that some of them are not present at that moment, we do not think it absolutely necessary to their Confirmation to make them wait till the administration is ended, and then to beg the bishop to begin over again for them the prayer and imposition of hands.

In the evening, vespers, a sermon on perseverance, and the *salut* of the Blessed Sacrament.

Article IX

Distribution of Memorials of First Communion and Confirmation

A few days after the Confirmation, the children are given memorials of the first Communion. It is a favourable opportunity for the pastor of the parish to give them useful advice and, for the last time, to point out to them the line of conduct they ought to follow in the world.

It is not necessary to give two separate pictures, one for first Communion and one for Confirmation,

MEMORIALS OF FIRST COMMUNION

but these pictures must be good ones, so that the children will be anxious to get them framed, and will take care of them. It is easy in these days to get such, not at a very high price, not very remarkable, artistically considered, but yet very suitable. Every pastor makes his own choice, according to the resources Providence gives him, and according to the general condition of the children in his parish. He considers how best to use the money he designs for these gifts: for they may do much good by the remembrance they keep up in families of a first Communion. Many times the sight of this memorial has awakened sentiments of faith which had become weakened by time.

Many children think much of having a medal and a cross in memory of their first Communion. They keep the medal among their most precious treasures, and they wear the cross.[1]

---

[1] We may mention to parents who wish to make this present to their children, the beautiful medal which has been engraved by one of the most skilful Parisian artists, according to the design of P. Arthur Martin; it was exhibited in the *Exposition Universelle* of 1855. Monsignor the Archbishop of Paris wrote to Madame Anger, by whose order this remarkable work of art was done: "This medal, commemorating the three great acts in the Christian life, will be eagerly received by many families. . . . With exquisite delicacy of feeling and most felicitous execution, you have known how to show forth the symbols of Baptism, of first Communion, and of Confirmation."

CHAPTER IV

CATECHISMS OF PERSEVERANCE

Article I

On the great importance of establishing Catechisms of Perseverance

It is unhappily only too common a thing that the children, very soon after their going out into the world, their first Communion made, are, so to speak, drawn away in the torrent of temptation and bad examples. The seeds of piety and virtue which have been sown in their hearts are soon choked by passions and vices. How rare it is to see children persevere in the practices of a Christian life, to find any who do not in youth falsify the hopes we had formed of their goodness! It is no less sad to reflect that many only abandon religion, because they have themselves been abandoned. In their childhood they were instructed, they were prepared worthily to approach the Holy Table. But this duty fulfilled, no one thinks any more about them; and yet, if ordinary catechisms are one of the most useful and important exercises in the ministry of souls, what must we not think of the higher catechisms, the object of which is to secure the perseverance of the children, to give to them a more extended knowledge of religion, and to inspire them with a sincere and lasting love for religion, for its precepts and its counsels, a love which will lead them gladly to practise them?

Public instructions and other exercises common to all do not sufficiently answer to this need. For the very reason that these exercises are held for everyone, many young lads do not feel drawn to them; there is nothing in them specially suited to their age; things which interest them more directly are not spoken of, such as their duties as students, their relations with the world, what they should do to amend the faults of their character, to finish their education. . . . The young girls go with their mothers to the parish church; they will be present with them at the *prône*, the sermons, the benedictions of the blessed sacrament, and we are far from thinking they will get no profit from all this; on the contrary, we advise them to get the habit early of frequenting the public services, which always leave salutary impressions on the heart. But, without speaking of a number of others who will only be taken to a Low Mass, and will pass the rest of the Sunday in frivolous amusements, if they do not come to the catechism, we can say for certain that those who are assiduous at the parish offices will profit much more by them if, at the same time, for several years they attend the catechism of perseverance: they will be better instructed, they will get a direction which answers more to the needs of their soul, they will more certainly be led on to piety. Experience leaves no doubt on this point.

It is desirable, therefore, that under one title or another, under the name of Confraternity, of Association, of Youthful Work, of Congregation, or of Higher Catechism, a catechism of perseverance should be formed. But in establishing it there is always some difficulty. There is more than one hindrance to be got rid of: hindrances on the part of the families, hindrances on the part of the children, hindrances sometimes on the part of our superiors, who may be afraid that a vicar will be absorbed by the cares of a catechism, and may a little neglect the other duties of his ministry. The essential thing is to go about it quite simply, to keep to the order prescribed by authority, not seeking to satisfy any personal interest, nor dreaming of making one's own influence greater in the parish, putting the chief pastor at the head of the work, as is fitting, so that everything is done in his name and under his authority. He who keeps to this way, as marked out by the Spirit of God, and who devotes himself to the children with a true and supernatural love, will certainly succeed. Even if at first he should only have a dozen well-disposed children, he should begin the good work; others will come to join them; every year the first Communion will bring in new elements, and in a few years the pastor will thank God for the con-

CATECHISMS OF PERSEVERANCE

solations brought to him by the catechism of perseverance.

In Paris, the catechisms of perseverance are frequented by many young women, who continue to come to them till their marriage. We have also had the comfort of seeing many young men regular at the meetings of their catechism for several years after their first Communion. These meetings must certainly interest them greatly, or they would not attend them for so long.

We have sometimes heard good people express a fear that the young women who have attended the catechisms of perseverance for several years will, when they are married and leave, not feel at home in the services of their parish church. There is no ground for this fear, though we respect the feeling which inspires it: to convince them it would be enough to examine with a little attention and to compare the parishes where the catechisms of perseverance are the most frequented, with those in which there are either no such catechisms, or where perhaps only a few children attend them. The parish of S. Sulpice would certainly, in Paris, be a good illustration. Everyone knows how zealously the young people come to the catechism, and no other parish could be named where all the public services are more frequented on Sundays and festivals. And the curés, too, of S. Sulpice have always shown the greatest satisfaction in seeing the work of the catechisms of perseverance more and more consolidated and extended. The pious M. Colin always rejoiced to say that these catechisms were the seminary of his parish, that is to say, they produced the best parishioners.

It must naturally be so, since the catechists are constantly exhorting the children to attend the services of their parish church. In a book which has been compiled for them, we say: "Though we advise you to come assiduously and for a long time to the catechisms of perseverance, we do not wish you to forget the parish church: on the contrary, we shall always endeavour to persuade you to attend the public services when there is no catechism, so that from this time you may begin to form good habits, which it would be very good for you to keep up all your life. You will notice that the meetings of the perseverance are suspended during four months of the year, from July to November; and moreover, they are not held on the days of the principal festivals—All Saints, Christmas, Easter, Pentecost, nor during the week. On Sunday itself it is always possible to assist at some of the holy offices, at High Mass, or at vespers, according to whether the catechism is held in the morning or afternoon. It is not very difficult then, as you see, to fit in everything; you can be constant at the catechism, and, at the same time, constant to the parish church."[1]

Those who frequent the catechisms for a long time do good in a twofold way, which is invaluable. They are themselves strengthened in solid piety by the exercises of the catechism; the counsels they receive are more suitable to them, and meet their

[1] *Persévérance Chretienne*, 3rd ed. p. 55.

needs more directly, than those which they hear addressed to an audience composed indifferently of all sorts of people. And further, by their example, by their assiduity, and by many services they are in a position to render, they contribute to the prosperity of a work which is so important for the younger children. Those who have any experience know well that the success of the great catechisms is due in great part to the old members, to the aspirants, and the associates.

Article II

Rule of the Catechisms of Perseverance

The exercises of the catechism of perseverance are not different from those of the ordinary catechisms. We use very nearly the same methods for making these exercises pleasant to the children; we try, as in the other catechisms, to give them such innocent pleasures as shall make them forget worldly pleasures, and lead them willingly to devote some hours every Sunday to their advancement in the knowledge and the love of religion. There are also the same means employed for emulation: pictures, prizes, dignities, etc. As the children are older, and in no way obliged to come to this catechism, we treat them with much consideration, and make every arrangement for them which Christian charity demands; but with regard to the observance of the rules, nothing is slackened. Severity on this point, however, by no means keeps the young people away from the catechism; experience teaches us, on the contrary, that it makes them love it more, and that it is inseparable from the best way of governing them. The elders among them, particularly, are strongly attached to their customs, and are distressed if they are departed from, in however small a degree.

All the children belonging to the catechism are present at the same exercises, and have the same things to do; but in what concerns the analyses and compositions, a distinction may be made in favour of the new members of the perseverance: those of the first year might only compete among themselves for the seals and prizes, not with the older members.

In the instructions there are two extremes to be avoided. Although they should be more advanced and fuller than in the other catechisms, they must not be above the level of many of the children. Although grounding the instruction on what will be to the general profit of the catechism, the catechists should add a certain number of questions and some rather more advanced developments, so that even the best informed children will find something to learn. It is more than ever necessary in a catechism of perseverance that the instructions should be marked by great distinctness in the ideas, great clearness and precision in their expression, and perfect exactness in doctrine. As these instructions, being deeper as well as higher, are generally more difficult to follow than those given in the other catechisms, it is necessary, in order to keep up attention, to make them attractive in various ways, bringing in illustrations and well-authenticated stories. One need not be afraid of saying something even to provoke a smile, keeping always within bounds.

It is not well, in catechisms of young people, to give proofs which are too scientific or too much reasoned out. Too much pains cannot be taken in choosing such as are suitable to them. Religion can offer reasons for belief adapted to all sorts of people, and fully sufficient to work entire conviction in those whose intellect is less cultivated. These are the sort of proofs we should keep to in the instructions of which we are speaking, and not those which are only good for a class of people whose intellect is of a higher order.

Above all, in the instructions, great care must be taken in speaking of objections which may be made against the truths we are teaching. Children, and even grown-up persons, often feel all the force of an objection, but are not equally struck by the answer, however satisfactory it may be. On this point the first rule is, to make as few objections as possible, and only to forewarn the children against such as they cannot help hearing in the world. The objection must be given out for what it is, that is to say, a mischievous thing, only produced by ignorance or want of faith, and the catechist must make sure that the answer shall be so clear that not a cloud is left on the children's mind. But no arrogant terms or triumphant manner must be assumed when giving the answer; this generally only tells against the preacher rather than in his favour, and sometimes damages what he says as well. If any objection is to be fully answered, and no bad impression left on the mind, it must be set forth in such a way that the answer shall be seen directly the objection is made: for instance, turn the objection into a proof in favour of the doctrine, and then dwell on the fact that unbelievers or heretics think we shall find a serious difficulty in their objection. By this means, whenever the children hear the objection brought forward, it can only have a good effect. This was the method which S. François de Sales employed for converting heretics.

Article III

Plan of Instructions for the Catechism of Perseverance

In the catechisms of perseverance the course of instruction, as a rule, lasts for three years. This time has been thought sufficient, supposing that we can have thirty meetings each year, independently of the festival days. The first year is devoted to the exposition of dogma; the second, we deal with morals; the third is kept for the sacraments and all which concerns public worship.

In some parishes, the course is distributed over

five or six years. We find that there are inconveniences in this plan. It must not be forgotten that the greater number of children will not remain so long at the catechism, and that, besides, it is well for them to hear the same questions treated more than once. In a course of five or six years, it must necessarily happen that many subjects and developments are brought in, which no doubt are interesting, but are yet only of secondary importance. It follows from this that children who only attend for one or two years at the perseverance are liable to get no instruction on much more important subjects; if, on the other hand, this course only lasts three years, these same children will receive complete instruction on one or two of the most essential points of Christian doctrine.

There is no reason to fear that those who come for five or six years, or more, will not be interested in instructions which they have already heard. Though the groundwork of the instructions is the same, they are never reproduced under the same form. There is always something new—different points of a doctrine, ideas, difficulties, practical solutions not observed at first, or else no longer remembered. Those who missed some analyses in a first course, those who made them too imperfectly, repair these defects when they hear a subject treated for the second time. If their collection is complete, they will dispense themselves from making analyses; but they can make synoptical charts, as the elder boys do in their catechism.

We give here a programme of instructions which

can be adopted for catechisms of perseverance; and at the same time we shall take the liberty of pointing out what corresponds to the different parts in the *Cours d' instruction*,[1] which has been published according to this plan. Nevertheless we must observe that in this work there are some questions of religious philosophy, of ecclesiastical history and of criticism, useful for those who wish to go deeply into the study of religion, but not equally suitable for all catechisms. It is for the catechist to find out what is best suited to his audience, and what should be reserved for instructions intended for more educated people.

First Year of the Course—Dogma

I. Instruction. On the study of religion.
  1. Excellence of the study of religion: how superior in its object to the study of human sciences; comforts it procures for us. 2. Necessity of the study of religion for ourselves and for those whom we may be able to enlighten on Christian doctrine; misfor-

---

[1] *Cours d' instruction religieuse, ou Exposition complète de la doctrine Chrétienne*, by the Director of the Catechisms of S. Sulpice, 4 vols. in 12mo. Equally may be used *Instructions Générales, en forme de Catéchisme*, by Charancy; the *Explication du Catéchisme*, by Guillois, 4 vols. in 12mo.; the *Catéchisme de Persévérance*, by M. l'Abbe Gaume, 8 vols. in 8vo. The *Catéchisme du Concile de Trente*, published by order of S. Pius V., is too well known for it to be necessary to mention it. In speaking of catechetical works, there is no book which possesses so great an authority, nor any from which we may draw with more certainty the teaching of the Church.

tune of those who know it not. 3. Method to be followed in the study of religion: study in succession, following the order of the catechism,—dogma, morals, worship; for this study only read well-chosen books; suffer ourselves to be guided by the teaching of the Church. (*Cours d' instruction*, vol. i. ch. i.).

II. On the Holy Scriptures and Tradition.
1. Concerning the Holy Scriptures and Tradition: what is understood by the Holy Books; how many there are; Books of the Old and New Testament; historical, prophetic, moral books; all that God has revealed to us is not in the Holy Scriptures. 2. Authority of the Holy Scriptures and of Tradition: it is the word of God, therefore, deep reverence; example given us in all ages by the truly faithful in this respect. 3. Interpretation of the Scriptures and of Tradition: it is from the Church that we must learn the true meaning of the divine Scriptures; read only translations approved by the Church. (*Cours d' instruction*, vol. i. ch. iv. secs. 2, 3.)

III. On God.
1. First proof of the existence of God: the revelation of Himself which He has made in manifesting Himself to men. 2. Proof drawn from the unanimous consent of all people: always and everywhere people have believed in divinity, though they may have been deceived as to the true idea we should have

of God. 3. Proof drawn from the wonderful order which reigns in the universe: this order and the very existence of the world can only be explained by going back to God, who has created everything and disposed everything with wisdom. (*Cours d' instruction*, vol. i. ch. i. sec. 1.)

IV. On the perfections of God.
 1. What God is in Himself: pure Spirit, eternal, infinitely perfect. 2. What God is in relation to us: He has created us, He preserves us, He watches over us. Proofs of divine Providence, drawn from the preservation of the world, from the universal belief of all people, and from the Holy Books. (Vol. i. ch. i. secs. 2, 3.)

V. On the angels.
 1. Existence of angels; proofs drawn from the Holy Scriptures, which speak of angels, also from the invariable traditions of all people. 2. Distinction between good and evil angels —all the angels were created good, but the good have remained faithful to God, the evil ones went astray by the abuse of their freedom. 3. Occupation of the angels: what the evil angels do; services rendered to us by the good angels, and specially by the guardian angels. (Vol. ii. ch. xii. secs. 1, 2, 3.)

VI. On the creation of man.
 1. Circumstances of the creation of man as they are related to us in Genesis. 2. Distinction

between soul and body, and their intimate union; by this show the spirituality of the soul. 3. Natural faculties of man—he is reasonable and he is free. Proofs of this liberty drawn from conscience and common sense. (Vol. i. ch. ii. secs. 1, 2, 3.)

VII. On primitive revelation.

1. God established a religion in the beginning of the world—there is nothing so contrary to the wisdom and goodness of God as to suppose that, in creating man, he left him to himself, without instructing him as to his origin and his end. 2. In what primitive religion consisted—truths that man must believe, and duties which he must fulfil. 3. How primitive religion was to be preserved and transmitted—the fathers to teach their families. (Vol. i. ch. iv. sec. 1; ch. vi. secs. 1, 2.)

VIII. On the sin of the first man, and the consequences of this sin.

1. Adam and Eve seriously offend God by doing what He had forbidden them to do; God punishes them by driving them out of the earthly Paradise, and condemning them to the miseries of life and death. 2. Adam's children are divided into two companies; some, who may be called the children of God, remain faithful; the others follow their own evil inclinations—Cain and Abel. 3. God punishes man by the Flood; certainty and universality of the Flood (this instruction

is entirely historical). (Vol. i. ch. v. sec. 3; ch. vii.)

IX. On the deterioration of primitive religion.

1. The greater part of the nations lose the knowledge of the true God—idolatry, its origin and its progress. 2. Religious worship is depraved by superstitions; human sacrifices. 3. Unhappiness of men who lived in the midst of this general corruption; nevertheless God did not deprive them of all means of salvation, as will be seen in the instructions which follow. (Vol. i. ch. ix. secs. 1, 2; ch. x. sec. 1.)

X. On the call of Abraham and the beginnings of the Hebrew people.

1. Call of Abraham; the design of God in the choice of this patriarch, to make him the head of a great people. 2. Isaac, Jacob, and the twelve sons of Jacob. 3. The family of Abraham come into Egypt; oppressed by their enemies. (Vol. i. ch. x. sec. 2; ch. xi.)

XI. On the revelation made to the Hebrew people and the divine law which was given to them.

1. God raises up Moses to deliver His people from the bondage of Egypt. 2. God appears to Moses on Mount Sinai; He renews the revelation made at the beginning of the world and gives a definite law to the Hebrew people. 3. The definite law given on Mount Sinai is only binding on the Hebrews; but it is for the good of all nations, since it tends to form a nation which will preserve true

FIRST YEAR—DOGMA

doctrines and propagate them in the world. (Vol. i. ch. xii. prelude; ch. xiii. secs. 1, 2.)

XII. On the divinity of the revelation made to the Hebrews.

1. Miraculous facts recorded in the Old Testament—plagues of Egypt; passage of the Red Sea. 2. Mount Sinai. 3. It is impossible, with any reason, to doubt the miracles reported by Moses—these miracles are a manifest proof of the divinity of the revelation made to the Hebrews. (Vol. i. ch. xii. secs. 1, 2, 3.)

XIII. On the prophecies relating to the Messiah.

1. God promises to Abraham, to Isaac, and to Jacob that the Messiah shall be born in their family. 2. By His prophets God proclaims that the Messiah will come before the destruction of the temple at Jerusalem, and before the entire dispersion of the Jewish people (Jacob, Daniel). 3. Prophecies as to the manner in which the Messiah will bring about the salvation of men (David, Isaiah). (Vol. i. ch. xv. secs. 1, 2.)

XIV. On the expectation of the Messiah and His coming.

1. Why did God delay so long before giving a Saviour to the world? 2. Expectation of the Messiah at the time when Jesus Christ came into the world. 3. The principal circumstances of the birth of Jesus Christ and His first manifestations. (Vol. i. ch. xv. sec. 2; vol. ii. ch. xiv. sec. 1.)

XV. On the divinity of Jesus Christ.

1. Jesus Christ declares publicly that He is the only Son of God. 2. The Eternal Father declares that Jesus Christ is His well-beloved Son; baptism of our Lord; transfiguration. 3. Jesus Christ works miracles which are a manifest proof of His divinity—multiplication of the loaves, curing the blind, resurrection of Lazarus. (Vol. i. ch. xvi. secs. 1, 2, 3.)

XVI. On the divinity of the Christian religion.

1. The Christian religion carries in itself the evident signs of its divinity—everything in it is worthy of God, both as to its dogmas and its morals. 2. The spread of Christianity in the world is another equally clear proof of its divinity; obstacles of all kinds; absence of all human means; supernatural success. (Vol. i. ch. xvi. secs. 5, 6.)

XVII. On the establishment and the constitution of the Church.

1. Jesus Christ established a body of shepherds, to teach, to propagate, and to preserve the Christian religion; S. Peter is appointed chief of the body of shepherds; he is the vicar of Jesus Christ, the father, the teacher, and the chief shepherd of all the faithful, and of the shepherds themselves. 2. The Apostles are all appointed shepherds; but they must remain united to their chief, and subject to his authority. 3. The constitution of the Church consists, therefore, in that it is governed by the Pope, the successor of

FIRST YEAR—DOGMA

S. Peter, and by the bishops, successors of the Apostles, united and subject to the Pope, supreme Pontiff. (Vol. ii. ch. i. secs. 2, 3.)

XVIII. On the authority of the Church, as regards doctrine.

1. Our Lord has given the Church the right to teach us with authority. 2. Our Lord has promised to the Church supernatural assistance which renders her infallible in teaching the true faith. 3. How the Church teaches us: councils; dogmatic decisions of the Holy See; catechisms. (Vol. ii. ch. iii. secs. 1, 3.)

XIX. On the authority of the Church with regard to discipline.

1. The Church has received from Jesus Christ the power to rule by laws things which concern good conduct and divine worship. 2. The authority to make laws, in spiritual things, is only possessed by the chief pastors, the Pope and the bishops. 3. Obligation which lies on us all to keep the commandments of the Church. (Vol. ii. ch. iv. secs. 1, 2.)

XX. On the properties or characters of the Church: unity and sanctity.

1. In what consists the essential unity of the Church—unity of faith, of worship, of ministry. 2. In what consists the sanctity of the Church —she is holy in her Head, in her belief, in her worship, in many of her members. (Vol. ii. ch. xviii.)

XXI. On the properties or characters of the Church—Catholic and Apostolic.
1. The true Church should spread herself everywhere; she will always be more vast than any other religious body. 2. The true Church is Apostolic—she comes from the Apostles, and continues without interruption by the pastors who have succeeded the Apostles. (Vol. ii. ch. xviii.)

XXII. On the axiom, *Outside the Church, no salvation*.
1. The Church cannot be distinguished from Christianity—they are one and the same thing. 2. Men are all bound to profess Christianity as far as they know it—that is to say, to believe what Jesus Christ teaches us by His Church, to perform the duties He lays upon us, to obey the pastoral ministry which He has appointed. 3. This is the true meaning of the axiom, *Outside the Church, no salvation*. (Vol. ii. ch. v. secs. 1, 2, 3.)

XXIII. On the Creed in general.
1. What is the Apostles' Creed? Does it come from the Apostles? Has it varied in the course of time? 2. The Creed contains truths or dogmas which are incomprehensible to us. 3. How reasonable it is to believe the mysteries of the Christian religion. (Vol. ii. chs. viii. ix.)

XXIV. On the 1st Article of the Creed—the Holy Trinity.

FIRST YEAR—DOGMA

1. There are Three distinct Persons in God : proofs of the faith of the Church regarding this article. 2. Relations of the Three Divine Persons among themselves — the Second Person, the Word, proceeds from the Father, of Whom He is the only Son; the Holy Spirit proceeds from the Father and the Son. 3. This mystery gives us a high idea of God, and leads us on to love one another. (Vol. ii. ch. xi. secs. 1, 2, 3.)

XXV. On the fall of the first man and on original sin.

1. Supernatural gifts which the first man received from God—he was innocent, united to God by love, exempt from the lusts of the flesh, immortal. 2. Man lost these gifts, together with the friendship of God, by sin ; circumstances of Adam's sin. 3. The whole human race is defiled by the sin of the first man, and is included in his misery. Proofs of original sin drawn from the Holy Scriptures and from the teaching of the Church. The dogma of original sin can be reconciled with the goodness and the justice of God. (Vol. ii. ch. xiii. secs. 3, 4, 5.)

XXVI. On the 2nd and 3rd Article of the Creed—the Incarnation.

1. Jesus Christ is God and Man—therefore there are in Him two distinct natures. 2. The Son of Mary is the same as the only Son of God—therefore in Jesus Christ there is only one Person, the Person of the Word.

3. Why the Son God became man. (Vol. ii. ch. xiv. secs. 2, 3.)

XXVII. On the 4th Article of the Creed—Redemption.

1. Jesus Christ worked the redemption of the world by His death. 2. Redemption is universal; it extends to all men, to those who lived before the coming of Jesus Christ as well as to those who will come into life till the end of the world. 3. The gratitude we should feel to our Lord. (Vol. ii. ch. xiv. secs. 1, 2.)

XXVIII. On the 5th, 6th, and 7th Articles.

1. Burial of our Lord and His descent into hell. The Divinity remained united to the body of Jesus Christ which was laid in the tomb, and to His soul which descended into limbo to visit and comfort the just ones. 2. Resurrection of our Lord; chief circumstances of this great event. 3. Ascension of our Lord into heaven. (Vol. ii. ch. xvi. secs. 1, 2, 3.)

XXIX. On the 8th Article of the Creed—the Holy Spirit, the Sanctifier.

1. Habitual grace which the Holy Spirit communicates to souls in sanctifying them; He infuses the virtues of faith, of hope, of charity. 2. Actual grace which He gives them to enlighten them, to lead them to good, and to enable them to do works of salvation. 3. Absolute necessity of this grace for doing good, or even for the desire of doing good, in the supernatural order. This grace for the

FIRST YEAR—DOGMA

fulfilment of laws is denied to no one. (Vol. ii. ch. xvii. secs. 1, 2, 3.)

XXX. On the 9th and 10th Articles—the Communion of Saints.

1. Links which unite all the faithful, those who are fighting on earth, those who are suffering in purgatory, and those who are triumphing in heaven. 2. In what sense the treasures of the Church are common to all the faithful. 3. Happiness we enjoy in belonging to the Church; it is in her bosom, by her prayers, and by the grace of the sacraments, that we receive forgiveness of sins. (Vol. ii. ch. xix.)

XXXI. On the resurrection of the body.

1. The Church has always believed in a future life. 2. All men will one day rise again. 3. Circumstances which must precede and follow the general resurrection: the last judgment. (Vol. ii. ch. xx.)

XXXII. On the 12th Article—Eternal Life.

1. Purgatory: state of transition, and purification of the just; holiness of God, Who cannot suffer the smallest defilement in souls. 2. Hell; permanent state of punishment for the reprobate; justice of God, Who punishes eternally those who have died in mortal sin. 3. Heaven; there only is the true life, the life eternal; goodness of God, Who calls us all to enjoy with Himself a happiness which will never end. (Vol. ii. ch. xxi.)

If there cannot be thirty-two meetings, those instructions which are thought least necessary can be left out; if there are more than thirty-two, it would be quite easy to add to them: for instance, among other subjects, the perpetuity of the Church might be treated of, or the reproach that is sometimes made against her of being intolerant; it would be useful to devote one instruction to showing that in the first year's course, everything may be traced to these three fundamental articles: God, Jesus Christ, and the Church.

Second Year of the Course—Morals

I. Instruction. On the relation between dogma and morals.
> 1. All morality of necessity supposes dogmas. 2. The more free from all error is dogma, so the purer and more efficacious will be morality in ruling the conduct of man. 3. Therefore the morality of Christianity is the most perfect. (Vol. iii. introduction.)

II. On the first of God's commandments—Faith or belief.
> 1. What faith is: its object, all the truths revealed by God; its foundation, the truth of God, Who cannot deceive us; its rule, the teaching of the Church, which teaches us infallibly what God has revealed. 2. Necessity of faith; without supernatural faith it is impossible to do one single action deserving of heaven. 3. Consequences of this doctrine: necessity of being instructed in the truths of the faith; serious sin which would be com-

mitted by doubting an article of faith; we should be careful not to read books against religion. (Vol. iii. ch. i. secs. 1, 2, 3.)

III. On the first of God's commandments—Hope.
1. What hope is: its object, heaven, and the graces we need to enable us to reach it; in what sense we may also hope for temporal benefits, and ask God for them; the ground of hope, the merits of Jesus Christ, and the promises which God has given us. 2. Necessity of hope: there is no situation in life in which we cannot hope in God. 3. Sins which may be committed against hope: presumption, despair. (Vol. iii. ch. iii. secs. 1, 2, 4.)

IV. On the first of God's commandments—Charity.
1. What it is; love of God for Himself, because He is infinitely lovable, and above everything. Charity is the highest of all the virtues. 2. Necessity of charity: charity is the end of the law; man has been created to love God; it is the first and chief commandment; all the others spring from it. 3. Effects of charity: it detaches us from all unruly affections towards created things. (Vol. iii. ch. iv.)

V. On the first of God's commandments—Charity to our neighbour.
1. Precept of loving our neighbour; in what sense does our Lord say that the second precept is like the first. 2. To obey this precept, how should we love our neighbour?

our love must be supernatural in its motive and universal in its object; love of our enemies. (*Same chapter.*)

VI. On the obligations laid on us by charity with regard to our neighbour.

1. Charity with regard to our neighbour cannot remain barren; it leads us to do good to our neighbour. 2. To strive for the salvation of our neighbour. 3. To be a help to our neighbour in his bodily wants; rules as to almsgiving. (Vol. iii. ch. iv. sec. 3.)

VII. On the virtue of religion.

1. What is worship and sacrifice: worship and sacrifice only due to God. 2. It is allowable to invoke the saints and to honour their relics. 3. Essential difference between the worship due to God alone, and the worship (*culte*) which the Church pays to the saints. (Vol. iii. ch. v. secs. 1, 2, 3.)

VIII. On prayer.

1. What prayer is. 2. Conditions necessary for prayer to be efficacious. Obligation of prayer; when we are bound to pray. (Vol. iii. ch. iii. sec 3.)

IX. On vows and oaths. Second commandment.

1. Of a vow: what distinguishes a vow from a simple intention; vows to be made with great caution. 2. Of oaths: under what circumstances it is allowable to take an oath. 3. How may the obligation of a vow or an oath be dispensed from? (Vol. iii. chap. vi. secs. 1, 2, 3.)

SECOND YEAR—MORALS

X. On the third commandment—Sanctification of Sunday.
   1. Reasons for keeping Sunday holy. 2. What divine law and ecclesiastical law demands with regard to the hallowing of Sunday. 3. Circumstances under which we may be dispensed from keeping the laws of the Church with regard to Sunday. (Vol. iii. ch. viii. secs. 2, 3, 4.)

XI. On sins against religion.
   1. Vain and superstitious worship. 2. Sacrilege. 3. Invoking the aid of the devil, as in magic and any other unlawful practice. (Vol. iii. ch. viii. secs. 1, 2, 3.)

XII. On the fourth of God's commandments.
   1. On the authority of fathers and mothers in their families. 2. Authority of bishops and other pastors in the Church. 3. Authority of princes and magistrates in civil society: what cases may arise in which we should not be bound to obey our superiors. (Vol. iii. ch. ix. secs. 1, 2, 3, 4.)

XIII. Duties of superiors to those who are subject to them.
   1. We should be just towards those under us. 2. We should love them. 3. We ought to take care of them: fathers and mothers absolutely bound to provide Christian education for their children (Vol. iii. ch. ix. sec. 5.)

XIV. On the fifth commandment—Duties which justice demands of us with regard to our neighbour.
   1. The right of our neighbour to have his

natural life preserved. 2. Obligation laid on us to preserve our own life. 3. Spiritual murders and suicides through sin, and causes of offence. (Vol. iii. ch. x. secs. 1, 2, 3 ; ch. xi. sec. 1.)

XV. On the sixth commandment.
1. What it is which the sixth commandment commands and forbids. 2. On the various occasions in which we may run the risk of breaking this commandment. (Vol. iii. ch. xi. secs. 1, 2.)

XVI. On the seventh commandment—Duties which justice requires towards our neighbour. (Temporal goods.)
1. Our neighbour has a right to keep those goods which he has lawfully acquired, hence results the obligation we are under to cause no damage to the temporal goods of our neighbour. 2. In what ways riches are lawfully acquired; the providence and wisdom of God, Who binds men to each other by their mutual needs, and arouses their diligence so that they may provide for themselves and their families such temporal good things as are necessary or useful to them. (Vol. iii. ch. xii. secs. 1, 2.)

XVII. On the obligation we are under to make restitution to our neighbour for any wrong we may have done him as regards his temporal goods.
1. In what way we may do harm to our neighbour's rights. 2. Obligation to make restitution for wrongs committed. 3. Causes which

may delay or put an end to this obligation. (Vol. iii. ch. xii. secs. 3, 4.)

XVIII. On the eighth commandment.
1. Slander. 2. Calumny. 3. Rash judgments. (Vol. iii. ch. xiii. secs. 1, 2, 3.)

XIX. Continuation of the eighth commandment.
1. Lies. 2. Mental reservations. 3. Revealing secrets. (Vol. iii. ch. xiii. sec. 4.)

XX. On the ninth and tenth commandments.
1. What are the thoughts, desires, and affections which God forbids in these two commandments? 2. Whence come bad thoughts, bad desires; bad thoughts which we instantly check, are merely temptations. 3. Necessity of Christian watchfulness and mortification, that we may keep ourselves pure in God's sight. (Vol. iii. ch. xiv.)

XXI. On the commandments of the Church in general.
1. Authority of the Church with regard to these commandments; recall here what was said the year before upon the legislative authority of the Church; they all tend to make it easier for us to keep the commandments of God. (Vol. ii. ch. iv. sec. 1; vol. iii. ch. xv. prelude.)

XXII. On the two first commandments of the Church.
1. Origin of festivals; festivals in the Old Testament; festivals appointed by the Apostles and by the Church. 2. Advantages of festivals; they teach us the mysteries of religion; they lead us to serve God better;

they encourage and strengthen us. 3. Obligation as to observing the festivals; there are festivals which are simply devotional, there are others which all the faithful should join in celebrating; what are these festivals? (Vol. iv. ch. xvi.)

XXIII. On the third and fourth commandments of the Church.

1. Obligation on all the faithful to come to the sacraments once a year; they should make their Easter Communion. 2. Useful and necessary for many, to confess and communicate more often. (Vol. iv. ch. viii. sec. 2; ch. ix. sec. 3.)

XXIV. On the fifth and sixth commandments of the Church—Fasting and abstinence.

1. These commandments order two things for us: fasting and abstinence. 2. Reasons for this obligation. 3. Circumstances which may dispense us from fasting and abstinence. (Vol. iii. ch. xv. secs. 1, 2, 3.)

XXV. On the evangelical counsels.

1. What distinguishes counsels from precepts? 2. Three chief evangelical counsels: chastity, poverty, obedience. 3. Rules to be followed with regard to the practice of evangelical counsels. (Vol. iii. ch. xvi.)

XXVI. On the means which God gives us of knowing the commandments and the counsels; conscience and pastoral teaching.

1. What conscience is; an upright conscience, a loose conscience, a scrupulous conscience.

SECOND YEAR—MORALS

2. Rules to be followed so that we may not be deceived as to our conscience; never go against our conscience, in doing what we believe to be wrong; in whatever we do, to have a proper feeling that we are not offending God; in doubt, consult a director, if we can. (Vol. xvii. secs. 1, 2.)

XXVII. On the goodness and merit of actions done by a man by means of grace and following the inspirations of his conscience.

1. Our actions are good when we do what God commands or counsels us, and do it from a good motive. 2. By our good works, we acquire a merit in God's sight; this merit, in the supernatural order, supposes that what we do is from motives of faith, and that we are in a state of grace; but yet one who is not in this state can do, and ought to do, actions which are good and profitable to his salvation. (Vol. iii. ch. xviii. sec. 1.)

XXVIII. On sin.

1. What sin is; for an action to be sinful in God's sight there must be certain conditions. 2. Distinction between mortal sin and venial sin; rules for distinguishing one from the other. (Vol. iii. ch. xvii. secs. 2, 3.)

XXIX. On the causes of sin.

1. Temptations of the devil. 2. Scandals of the world. 3. Concupiscence; consequence of original sin; it is an unruly love of self; whence proceed pride, sensuality, and slothfulness. (Vol. iii. ch. xvii. sec. 4.)

XXX. On the means we possess for avoiding sin and doing rightly.
>   1. Watchfulness over ourselves. 2. Frequent recourse to prayer and to the sacraments. 3. Mortification of our unruly inclinations. (*Persévérance Chrétienne*, ch. iii. secs. 4, 5, 6.)

If there are more meetings, some Christian virtue may very profitably be treated of, as, for instance, humility (*Cours d'instruction*, vol. iii. ch. xvi. sec. 2), or the most common hindrances to a really virtuous life, such as frivolity of mind, idleness, certain defects of character. (*Persévérance Chrétienne*, ch. ii. sec. 3.)

Third Year of the Course—Worship

I. Instruction on public worship.
>   1. What public worship is. 2. Necessity of it for individuals, for the family, and for society. 3. Essential parts of public worship: prayers, sacrifices. (Vol. iv. introduction.)

II. On churches, religious buildings destined for the exercise of public worship.
>   1. The most ordinary form of churches: altar, holy table, nave, side aisles. . . . 2. Consecration of churches; rites of consecration. 3. Benediction of bells; what is intended by this benediction; feelings which the sound of the bells should excite in us. (Vol. iv. ch. i. secs. 1, 2, 3.)

III. On the sign of the cross.
>   1. Antiquity of the sign of the cross in all acts of private or public worship. 2. Virtue of

the sign of the cross. 3. Reverence we should have for the cross. (Ch. ii. secs. 1, 2, 3.)

IV. On public prayer.
1. Efficaciousness of public prayer, according to our Lord's promises. 2. Different parts of public prayer: the *prône*, vespers, benediction of the Blessed Sacrament. 3. Devotion which faithful Christians have always had for public worship. (Ch. iii. secs. 1, 2.)

V. On some customs of the Church in public worship.
1. Why the Church does not use the vulgar tongue in public worship. 2. Why the Church allows variety as to customs in public worship in different countries. 3. These varieties are not contrary to the unity of Catholic worship, if they are authorised by the Church. (Ch. iv. secs. 3, 4.)

VI. On ceremonies which take place in public worship.
1. Sprinkling of the consecrated water. 2. Illumination of the altar. 3. Censing. 4. Processions. (Ch. iv. secs. 1, 2, 3, 4.)

VII. On the sacraments in general.
1. Institution of the sacraments; tradition of the Church on the seven sacraments. 2. Effects of the sacraments: sanctifying grace, sacramental grace, character. 3. God has provided for all the spiritual needs of men by the different effects of the seven sacraments. (Ch. v. secs. 1, 2, 3.)

VIII. On baptism.

    1. Institution of baptism. 2. Three effects of baptism: it purifies us from the stain of sin, and remits us from the punishment of sin; it gives us the right of obtaining, as we need it, the grace necessary for leading a Christian life; it impresses on us the Christian mark (*caractère*) which cannot be effaced. 3. How is it that baptism, which regenerates us, does not set us free from concupiscence and other effects of original sin? (Ch. vi. secs. 1, 2.)

IX. Necessity of baptism and obligations which it imposes.

    1. Baptism is necessary to salvation, for children as well as for adults; perfect charity or martyrdom may nevertheless supply the place of baptism, in cases where it could not be received. 2. Baptism imposes on all those who receive it the obligation to live according to the precepts of the Christian religion; why this obligation extends to children baptized before they have come to the use of their reason. (Ch. vi. secs. 3, 4.)

X. On the ceremonies of baptism.

    1. Ceremonies which precede baptism: the catechumenate, exorcisms. 2. Ceremonies which accompany baptism and are the essential parts of the sacrament. 3. Ceremonies which follow baptism: anointings, lighted candle, white robe. (Ch. vi. sec. 3.)

XI. On Confirmation.

    1. Institution of the sacrament. 2. Effects

which it produces: in what sense it is said to make us perfect Christians; gifts of the Holy Spirit, some of which help in perfecting the understanding, while others strengthen the will. (Ch. vii. secs. 1, 2.)

XII. On Confirmation.
1. Obligation which lies on the faithful to receive this sacrament. 2. Dispositions they must bring to it. 3. Ceremonies: imposition of hands; invocation of the Holy Spirit: anointing with the holy chrism. (Ch. vii. secs. 3, 4.)

XIII. On the Sacrament of the Eucharist.
1. Promise of the Holy Eucharist, and its institution, as related to us in the Gospel. 2. Real presence of Jesus Christ in the Eucharist. 3. Consequences of this Presence in the adoration paid to the Holy Eucharist. (Ch. viii. sec. 1.)

XIV. On Communion.
1. Necessity of receiving the Holy Eucharist at certain times; the desires of the Church with regard to frequent Communion. 2. Effects which the Holy Eucharist produces in souls. (Ch. viii. sec. 2.)

XV. On the dispositions required for Communion.
1. Dispositions of the soul: state of grace: necessity of confession for those who have committed any mortal sin. 2. Bodily preparation—fasting Eucharist; modesty. (Ch. viii. sec. 3.)

XVI. On the Sacrament of Penitence.

1. Jesus Christ gave to His Apostles and to their successors the power to remit sins committed after baptism. 2. Jesus Christ gave them this power on the condition that they should only exercise it towards those who should confess their sins. 3. It is absolutely necessary to all men to have recourse, by confession, to the Sacrament of Penitence, that they may receive pardon for mortal sins committed after baptism. (Ch. ix. secs. 1. 2, 3.)

XVII. On the precept of confession.

1. When are we bound to confess? annual confession; usefulness of more frequent confession. 2. To whom must we confess? necessity of experience for the priests. 3. How must we confess? recall briefly the qualities of a good confession. (Ch. ix. sec. 3.)

XVIII. On contrition.

1. What real contrition is; conditions it should have: dwell chiefly on supernatural motives and on the necessity of having a true sorrow for all mortal sins, with a firm resolution of never committing them again. 2. Two sorts of contrition, perfect and imperfect; difference between them arising from the difference of motive; perfect love the motive in one case; fear or hope, with a beginning of the love of God in the other: effects of each. (Ch. ix. sec. 4.)

XIX. Sacramental satisfaction.

1. It is necessary to do penance, even on account of those sins for which we have

received absolution. 2. Different works of satisfaction: prayers, alms, mortification of the senses, Christian patience in bearing the ills of life. 3. How to fulfil the penance imposed by the confessor. (Ch. ix. sec. 6.)

XX. On indulgences.
1. What the Church means by the indulgences which she gives us, plenary and partial indulgences. 2. Power the Church has received to remit, by way of indulgences, the punishments due to our sin. 3. Necessary conditions for obtaining indulgences. (Ch. ix. secs. 7, 8.)

XXI. On extreme unction.
1. Institution of the sacrament. 2. Ceremonies used in its administration; oil of the sick; what it signifies; what parts are anointed. 3. Effects it produces: purification of the soul; consolation and strength in the trials of sickness, and at the approach of death. (Ch. x. secs. 1, 2, 3.)

XXII. On the Sacrament of Order.
1. Origin of the Christian priesthood. 2. Hierarchy of order established in the Church: minor orders; greater orders; the episcopate. 3. What an honour it is to a family if God chooses one of its members for the priesthood. Duties of parents with regard to the vocation of their children. (Ch. xi. secs. 1, 2.)

XXIII. On the Sacrament of Marriage.
1. Our Lord raised marriage to the dignity of

a sacrament; tradition of the Church with regard to this. 2. Necessary conditions for the valid and legitimate celebration of marriage; in what parish the marriage should take place. 3. Sin and misfortune of those who are not married by their pastors; these purely civil unions are not true marriages in the eyes of God. (Ch. xii. secs. 1, 2.)

XXIV. On the holy sacrifice.

1. Relation of the sacrifice of the cross with the Eucharistic sacrifice. 2. Effects of the holy sacrifice; its virtue. 3. How we should assist at it. (Ch. xiii. secs. 1, 2.)

XXV. On the arrangements for the sacrifice.

1. Sacred vessels. 2. Vestments of the priests and others who serve at the holy sacrifice. (Ch. xiv. secs. 1, 2, 3.)

XXVI. On the ceremonies of the holy sacrifice.

1. First part of the Mass, from the beginning to the offertory: prayers at the foot of the altar, introit, epistle, Gospel. 2. Second part, from the offertory to the consecration: offertory, preface, canon of the Mass. (Ch. xv. secs. 1, 2.)

XXVII. Continuation of the ceremonies of the Mass.

1. From the consecration to the Communion: adoration, *Memento* of the dead, *Pater*, *Agnus Dei*. 2. From the Communion to the end: Communion under two kinds, prayers, the priest's blessing, Gospel of S. John. (Ch. xv. secs. 2, 3.)

XXVIII. On the festivals: festivals of our Lord.
1. Festivals appointed in honour of the coming of our Lord and His manifestation to the world: Christmas, Circumcision, the Epiphany. 2. Festivals to celebrate the work of redemption: Holy Week, Easter. 3. Festivals in celebration of the continuation of the work of redemption: Ascension, Pentecost, *Fête Dieu* (Corpus Christi).[1] (Ch. xvii. secs. 2, 3, 4.)

XXIX. On the festivals of the Blessed Virgin.
1. Festivals which recall to us how God prepared Mary for the accomplishment of His designs for her: Immaculate Conception, Presentation, Annunciation. 2. Festivals which recall to us the part which the Holy Virgin had in the work of our redemption: Visitation, Presentation of the Child Jesus in the temple, Compassion. 3. Festival for celebrating the glory and the triumph of the Holy Virgin: Assumption. (Ch. xviii. secs. 1, 2, 3.)

XXX. On the festivals of the saints.
1. Various festivals appointed in honour of the saints: All-Saints. 2. Advantages we receive from the festivals of the saints: instruction, edification, confidence. (Ch. xix.)

[1] In this and the following instructions, it is sufficient to explain the general plan of the Church in the appointment and celebration of festivals. A more detailed explanation of each of these festivals is given at the catechism on the days when they are celebrated. For the festivals, refer to the *Instructions historiques, dogmatiques et morales, sur les principales fêtes*, by a director of the seminary; 3 vols. in 12mo.

XXXI. On the commemoration of the faithful departed.

1. Reverence the Church has always had for the mortal remains of the faithful departed in her communion: cemeteries. 2. Her zeal in offering prayers to God for the faithful departed: virtue of the holy sacrifice for the consolation of souls in purgatory. 3. Festival of commemoration of the dead. (Ch. xx.)

Article IV

Methods of Sanctification employed in Catechisms of Perseverance

If, in a catechism of perseverance, we strive to give the young people a sound and sufficiently wide instruction on religion, we strive with not less care to strengthen them in Christian virtues. The more liable they are to lose the grace of God in the midst of the dissipations of the world and the grievous influence of bad examples, the more important it is to strengthen them in those good habits which at a more tender age we trained them in. Four sorts of exercises tend directly to this object: the counsels, monthly Communions, festivals, and retreats. We have besides, associations and works of charity.

The counsels (*avis*) and the homilies are very important in these catechisms, because they are intended to give safe directions to the children for the

METHODS OF SANCTIFICATION

most delicate and the most critical time of their life. These counsels must be so arranged as to include all essential things; there must be discernment and tact, so as only to say what is fitting, and in a way best fitted to make the hearers delight in the maxims of the Gospel; the catechist must study his own heart, must go back to the recollections of his youth, and what he has observed in his own family and in the world, so that he may go into such practical details as shall best teach the duties of a Christian life. The three years devoted to the course of instruction abundantly suffice for giving all these counsels; there are many to which we often return, and, outside the bounds which the catechist has marked out for himself, there are counsels arising from special circumstances, for which he should provide, as far as possible.[1]

The *monthly Communions*, so called because they take place, as a rule, once a month, in the catechisms of perseverance, produce an excellent effect. They contribute very much to keep up piety in the children's hearts.

The Holy See has granted a plenary indulgence in perpetuity to the children of the catechisms of S. Sulpice, and to children of other catechisms in France which are affiliated to S. Sulpice, every

---

[1] All the most important counsels which should be given in a catechism of perseverance are brought together in a book entitled, *Persévérance Chrétienne, ou Moyens de conserver les fruits de la première communion*, 1 vol. in 12mo. The catechist will also find material for excellent counsels in *Vraie et solide Piété d'après Saint François de Sales*, 1 vol. in 18mo, in the *Combat Spirituel*, and other well-known books.

time that they communicate at the monthly Communions in their respective parishes, as well as to their fathers and mothers when they communicate there. We cannot strive too much to bring the children to love this practice, for it has more power than any other to entirely change the aspect and the heart of a parish. It was by the catechisms and the *monthly Communions* that the parish of S. Sulpice, once the very sink of Paris and the resort of all the worst characters, attained to be looked upon as the most exemplary parish in the capital. In the space of fifty years piety had so increased there that, as a rule, 200,000 communions were made in the year in the one parish church, though there were thirty communities resident in this parish, and their churches were mostly much frequented.

The exercise of the monthly Communion begins with a meditation, which is immediately followed by the Holy Mass. After the communion of the priest, the officiant, passing to the Gospel side, turns to the children, who will be seated, and gives them a preliminary exhortation, as a kind of preparation for Holy Communion. He exhorts them to make acts of faith, of love, and of desire. Then some one person, appointed by the chief of the catechism, reads aloud, on his knees and a lighted candle in his hand, an act of *amende honorable*. While the priest is distributing the Holy Communion, hymns are sung in honour of the Blessed Sacrament. When the Communion is ended, the children again sit down ; the priest then again gives them an address, in which, after having suggested acts which it is right to make after Holy Communion, he exhorts them inwardly to renew their baptismal promises, and gives them certain rules to help them to keep up through the month, the fruit of this Communion. Finally, after the Mass, the customary prayers are recited for gaining the plenary indulgence.

The children must quite understand that they are in no way bound to communicate at the catechisms, that no remark will be made on those who communicate and those who do not; that, in short, they are left perfectly free on this point. It will hardly be believed how important this is, but they ought, nevertheless, to be pressed to assist at the monthly Communions, though they may not communicate then; we can tell them that it is the custom, and that mutual edification demands it. Their presence helps to increase the fervour of the communicants, and sometimes it stirs them up to get over their own indifference, and becomes a motive to lead them on to make themselves worthy to approach the Holy Table.

The celebration of the festivals contributes no less than the monthly Communion to the edification of the children. All the great festivals of the Church are celebrated in the catechisms, but there are also more special festivals which are celebrated with a greater amount of pomp. In the girls' catechism there are the Immaculate Conception of the Blessed Virgin, the Epiphany, and the *Sacré Cœur;* in the boys' catechism, Christmas, Pentecost, and the first Sunday in the month of May.

Many children, particularly in the girls' perseverance, write a little account of what has most struck them in these festivals; they give their personal impressions, they write down the counsels which were given them either by the chief or by the president, and various incidents which seem to them worthy of remembrance. These little works may very well be encouraged, provided they are done with simplicity and devotion. But if they are only a *jeu d'esprit*, or pictures of an excited imagination or other things of this kind, as has happened sometimes, the chief ought to give them advice privately and tell the children that we have no fancy for these sort of compositions, and see in them nothing but mere amusement or vanity. What we wish to see is a work of piety which the children may read over again at a future time with interest and with profit.

Article V

Retreats

Retreats are a yet more powerful means of edification, because they embrace all the other means of which we have just been speaking, and bring them to bear on the soul when it is most recollected, more in a condition, consequently, to listen to the voice of God, and to follow His holy inspirations.

At S. Sulpice, for the girls' catechism of perseverance, we hold a little retreat on the Sunday, Monday, and Tuesday of Quinquagesima. Both catechisms of perseverance have another retreat at the time of first Communion.

The object of the first retreat is chiefly to turn the young girls away from the vanities of the world and to interest them in works of charity. Every year we have the comfort of seeing, morning and evening, for these three days, a great many members of the perseverance attending the exercises of the catechism with great assiduity. On Sunday morning a meditation is made, then follows the Holy Mass, after which the chief of the catechism gives some pious counsels. In the evening, after the report of the analyses, vespers are sung, and followed by an exhortation from some ecclesiastic who is a stranger. When the exhortation is ended, preparation is made for the *salut* of the Blessed Sacrament: three members of the perseverance, chosen out beforehand, one associate, one aspirant, and one child, all on their knees, their heads covered with a white veil and holding a candle, recite the acts of public confession (*amende honorable*), then the benediction is given, and the whole concludes with the adoration of the cross, which all persons present come to kiss at the railing, on their knees, while the psalm *Miserere* is chanted.

Monday and Tuesday morning everything is done as on Sunday. In the evening there is no sermon. Vespers are sung, and the chief of the catechism gives some holy advice, or tells the children something which may interest and edify them. On Monday the lottery of the *Petite-Œuvre* is drawn.

On Tuesday there is generally the admission of a child to the *Petite-Œuvre*, and on the two days these fill up part of the time. The two meetings conclude, as on Sunday evening, with the *salut* of the Blessed Sacrament, and the acts of *amende honorable*.

The second retreat lasts a little longer, and is of a more serious character. Beginning on Sunday evening, it ends on Friday morning with the Mass of thanksgiving. The order of the exercises has been already given (ch. iii. art. vi. p. 288): in the morning, meditation, Holy Mass, counsels, sermon; in the evening, vespers, reading with explanation or counsels, sermon. On Thursday, the day on which the children make their communion, the priest gives them a short exhortation during the Mass, before and after Communion; in the evening there is a sort of conference and the *salut* of the Blessed Sacrament.

There are great advantages in being able to give a special retreat for the catechisms of perseverance. The meditations, the counsels, the conferences are better suited to the age and to the spiritual needs of the hearers; they understand and they feel that it is all meant for them. We speak to them in succession of the necessity of renewing in themselves Christian piety, and of strengthening the resolutions they made at the time of first Communion; of the danger of the abuse of grace, and the danger of the bad habits which may be formed in youth; we tell them that every one should study the faults of their own character, that they may correct them; we speak to them of the spirit of faith, of the dispositions necessary when we approach the sacraments, of the conduct they should observe in the world, on the choice of intimate acquaintances, on what they should read,—in short, we trace out for them the plan of a Christian life. These exercises always, in very many cases, are an epoch in the renewal of their life, and it has become a custom in a great many parishes to give retreats not only for the catechisms of perseverance, or for the congregations of women and girls, but for all the faithful.

Article VI

Associations

In many catechisms of perseverance, associations have been formed for keeping up the zeal and ardour of the children. We may be allowed here, once more, to say what is done in the parish of S. Sulpice.

In the girls' catechism, the association is composed of not less than forty, not more than fifty associates, thirty aspirants, and an unlimited number of affiliated members. These last are admitted on their own request, after deliberation of the associates; they have the privilege of being present at the *ordinary* meetings of the association. The aspirants form the noviciate of the associates; they are taken from the children who have attended the catechism of perseverance for at least two years since their first Communion, and who have set a good example to their companions. The associates are always consulted as to the choice of aspirants. They must be aspirants for at least two years before they can be elected associates. Generally there is only one election in the year, and only sufficient aspirants and associates are elected to fill up the prescribed number, if vacancies have been caused by the death, or marriage, or resignation of one or more associates or aspirants.

The associates, without making any vow, devote themselves to the honour (*culte*) of the Blessed Sacrament; they are closely bound amongst themselves to do all charitable offices to one another; and lastly, they devote themselves to the instruction of the children of the catechisms of S. Sulpice. The principal object of the association is to honour Jesus Christ abiding in our tabernacles; and every associate who is faithful to the grace of her vocation, is intended both to fill up the piety of the parishioners, and to show what reverence is due to our Lord in this mystery. All the prayers of the associates, their sacrifices, their mortifications, their communions, and all their good works, are held to be in common: they all have the right to draw out of this treasury, where each can make herself rich, even out of that which she gives. They relieve each other in their temporal wants, they nurse each other in sickness, and do all other charitable duties. Lastly, they devote themselves to teaching the children. S. Paul speaks often in his Epistles of the holy women who helped him in the work of the Gospel, and who, according to the holy Fathers, explained in private what the Apostles had taught in public. Such is now the ministry which the associates exercise in the parish of S. Sulpice, particularly at the time of the first Communions. The Holy Apostolic See, to encourage a work so valuable for the salvation of souls, grants several plenary indulgences to associates who have taught children in the course of one year.

Every month, generally on the Sunday preceding the Communion of which we have spoken in Article IV., the associates come together for a special meeting. After the prayers appointed for these kind of meetings, whoever is presiding gives the associates an address, and at the end suggests to them a spiritual *banquet*, a prayer and a practice for the month which is beginning. Other prayers follow, and the meeting ends with a distribution of *billets* containing the names of the saints of the month. In the course of the following week, a Mass is celebrated for the association, at which all the associates are expected to assist. The aspirants also have meetings and special Masses, but only once in three months. The Holy See grants a plenary indulgence once a month to all of them, if they have not been absent from any of their respective exercises, nor from those of the catechism of perseverance.

The ceremony for the reception of associates and aspirants is the most solemn festival which the catechism of perseverance has. After vespers, the new associates, dressed in white, each holding a lighted candle, come from the sacristy, led by their president, and range themselves round the balustrade. The officiating priest, on his knees, at the foot of the altar, intones the hymn *Veni Creator*; afterwards, standing at the Gospel corner, he gives a short address to the future associates and aspirants. When he has finished speaking, one of the new associates recites an act of consecration, in the name of her companions; after which the secretary hands the register and a pen to each of them, and on her knees she signs the act of her reception. Then the officiant, leaving the altar, comes to the associates and gives them a seal, framed, and says to each, "*Receive this pledge of the engagements you have just entered into with Jesus Christ in the Blessed Sacrament of the altar.*" He also gives the aspirants their seals of admission, saying these words, "*For Jesus Christ and for ever.*" Then he goes back to the Gospel corner, and stands, turning towards the children, while the president who is going out of office recites, in the name of the old associates, an act of renewal of their promises. Lastly, he says a few words to the whole association, to encourage them to new earnestness in the spirit of their vocation, and the faithful fulfilment of all its duties. The regular prayer is chanted for the *salut* of the Blessed Sacrament, and after the benediction, the *Te Deum* is sung as an act of thanksgiving.

There are eight dignitaries of the association: the President, the *Surveillante* of the sick, the *Zélatrice*, the Secretary, the Treasurer, the Librarian, and the two Sacristans. Each dignitary, except the President, has an assistant who takes her place when she is obliged to be absent. The dignitaries are chosen newly once a year, on the day of the festival of the association.

The President has the charge of watching over the association and the aspirants, and of giving notice to the chief of the catechism, who is *ex-officio* superior of the association, of any abuses she may observe; lastly, she has certain functions to perform which tend to the good observance of the rules, the edification of the associates, and the good order of the catechism.[1]

The *Surveillante* of the sick has the charge of visiting associates and aspirants who are ill, of bringing them the consolations of religion, and, above all, she has to see that they do not die without receiving the sacraments of the Church. She commends them to the prayers of the catechism, and asks the associates to visit them. She looks also to the temporal wants of the sick, and gives them such help as may be necessary.

The *Zélatrice* has the special charge of finding instruction for the more backward girls; it is she who sends them to the associates who will instruct them. She finds out the needs of the poor children, and reports them to those people whose business it will be to provide these children with suitable clothes for the day of first Communion.

---

[1] The functions of the dignitaries, and generally all the usages which concern the association, are more fully described in the *Directoire des Associées du Catéchisme de Persévérance de S. Sulpice*, 1 vol. in 18mo.

The Secretary writes an account of every meeting; in her register, she reports any interesting circumstances of the festivals of the catechism, and all the changes of superiors, catechists, and dignitaries. She also keeps all writings connected with the association. The Treasurer receives the offerings of those who are in the habit of giving. The Librarian has the charge of the library belonging to the associates; she lends books and receives them back.

The Sacristans decorate the altar; they prepare the linen and the vestments for the holy sacrifice, and even the sacred vessels, which they are allowed to handle by the special favour of Monseigneur the Archbishop of Paris. One of them must always be at the Mass of the girls' catechism, and be in the chapel a quarter of an hour before. After the holy sacrifice, they fold up the vestments and the linen; they take care that the napkins, the corporals, and the purificators are always clean, and change them when they cease to be so.

It is easy to understand that an association such as this must be the strongest possible support to a catechism of perseverance. There are three things which are apt to make children leave the catechism: the natural distaste which comes unconsciously to those who are not bound to it by any special link; the example of the children who leave it, particularly if they have influence over the others; and lastly, a change of catechists. Now all these obstacles disappear when the catechism itself contains an association such as we have been describing, or some other similar institution. The change of catechists can nowhere be more frequent than it is at S. Sulpice; yet we have never found that their departure has caused any blank in the catechism. The reason is, that most of the children are attached to it by purely personal motives. In the first place, the associates, forty or fifty in number, are attached to it by the strongest possible ties, because they have so great a share in the administration of the catechism, having in charge so many things which contribute to the success of this good work. The thirty aspirants show a great zeal for the catechism, because every one of them hopes to become an associate; and a great number of children, hoping that they may be elected aspirants, equal them in zeal and regularity. Lastly, as the body of associates and aspirants is composed of the best children, their example must necessarily influence the mass of the catechism. Their attention, their modesty, their piety, their zeal, the esteem in which they hold the catechism, —all these are examples for the younger ones, and attract them to the catechisms.

The boys' catechism has a similar association. The rules are very nearly the same. The dignities of President, of *Zélateur*, of Sacristan, of Secretary, of Treasurer, and of Librarian, with their respective offices and the exercises of the association, are all noted in a special *Directoire*.

This association, composed of the very best of the youths, is, as it were, the heart of the catechism. We have the comfort of seeing young lads, going on for several years, and even after they have ended their classical studies, giving an example of diligence and of a holy zeal in drawing their friends into the *persévérance*.

The sovereign Pontiffs, Pius VIII. and Gregory XVI., in consideration of this, and still further to excite the associates of S. Sulpice to the faithful performance of their duties, graciously granted the following indulgences, desiring also that they should include all the other catechisms of the same kind which should be associated with that of S. Sulpice:—[1]

1. A plenary indulgence, once every month, to the members of perseverance, and to the aspirants and associates who, being penitent, and having made their confession not more than a week ago, make their Communion in their catechism.

2. An indulgence of three hundred days to the same, every time that they take part in the general meetings of the catechism, or in the private meetings of the association.

---

[1] In order to affiliate a boys' catechism of perseverance to that of S. Sulpice, it is not necessary that there should be an association of the Blessed Sacrament in this catechism, nor that only young lads should be admitted to the exercises of this catechism. So it was decided by the Sacred Congregation of Indulgences, when consulted on some doubts relating to the brief of Gregory XVI. To obtain an affiliation, the catechism, through its president and its secretary, writes to the associates of the catechism of S. Sulpice: this letter explains the condition of the catechism; it is sent to Paris, enclosed under cover, addressed to M. the Director of the Catechisms of S. Sulpice, at the great seminary. The reply contains the authentic act of affiliation. The same course is followed in order to affiliate a girls' catechism to that of the perseverants of S. Sulpice; but with this difference, that, according to the terms of the brief of the Holy See, it is necessary that there should be a body of associates and aspirants in the catechism of girls which asks to be affiliated.

3. A plenary indulgence, twice every month, and under the same conditions, to the catechists of these children or associates; and the same partial indulgence, as above, every time that they preside over either the general or the special meetings.

These indulgences are granted in perpetuity, and are applicable to the departed.

Article VII

Works of Charity instituted in Catechisms of Perseverance

It is a very fitting thing to institute works of charity in catechisms of perseverance. They are very valuable to the poor in the help they receive from them; but they have a much wider effect, and a much more important result, they accustom the children early to exercises of charity; they teach them the secret of doing good.

The catechism of girls have the work of the *Sainte Enfance de Marie*, better known under the name of *Petite-Œuvre*. It is intended to gather in a certain number of poor little girls, some of those who are most neglected, and to secure for them the invaluable benefit of a Christian education, together with suitable instruction and an employment which will enable them some day to earn their living honourably.

The resources for this work are provided by

subscriptions, by a lottery which is drawn every year, by collections which are made every month, and by special gifts. Subscribers are expected to give at least thirty centimes a month; in the month of January they are asked to give sixty, and also in the month of May, consecrated to Mary. They are asked also to recite every day the prayer *Sonvenez-vous*, etc., that the work may be under the protection of the Blessed Virgin, patron-saint of childhood.

The *Petite-Œuvre* is administered by two councils; the object of the first is to decide on the admission of the children who are brought to it, and to provide the means necessary for the keeping of these children and for the house of the *Petite-Œuvre*; the other is chiefly concerned in the administration of the funds. These two councils are presided over by the chief of the girls' catechism of perseverance, in the absence of the Superior of the *Petite-Œuvre*.

The general council is composed of dignitaries of the *Petite-Œuvre* and of simple members of council. The dignitaries are:—

The Directress of the house of the *Petite-Œuvre* and her Assistant; a Treasurer and two Assistant Treasurers; a Secretary and an Assistant Secretary.

The members of council are:—The associates and the aspirants of the catechism of perseverance, and children from other catechisms. These are chosen from among those who subscribe; their number is not limited. Amongst them, some are

CHARITABLE WORKS: GIRLS

simple members of council, others are certificated members: these are called also Special Treasurers; they devote themselves to obtain subscriptions from people who are strangers to the catechisms.

The Directress and the Treasurer, as well as their chief Assistants, are always taken from the associates of the catechism of perseverance; the others may be chosen indifferently from the associates or other children of the catechisms.

The dignitaries and certificated councillors are chosen afresh every year, with the exception of the Directress and the Treasurer; these may hold office for several years.

The most important work of this council is the choice of the children who are offered to them, and in order to give more solemnity to this, the choice is generally made at a meeting of the catechism of perseverance.

All the members of the council have the right to propose a child, provided that this child fulfils the following conditions:—1. She must be at least seven years old, and not yet ten; 2. She must belong to the parish of S. Sulpice, or at least have lived in the parish for a year; 3. Her admission must be approved by the doctor of the *Petite-Œuvre*; 4. She must have the consent of her parents or guardians, who must themselves be subject to the rules in force regarding the keeping of the children, their stay in the institution, and what communications they may hold with the outside world. When everything is ready, the President announces the number and the names of the children who are proposed; any notes which have been made about them are read, and any information, and then the election is proceeded with. Each member of the council receives a counter or *billet*, and they come up in order, as arranged by the president, to cast their vote into the ballot-box: the child who receives the greatest number of votes is elected. Should it happen that her parents withdraw their consent before the child is admitted into the institution, her right passes on to the next child who has received the greatest number of votes.

The Secretary makes minutes of the election; she mentions expressly the names of the children who competed, and the number of votes which each one received.

The general council being much too numerous for it to be possible to treat in detail the affairs which concern the interest of the *Petite-Œuvre*, particularly the administration of its funds, it has been found necessary to have a small council specially charged with this business: this was done in 1840, by the Director of the Catechisms, after he had taken counsel with the dignitaries and certificated counsellors. This council, as now organised, is composed of five members at least, and of eight at most.

The Assistant of the Directress, the Treasurer, and the Secretary of the *Petite-Œuvre* are members; they are represented, in case of absence, by those who assist them in their offices; the other members may be drawn indifferently from among the associates, the aspirants, the affiliated members, from the children of the perseverance, and from teachers whose schools attend the catechism.

The choice of dignitaries and simple counsellors is made every year, but so arranged that there shall always be two members of the old council, and all may be re-elected, if it is thought good for the interests of the work.

The Directress of the house of the *Petite-Œuvre* assists at the council; she may be represented by one of the mistresses who are associated with her in the education of the children.

As a rule, the council meets twice a year—the first meeting takes place on one of the days in the week preceding the festival of the *Petite-Œuvre*; the second, a few days before Pentecost. After reading the minutes of the last meeting, the President informs the meeting of what subjects will be offered for their consideration. The Directress gives an account of the condition of the institution, so that the members of the council may know what it needs; then every one takes a part, and makes such observations on the work as she thinks will be useful. Lastly, the Treasurer gives in the account of receipts and expenses, as well as the actual balance in hand. The receipts and expenses are given out, but without going into detail. Under the head of receipts, the results of collections, of subscriptions, of lotteries, of the children's work, of special gifts, are given separately. Under the head of expenses are included the sums employed for the clothing and feeding the community, the keeping up of the house, and the taxes. This account is verified and approved by the Assistant of the Directress, and the Secretary.

Independently of this rendering of accounts, the council enters also into the most important affairs which concern the work; such as an increase in the staff of mistresses, the reception of the children, the extra expenses which may be thought necessary or useful. Care is always taken to have sufficient funds in reserve for one whole year.

The children adopted by the council are lodged, fed, and kept in the institution of the *Petite-Œuvre* till they attain the age of twenty-one; their parents or guardians enter into an engagement with the Directress by which they bind themselves not to take them away before this time. The children are brought up according to the rules and practices of Christian piety; they are taught reading, writing, arithmetic, and needlework, and are instructed also in household cares and details. In case of illness, they are treated with all the care their condition demands: if the illness becomes serious, they are sent back to their parents if they wish it.

The interior government of the institution is intrusted to the charge of the Directress and to those associates who she joins with herself. She has the right to send away children who behave badly; but she cannot decide upon this unless there is a majority of votes from the mistresses, and it must also be done with the advice of the Superior.

In the case of sending away a child, the private council are told of it, and after having heard the report which the Directress gives them of the child's behaviour, they see if it is better to send her back to her parents or to commend her to the care of some charitable person who will try to place her elsewhere.

The Directress arranges in her own name all things connected with the institution, such as the engagements with the children's parents.

The Directress should, a fortnight before each election of children, request the chiefs of the girls' catechisms to announce the day and hour of this election, and also to urge the members of the council to come to it punctually, and even to propose children, as they have a right to do. She takes down all the necessary information concerning the proposed children, their age, their abode, the condition of their families; she commits all this to writing, in order to present it to the chief of the perseverance, at the time of the balloting.

The Treasurer has two registers—in one the Directress writes and signs the orders which she gives to the Treasurer for expenditure; the other register is for receipts and disbursements.

The Treasurer receives all the funds of the *Petite-Œuvre*. The members of council whose business it is to collect subscriptions remit the sum to her, with a list, which they sign.

As to voluntary gifts, they are given into the hands of a member of the council who is appointed for this purpose every month by the chief of the catechism. She also remits to the Treasurer everything she receives.

The Directress and the Treasurer go through

together the accounts of receipts and expenses, twice a year, before each of the meetings of the council which overlooks the administration of the funds, so that they may be presented in a condensed form.

On leaving office, the Treasurer gives in a general note of the expenses and receipts, and the actual state of the funds of the institution; the Superior verifies this account and signs it, together with the Directress or her Assistant; the new Treasurer acknowledges it and signs it also on entering into office.

The Treasurer's Assistant takes her place in all these functions in case of absence or illness; she has the charge also of the necessary preparations for the lottery, the writing the tickets, and the arrangement and disposition of the lots; for things relating to the lottery she brings the second Assistant to her help, or any other she may think best.

The Secretary ought to have two registers; in one she writes the minutes of each meeting of the great council, and in the other she writes all the deliberations of the private council. She keeps an exact list of all the members of both councils, so that she may summon them when necessary.

Every year, on the Monday of Quinquagesima, the chief of the girls' perseverance has a Mass celebrated for all the present members of the *Petite-Œuvre*—that is to say, for all the dignitaries, the members of council, and for all those who subscribed; another Mass will be celebrated for the departed members; this generally takes place a few days before the vacation of the seminary begins.

The boys' catechism of perseverance has a work similar to that of the girls, though a little different in some points; it is called the *Petite-Conférence* of S. Vincent de Paul.

In creating this new work, one object has been the relief of some unfortunate families, chosen as much as possible from those whose children attend the catechism. But still more, we have in view the training these young people early in the sweet habits of charity, of love for the suffering members of our Lord; we wish them to feel by their own personal experience the pure joy that is experienced in drying the tears of the poor, in comforting them in their sorrow, in cheering them in their sadness, by showing them that God is watching over them, since He inspires even young children with the thought of visiting them.

All those who support the work by their subscription are members of it, whether they belong to the catechism or not, such as the parents of the children. The minimum of the subscription is fixed at thirty centimes a month. The subscribers give their names, and, if they wish it, they may give their whole subscription to the Treasurer-General, or else they can pay it, the second Sunday in each month, to the ordinary Treasurer, whose name will be given them.

From the members of the *Œuvre* are chosen those who are to visit the families adopted by the council, and to take them such help as the *Œuvre* can dispose of. Children who are remarkable for their zeal and for their piety, and who have their parents' permission, are elected and appointed visitors, being proposed by the chief of the catechism. This very honourable function they are to fulfil with zeal, and according to the advice and the rules which will be given them. To this end, they will visit regularly the family which is intrusted to them; they will ask their parents or their teachers, or one of the old members of the council, to go with them, unless, in consideration of their age and steadiness, the chief of the catechism authorises them to go alone. They must look on the poor with respect when they go to them, remembering our Lord's words: "*Inasmuch as ye have done it unto one of the least of these . . . ye have done it unto Me*": words which show us that our Lord is pleased to be visited and honoured in the person of the afflicted, the poor, and the unhappy.

The members of the *Petite-Conférence*, when they visit the poor, take pains to find out their needs, so that they may report them, and may ask, if need be, for extra help; they give them tickets for bread, or meat, or any help in money which has been agreed upon in the council of the *Œuvre*. When they come to know the children of the family a little, they can ask them if they go to the catechism; they can teach them some prayers, they can inspire them with devotion for the Holy Virgin, or they can put some holy thought into their minds which may help them to become good.

As the subscriptions would not suffice for the needs of the work, the children of the catechism make it their duty to procure other help, either in money or clothes, according to what is in their power to do, and with the advice of their parents; they bring the clothes which they have no further use for, but which can always in some way be made useful to the poor. Moreover, every year, as a rule, a lottery is held, and consequently they all try to get their family to take tickets, and also to persuade their friends and acquaintances to take shares. These are all taken to the catechists one week before the lottery is drawn, so that those persons who have the management of it may have time to number and arrange them, and to prepare everything properly.

For the disposal of its funds, the *Petite-Conférence* has dignitaries, and holds regular meetings, at which the choice of families to be adopted is agreed on; and the amount of help which can be given.

The dignitaries are:— 1. A Secretary and a Vice-Secretary; 2. A Treasurer-General and ordinary Treasurer; 3. One member to have charge of the clothing. All these dignitaries are nominated by the chief of the catechism, who is the director of the *Œuvre*: he announces them on the Sunday on which is celebrated the feast of the Purification, and they begin their functions on the following Sunday.

The Secretary, at the beginning of each year, writes a list of the members, and in the course of the year adds to it those who are newly admitted. He keeps a register of the families who are helped, writing—1. The name and address, which he is careful to change when the poor people go to live elsewhere; 2. The date when the family began to be visited by the *Œuvre*; 3. A short account of the family and its condition; 4. The extra help which may be given to it.

If anything happens at the meeting or outside which interests the *Œuvre*, the Secretary enters it in the minutes, which he reads at the next meeting. On the day of the Purification, he gives a report of the proceedings of the *Petite-Conférence* throughout the year; in this he shows what has been received and what each Treasurer has specially collected. This report, before being read, has to be submitted to the chief of the catechism.

The Vice-Secretary helps the Secretary, and takes his place in all his functions, when he is unable to execute them.

The ordinary Treasurers are intrusted with the charge of collecting, as they are able, the subscriptions and voluntary donations for the *Œuvre*. On the day of the Purification, they receive their account-books: on the following Sunday they divide between them all the members of the catechism who belong to the *Œuvre*; and if they have forgotten to bring their offering, they take care to give them a gentle reminder afterwards. Outside the catechism, they endeavour to obtain subscriptions; they enter everything they receive in their books, and remit it to the Treasurer-General of the *Petite-Conférence* every month. He writes a receipt in the book.

The Treasurer-General sits at the bureau during the meetings of the *Œuvre*, and distributes the tickets (for bread, meat, etc.). If any extra help is voted, he gives the different sums to the visitors, and makes a note of it in his register. During the week preceding the last Sunday in the month, he goes to the tradesmen who supply the *Œuvre*, to take back the tickets; he pays the value which they represent, and receives a receipt, which he keeps for the making up of his own accounts. He always carefully makes out the balance of what the *Œuvre* has received, and what it has spent in gifts of bread or extra help, so that it may be easily known how things stand, and what there is to spare.

Three times a year, the last Sunday in January before the feast of the Purification, at Easter, and at the end of the year, the Treasurer gives in his accounts to the chief of the catechism, or to the catechist who habitually has the direction of the *Petite-Conférence*, that they may be verified and approved: he also prepares a general account for the whole year, which he gives in to the Secretary, as has been said above.

The Vice-Treasurer takes the place of the Treasurer-General when he cannot execute his functions. His more special charge is all that concerns the lottery, numbering the tickets, writing the lots, arranging them in the chapel, the distribution at the time of the drawing.

The member who has charge of the clothing department receives at his own house all which is given him for the poor of the *Œuvre*; he numbers them and keeps them carefully in a cupboard. He keeps a register in which all these clothes are classed under certain heads as *clothes for men, boots and shoes*, etc. etc., and he writes whatever he receives under these heads, so that he can find them again easily. He takes his book to the meetings, sits at the bureau, and when any demands are made for certain clothes, he sees if he has what is wanted. During the meeting, he makes a collection towards the keeping up of the clothing store.

This meeting of which we have been speaking is held, as a rule, every fortnight. The dignitaries and the visitors meet at the appointed place, and are presided over by the chief, or by one of the catechists. The dignitaries are at the bureau; the others take the places assigned to them at the beginning of the year. All kneel, and the *Veni Sancte* is recited, together with the invocations: "*Jesus, Father of the poor, have mercy upon us; Holy Virgin, comforter of the afflicted, pray for us; S. Vincent de Paul, pray for us.*" Then all rise, and sit down, silent.

The Secretary reads the minutes of the last meeting. Whoever is presiding addresses a few words to the *Conférence*; he tells them anything of interest, or else gives some advice to the members as to the way they should discharge their functions and practise the duties of charity with regard to the poor. The Treasurer gives out the needful gifts for the families to be visited. Those who wish to ask for any extra help should do so in a note which they hand to the chief of the catechism before the meeting. If a new family is to be adopted, the choice is made

CHARITABLE WORKS: BOYS

by a majority of votes, but only after all necessary information has been obtained.

The families that are chosen are some of the poorest, and in which there are old men, or quite young children, or boys, but never if there are others in the family whom it would not be fit for the young members of the perseverance to visit. Religious families are preferred, so that the children may themselves be edified, or at least may be able to say some word touching religion. After preliminary information has been obtained, either from sisters of charity or anyone else, one member of the *Conférence*, of the most experience, is chosen to pay a visit to the family proposed, and on his report the *Conférence* decides on its admission. When all the business has been transacted, everyone kneels down, the *Sub-tuum* is recited, together with the invocations used at the beginning, and the meeting separates.

Every catechism could have similar works of charity, modified in form according to the needs, the resources, and the customs of the place. In one place, there may be *patronages* (benevolent societies); in another place, the young girls may meet once a week or oftener, to work together for the poor. Experience has long ago shown that these works of charity, when well organised and arranged, are very attractive to the children; they touch their hearts, and are another link to attach them to the catechism. The trouble they give themselves in getting subscriptions, in circulating lottery tickets, in working with their own hands to make clothes for the poor, causes them to spend many happy hours, and makes them care about these things in a way which delights us to see. Happy children, whose chief anxiety is to provide good things for other children who are poor!